CoNLL SIGMORPHON 2017
Shared Task: Universal Morphological Reinflection

Vancouver, Canada
3 – 4 August 2017

ISBN: 978-1-5108-4566-4

CoNLL 2017

Proceedings of the

CoNLL SIGMORPHON 2017 Shared Task: Universal Morphological Reinflection

August 3–4, 2017
Vancouver, Canada

Support:

Google

Preface

This volume contains the system description papers associated with the CoNLL-SIGMORPHON shared task in morphological reinflection held at CoNLL 2017. This is the first time a CoNLL shared task has directly addressed the learning of morphology from examples—a fundamental task in NLP where good solutions promise to benefit many downstream tasks. Moreover, models that learn complex morphological patterns from example data are also of significant linguistic interest.

To support the task, we collected and curated data from 52 languages, forming a typologically and genealogically diverse data set against which to evaluate performance of the systems. We divided the learning challenge into two sub-tasks: (1) learning to inflect nouns, adjectives, and verbs from their lemmata (citation forms) into a desired target form, and (2) completing partially filled inflection tables or paradigms. Both of these tasks have been discussed in the NLP and linguistics literature. Participants were further asked to complete each sub-task under a variety of different data conditions.

A total of 12 teams with members from 15 institutions participated in the shared task with a total of 27 system submissions. Of these, 11 submitted system description papers, which are included here. Consistent with last year's SIGMORPHON 2016 shared task results, neural network models performed very well in each data condition, including with a very low-resource training set. Another noteworthy aspect of the results is formed by the various biasing and data augmentation solutions that the different teams exploited to yield good performance with scarce examples.

The creation of several components in the shared task received support from DARPA I20 in the program Low Resource Languages for Emergent Incidents (LORELEI). We wish to thank Google for sponsoring an award given to the strongest overall system(s) and the organizers of CoNLL 2017 for their help. We also want to thank the participants and other members of the community who often provided thoughtful commentary on the data and the task itself.

We hope the data sets, which are now available, will serve as a useful resource to develop further techniques and research into morphological learning.

Mans Hulden, on behalf of the shared task organizers
June 2017
Boulder, CO

Organizers:

Mans Hulden (chair)	University of Colorado
Ryan Cotterell	Johns Hopkins University
Jason Eisner	Johns Hopkins University
Manaal Faruqui	Google
Christo Kirov	Johns Hopkins University
Sandra Kübler	Indiana University
John Sylak-Glassman	Johns Hopkins University
Ekaterina Vylomova	University of Melbourne
Géraldine Walther	University of Zurich
Patrick Xia	Johns Hopkins University
David Yarowsky	Johns Hopkins University

Table of Contents

Conference Program

Thursday, August 3rd, 2017

11:00–11:30   *CoNLL-SIGMORPHON 2017 Shared Task: Universal Morphological Reinflection in 52 Languages*
Ryan Cotterell, Christo Kirov, John Sylak-Glassman, Géraldine Walther, Ekaterina Vylomova, Patrick Xia, Manaal Faruqui, Sandra Kübler, David Yarowsky, Jason Eisner and Mans Hulden

11:30–12:30: Poster session: shared task systems

Training Data Augmentation for Low-Resource Morphological Inflection
Toms Bergmanis, Katharina Kann, Hinrich Schütze and Sharon Goldwater

The LMU System for the CoNLL-SIGMORPHON 2017 Shared Task on Universal Morphological Reinflection
Katharina Kann and Hinrich Schütze

Align and Copy: UZH at SIGMORPHON 2017 Shared Task for Morphological Reinflection
Peter Makarov, Tatiana Ruzsics and Simon Clematide

Morphological Inflection Generation with Multi-space Variational Encoder-Decoders
Chunting Zhou and Graham Neubig

ISI at the SIGMORPHON 2017 Shared Task on Morphological Reinflection
Abhisek Chakrabarty and Utpal Garain

Experiments on Morphological Reinflection: CoNLL-2017 Shared Task
Akhilesh Sudhakar and Anil Kumar Singh

If you can't beat them, join them: the University of Alberta system description
Garrett Nicolai, Bradley Hauer, Mohammad Motallebi, Saeed Najafi and Grzegorz Kondrak

Character Sequence-to-Sequence Model with Global Attention for Universal Morphological Reinflection
Qile Zhu, Yanjun Li and Xiaolin Li

Data Augmentation for Morphological Reinflection
Miikka Silfverberg, Adam Wiemerslage, Ling Liu and Lingshuang Jack Mao

Seq2seq for Morphological Reinflection: When Deep Learning Fails
Hajime Senuma and Akiko Aizawa

CoNLL-SIGMORPHON 2017 Shared Task:
Universal Morphological Reinflection in 52 Languages

Ryan Cotterell[1] and **Christo Kirov**[1] and **John Sylak-Glassman**[1] and
Géraldine Walther[2] and **Ekaterina Vylomova**[3] and **Patrick Xia**[1] and **Manaal Faruqui**[4]
and **Sandra Kübler**[5] and **David Yarowsky**[1] and **Jason Eisner**[1] and **Mans Hulden**[6]
Johns Hopkins University[1] University of Zurich[2] University of Melbourne[3]
Google[4] Indiana University[5] University of Colorado[6]

Abstract

The CoNLL-SIGMORPHON 2017 shared task on supervised morphological generation required systems to be trained and tested in each of 52 typologically diverse languages. In sub-task 1, submitted systems were asked to predict a specific inflected form of a given lemma. In sub-task 2, systems were given a lemma and some of its specific inflected forms, and asked to complete the inflectional paradigm by predicting all of the remaining inflected forms. Both sub-tasks included high, medium, and low-resource conditions. Sub-task 1 received 24 system submissions, while sub-task 2 received 3 system submissions. Following the success of neural sequence-to-sequence models in the SIGMORPHON 2016 shared task, all but one of the submissions included a neural component. The results show that high performance can be achieved with small training datasets, so long as models have appropriate inductive bias or make use of additional unlabeled data or synthetic data. However, different biasing and data augmentation resulted in non-identical sets of inflected forms being predicted correctly, suggesting that there is room for future improvement.

1 Introduction

Morphology interacts with both syntax and phonology. As a result, explicitly modeling morphology has been shown to aid a number of tasks in human language technology (HLT), including machine translation (MT) (Dyer et al., 2008), speech recognition (Creutz et al., 2007), parsing (Seeker and Çetinoğlu, 2015), keyword spotting (Narasimhan et al., 2014), and word embedding (Cotterell et al., 2016b). Dedicated systems for modeling morphological patterns and complex word forms have received less attention from the HLT community than tasks that target other levels of linguistic structure. Recently, however, there has been a surge of work in this area (Durrett and DeNero, 2013; Ahlberg et al., 2014; Nicolai et al., 2015; Faruqui et al., 2016), representing a renewed interest in morphology and the potential to use advances in machine learning to attack a fundamental problem in string-to-string transformations: the prediction of one morphologically complex word form from another. This increased interest in morphology as an independent set of problems within HLT arrives at a particularly opportune time, as morphology is also undergoing a methodological renewal within theoretical linguistics where it is moving towards increased interdisciplinary work and quantitative methodologies (Moscoso del Prado Martín et al., 2004; Milin et al., 2009; Ackerman et al., 2009; Sagot and Walther, 2011; Ackerman and Malouf, 2013; Baayen et al., 2013; Blevins, 2013; Pirrelli et al., 2015; Blevins, 2016). Pushing the HLT research agenda forward in the domain of morphology promises to lead to mutually highly beneficial dialogue between the two fields.

Rich morphology is the norm among the languages of the world. The linguistic typology database WALS shows that 80% of the world's languages mark verb tense through morphology while 65% mark grammatical case (Haspelmath et al., 2005). The more limited inflectional system of English may help to explain the fact that morphology has received less attention in the computational literature than it is arguably due.

The CoNLL-SIGMORPHON 2017 shared task worked to promote the development of robust systems that can learn to perform cross-linguistically

1

Proceedings of the CoNLL SIGMORPHON 2017 Shared Task: Universal Morphological Reinflection, pages 1–30,
Vancouver, Canada, August 3–4, 2017. ©2017 Association for Computational Linguistics

Lang	Lemma	Inflection	Inflected form
en	hug	V;PST	hugged
	spark	V;V.PTCP;PRS	sparking
es	liberar	V;IND;FUT;2;SG	liberarás
	descomponer	V;NEG;IMP;2;PL	no descompongáis
de	aufbauen	V;IND;PRS;2;SG	baust auf
	Ärztin	N;DAT;PL	Ärztinnen

Table 1: Example training data from sub-task 1. Each training example maps a *lemma* and *inflection* to an *inflected form*. The inflection is a bundle of *morphosyntactic features*. Note that inflected forms (and lemmata) can encompass multiple words. In the test data, the last column (the inflected form) must be predicted by the system.

Lemma	Inflections	Inflected forms
Train		
afrontar	V;IND;PST;1;PL;IPFV	afrontábamos
afrontar	V;SBJV;PST;3;PL;LGSPEC1	afrontaran
afrontar	V;NEG;IMP;2;PL	no afrontéis
afrontar	V;NEG;IMP;3;SG	no afronte
afrontar	V;COND;2;SG	afrontarías
afrontar	V;IND;FUT;3;SG	afrontará
afrontar	V;SBJV;FUT;3;PL	afrontaren
	…	
Test		
revocar	V;IND;PST;1;PL;IPFV	revocábamos
revocar	V;SBJV;PST;3;PL;LGSPEC1	—
revocar	V;NEG;IMP;2;PL	no revoquéis
revocar	V;NEG;IMP;3;SG	—
revocar	V;COND;2;SG	revocarías
revocar	V;IND;FUT;3;SG	—
revocar	V;SBJV;FUT;3;PL	—
	…	

Table 2: Example training and test data from sub-task 2 in Spanish. At training time, the system is provided with complete paradigms, i.e., tables of all inflections for a given lemma, like the example at top. At test time, the system is asked to complete partially filled paradigms, like the example at bottom; note that the inflectional features for the missing paradigm cells are provided in the input.

reliable morphological inflection and morphological paradigm cell filling using varying amounts of training data. We note that this is also the first CoNLL-hosted shared task to focus on morphology. The task itself featured training and development data from 52 languages representing a range of language families. Many of the languages included were extremely low-resource, e.g., Quechua, Navajo, and Haida. The chosen languages also encompassed diverse morphological properties and inflection processes. Whenever possible, three data conditions were given for each language: low, medium, and high. In the inflection sub-task, these corresponded to seeing 100 examples, 1,000 examples, and 10,000 examples respectively in the training data for almost all languages. The results show that encoder-decoder recurrent neural network models (RNNs) can perform very well even with small training sets, if they are augmented with various mechanisms to cope with the low-resource setting. The shared task training, development, and test data are released publicly.[1]

2 Task and Evaluation Details

This year's shared task contained two sub-tasks, which represented slightly different learning scenarios that might be faced by an HLT engineer or (roughly speaking) a human learner. Beyond manually vetted[2] data for training, development and test, monolingual corpus data (Wikipedia dumps) was also provided for both of the sub-tasks. Figure 1 illustrates the two tasks and defines some terminology.

The CoNLL-SIGMORPHON 2017 shared task is the second shared task in a series that began with the SIGMORPHON 2016 shared task on morphological reinflection (Cotterell et al., 2016a). In contrast to 2016, it happens that both of the 2017 sub-tasks actually involve only inflection, not reinflection.[3] Nonetheless, we kept "reinflection" in this year's title to make it easier to refer to the series of tasks.

2.1 Sub-Task 1: Inflected Form from Lemma

The first sub-task in Figure 1 required morphological generation with sparse training data, something that can be practically useful for MT and other downstream tasks in NLP. Here, participants were given examples of inflected forms as shown in Table 1. Each test example asked them to produce some other inflected form when given a lemma and a bundle of morphosyntactic features.

The training data was sparse in the sense that it included only a few inflected forms from each lemma. That is, as in human L1 learning, the learner does not necessarily observe any complete paradigms in a language where the paradigms are

---

[1] https://github.com/sigmorphon/conll2017

[2] Thanks to: Iñaki Alegria, Gerlof Bouma, Zygmunt Frajzyngier, Chris Harvey, Ghazaleh Kazeminejad, Jordan Lachler, Luciana Marques, and Ruben Urizar.

[3] Cotterell et al. (2016a) defined the term: "Systems developed for the 2016 Shared Task had to carry out *reinflection* of an already inflected form. This involved *analysis* of an already inflected word form, together with *synthesis* of a different inflection of that form." In 2016, sub-task 1 involved only inflection while sub-tasks 2–3 required reinflection.

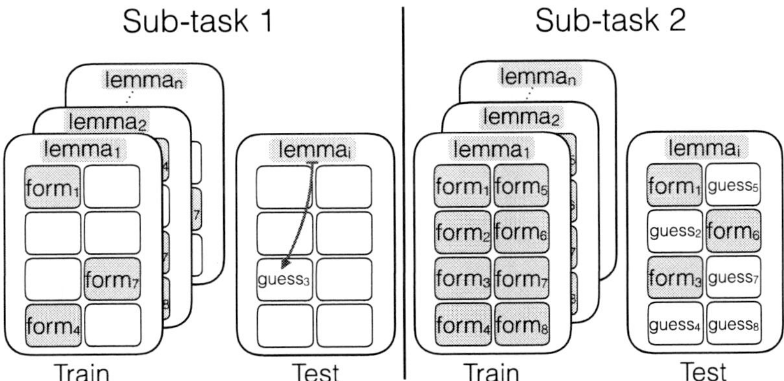

Figure 1: Overview of sub-tasks. Each large rectangle represents a **paradigm**, i.e., the full set of inflected forms for some lemma. Each small rectangle within the paradigm is a **cell** that is associated with a known morphological feature bundle, and lists a string that either is observed (shaded background) or must be predicted (white background). Sub-task 1 featured sparse training data and asked systems to inflect individual forms at test time. Sub-task 2 provides dense paradigms as training data and asks for full paradigm completion of unseen items.

large (e.g., dozens of inflected forms per lemma).[4] Key points:

1. Our sub-task 1 is similar to sub-task 1 of the SIGMORPHON 2016 shared task (Cotterell et al., 2016a), but with structured inflectional tags (Sylak-Glassman et al., 2015a), learning curve assessment, and many new typologically diverse languages, including low-resource languages.

2. The task is inflection: Given an input lemma and desired output tag, participants had to generate the correct output inflected form (a string).

3. The supervised training data consisted of individual forms (Table 1) that were sparsely sampled from a large number of paradigms.

4. Forms that are empirically more frequent were more likely to appear in both training and test data (see §3 for details)

5. Unannotated corpus data was also provided to participants.

6. Systems were evaluated after training on 10^2, 10^3, and 10^4 forms.

---

[4] Of course, human L1 learners do not get to observe explicit morphological feature bundles for the types that they observe. Rather, they analyze inflected tokens in context to discover both morphological features (including *inherent* features such as noun gender (Arnon and Ramscar, 2012)) and paradigmatic structure (number of forms per lemma, number of expressed featural contrasts such as tense, number, person...).

2.2 Sub-Task 2: Paradigm Completion

The second sub-task in Figure 1 focused on paradigm completion, also known as "the paradigm cell filling problem" (Ackerman et al., 2009).

Here, participants were given a few complete inflectional paradigms as training data. At test time, partially filled paradigms, i.e. paradigms with significant gaps in them, were to be completed by filling out the missing cells. Table 2 gives examples.

Thus, sub-task 2 requires predicting many inflections of the same lemma. Recall that sub-task 1 also required the system to predict several inflections of the same lemma (when they appear as separate examples in test data). However, in sub-task 2, one of our test-time evaluation metrics (§2.3) is full-paradigm accuracy. Also, the sub-task 2 training data provides full paradigms, in contrast to sub-task 1 where it included only a few inflected forms per lemma. Finally, at test time, sub-task 2 presents each lemma along with some of its inflected forms, which is potentially helpful if the lemma had not appeared previously in training data.

Apart from the theoretical interest in this problem (Ackerman and Malouf, 2013), this sub-task is grounded in the practical problem of extrapolation of basic resources for a language, where only a few complete paradigms may be available from a native speaker informant (Sylak-Glassman et al., 2016) or a reference grammar. L2 classroom instruction also asks human students to memorize example paradigms and generalize from them.

Key points:

1. The training data consisted of complete paradigms.

2. Not all paradigms within a language have the same shape. A noun lemma will have a different set of cells than a verb lemma does, and verbs of different classes (e.g., lexically perfective vs. imperfective) may also have different sets of cells.

3. The task was paradigm completion: given a sparsely populated paradigm, participants should generate the inflected forms (strings) for all missing cells.

4. The task simulates learning from compiled grammatical resources and inflection tables, or learning from a limited time with a native-language informant in a fieldwork scenario.

5. Three training sets were given, building up in size from only a few complete paradigms to a large number (dozens).

2.3 Evaluation

Each team participating in a given sub-task was asked to submit 156 versions of their system, where each version was trained using a different training set (3 training sizes $\times$ 52 languages) and its corresponding development set. We evaluated each submitted system on its corresponding test set, i.e., the test set for its language.

We computed three evaluation metrics: (i) Overall 1-best test-set accuracy, i.e., *is the predicted paradigm cell correct?* (ii) average Levenshtein distance, i.e., *how badly does the predicted form disagree with the answer?* (iii) Full-paradigm accuracy, i.e., *is the complete paradigm correct?* This final metric only truly makes sense in sub-task 2, where full paradigms are given for evaluation. For each sub-task, the three data conditions (low, medium, and high) resulted in a learning curve. For each system in each condition, we report the average metrics across all 52 languages.

3 Data

3.1 Languages

The data for the shared task was highly multilingual, comprising 52 unique languages. Data for 47 of the languages came from the English edition of Wiktionary, a large multi-lingual crowd-sourced dictionary containing morphological paradigms for many lemmata.[5] Data for Khaling, Kurmanji Kurdish, and Sorani Kurdish was created as part of the Alexina project (Walther et al., 2013, 2010; Walther and Sagot, 2010).[6] Novel data for Haida, a severely endangered North American language isolate, was prepared by Jordan Lachler (University of Alberta). The Basque language data was extracted from a manually designed finite-state morphological analyzer (Alegria et al., 2009).

The shared task language set is genealogically diverse, including languages from 10 language stocks. Although the majority of the languages are Indo-European, we also include two language isolates (Haida and Basque) along with languages from Athabaskan (Navajo), Kartvelian (Georgian), Quechua, Semitic (Arabic, Hebrew), Sino-Tibetan (Khaling), Turkic (Turkish), and Uralic (Estonian, Finnish, Hungarian, and Northern Sami). The shared task language set is also diverse in terms of morphological structure, with languages which use primarily prefixes (Navajo), suffixes (Quechua and Turkish), and a mix, with Spanish exhibiting internal vowel variations along with suffixes and Georgian using both infixes and suffixes. The language set also exhibits features such as templatic morphology (Arabic, Hebrew), vowel harmony (Turkish, Finnish, Hungarian), and consonant harmony (Navajo) which require systems to learn non-local alternations. Finally, the resource level of the languages in the shared task set varies greatly, from major world languages (e.g. Arabic, English, French, Spanish, Russian) to languages with few speakers (e.g. Haida, Khaling).

3.2 Data Format

For each language, the basic data consists of triples of the form (lemma, feature bundle, inflected form), as in Table 1. The first feature in the bundle always specifies the core part of speech (e.g., verb). All features in the bundle are coded according to the UniMorph Schema, a cross-linguistically consistent universal morphological feature set (Sylak-Glassman et al., 2015a,b).

---

[5] https://en.wiktionary.org/ (08-2016 snapshot)

[6] https://gforge.inria.fr/projects/alexina/

3.3 Extraction from Wiktionary

For each of the 47 Wiktionary languages, Wiktionary provides a number of tables, each of which specifies the full inflectional paradigm for a particular lemma. These tables were initially extracted via a multi-dimensional table parsing strategy (Kirov et al., 2016; Sylak-Glassman et al., 2015a).

As noted in §2.2, different paradigms may have different shapes. To prepare the shared task data, each language's parsed tables from Wiktionary were grouped according to their tabular structure and number of cells. Each group represents a different type of paradigm (e.g., verb). We used only groups with a large number of lemmata, relative to the number of lemmata available for the language as a whole. For each group, we associated a feature bundle with each cell position in the table, by manually replacing the prose labels describing grammatical features (e.g. "accusative case") with UniMorph features (e.g. acc). This allowed us to extract triples as described in the previous section.

By applying this process across the 47 languages, we constructed a large multilingual dataset that refines the parsed tables from previous work. This dataset was sampled to create appropriately-sized data for the shared task, as described in §3.4.[7] Full and sampled dataset sizes by language are given in Table 3.

Systematic syncretism is collapsed in Wiktionary. For example, in English, feature bundles do not distinguish between different person/number forms of past tense verbs, because they are identical.[8] Thus, the past-tense form went appears only once in the table for go, not six times, and gives rise to only one triple, whose feature bundle specifies past tense but not person and number.

3.4 Sampling the Train-Dev-Test Splits

From each language's collection of paradigms, we sampled the training, development, and test sets as follows. These datasets can be obtained from http://www.sigmorphon.org/conll2017.

Our first step was to construct probability distributions over the (lemma, feature bundle, inflected form) triples in our full dataset. For each triple, we counted how many tokens the inflected form has in the February 2017 dump of Wikipedia for that language. Note that this simple "string match" heuristic overestimates the count, since strings are ambiguous: not all of the counted tokens actually render that feature bundle.[9]

From these counts, we estimated a unigram distribution over triples, using Laplace smoothing (add-1 smoothing). We then sampled 12000 triples without replacement from this distribution. The first 100 were taken as the low-resource training set for sub-task 1, the first 1000 as the medium-resource training set, and the first 10000 as the high-resource training set. Note that these training sets are nested, and that the highest-count triples tend to appear in the smaller training sets.

The final 2000 triples were randomly shuffled and then split in half to obtain development and test sets of 1000 forms each. The final shuffling was performed to ensure that the development set is similar to the test set. By contrast, the development and test sets tend to contain lower-count triples than the training set.[10] In those languages where we have less than 12000 total forms, we omit the high-resource training set (all languages have at least 3000 forms).

To sample the data for sub-task 2, we perform a similar procedure. For each paradigm in our full dataset, we counted the number of tokens in Wikipedia that matched any of the inflected forms in the paradigm. From these counts, we estimated a unigram distribution over paradigms, using Laplace smoothing. We sampled 300 paradigms without replacement from this

---

[7]Full, unsampled Wiktionary parses are made available at unimorph.org on a rolling basis.

[8]In this example, Wiktionary omits the single exception: the lemma be distinguishes between past tenses was and were.

[9]For example, in English, any token of the string walked will be double-counted as both the past tense and the past participle of the lemma walk. This problem holds for all regular English verbs. Similarly, when we are counting the present-tense tokens lay of the lemma lay, we will also include tokens of the string lay that are actually the past tense of lie, or are actually the adjective or noun senses of lay. The alternative to double-counting each ambiguous token would have been to use EM to split the token's count of 1 unequally among its possible analyses, in proportion to their estimated prior probabilities (Cotterell et al., 2015).

[10]This is a realistic setting, since supervised training is usually employed to generalize from frequent words that appear in annotated resources to less frequent words that do not. Unsupervised learning methods also tend to generalize from more frequent words (which can be analyzed more easily by combining information from many contexts) to less frequent ones.

distribution. The low-resource training sets contain the first 10 paradigms, the medium-resource training set contains the first 50, and high-resource training set contains the first 200. Again, these training sets are nested. Note that since different languages have paradigms of different sizes, the actual number of training exemplars may differ drastically.

With the same motivation as before, we shuffled the remaining 100 forms and took the first 50 as development and the next 50 as test. (In those languages with fewer than 300 forms, we again omitted the high-resource training setting.) For each development or test paradigm, we chose about $\frac{1}{5}$ of the slots to provide to the system as input along with the lemma, asking the system to predict the remaining $\frac{4}{5}$. We determined which cells to keep by independently flipping a biased coin with probability 0.2 for each cell.

Because of the count overestimates mentioned above, our sub-task 1 dataset overrepresents triples where the inflected form (the answer) is ambiguous, and our sub-task 2 dataset overrepresents paradigms that contain ambiguous inflected forms. The degree of ambiguity varied among languages: the average number of triples per inflected form string ranged from 1.00 in Sorani to 2.89 in Khaling, with an average of 1.43 across all languages. Despite this distortion of true unigram counts, we believe that our datasets captured a sufficiently broad sample of the feature combinations for every language.

4   Previous Work

Most recent work in inflection generation has focused on sub-task 1, i.e., generating inflected forms from the lemma. Numerous, methodologically diverse approaches have been published. We highlight a representative sample of recent work. Durrett and DeNero (2013) heuristically extracted transformation rules and trained a semi-Markov model (Sarawagi and Cohen, 2004) to learn when to apply them to the input. Nicolai et al. (2015) trained a discriminative string-to-string monotonic transduction tool—DIRECTL+ (Jiampojamarn et al., 2008)—to generate inflections. Ahlberg et al. (2014) reduced the problem to multi-class classification, where they used finite-state techniques to first generalize inflectional patterns and then trained a feature-rich classifier to choose the optimal such pattern to inflect

unseen words (Ahlberg et al., 2015). Finally, Malouf (2016), Faruqui et al. (2016) and Kann and Schütze (2016) proposed a neural-based sequence-to-sequence models (Sutskever et al., 2014), with Kann and Schütze making use of an attention mechanism (Bahdanau et al., 2015). Overall, the neural approaches have generally been found to be the most successful.

Some work has also focused on scenarios similar to sub-task 2. For example, Dreyer and Eisner (2009) modeled the distribution over the paradigms of a language as a Markov Random Field (MRF), where each cell is represented as a string-valued random variable. The MRF's factors are specified as weighted finite-state machines of the form given by Dreyer et al. (2008). Building upon this, Cotterell et al. (2015) proposed using a Bayesian network where both lemmata (repeated within a paradigm) and affixes (repeated across paradigms) were encoded as string-valued random variables. That work required its finite-state transducers to take a more restricted form (Cotterell et al., 2014) for computational reasons. Finally, Kann et al. (2017a) proposed a multi-source sequence-to-sequence network, allowing a neural transducer to exploit multiple source forms simultaneously.

SIGMORPHON 2016 Shared Task.   Last year, the SIGMORPHON 2016 shared task (`http://sigmorphon.org/sharedtask`) focused on 10 languages (including 2 surprise languages). As for the present 2017 task, most of the 2016 data was derived from Wiktionary. The 2016 shared task had submissions from 9 competing teams with members from 11 universities. As mentioned in §2.1, our sub-task 1 is an extension of sub-task 1 from 2016. The other sub-tasks in 2016 focused on the more general reinflection problem, where systems had to learn to map from any inflected form to any other with varying degrees of annotations. See Cotterell et al. (2016a) for details.

5   The Baseline System

The shared task provided a baseline system to participants that addressed both tasks and all languages. The system was designed for speed of application and also for adequate accuracy with little training data, in particular in the low and medium data conditions. The design of the baseline was inspired by the University of Colorado's submission (Liu and Mao, 2016) to the SIGMORPHON 2016

Language	Family	Lemmata / Forms	High	Medium	Low	Dev	Test	Pr	Su	Ap
Albanian	Indo-European	589 / 33483	587	379	82	384	369	56.24	95.14	1.09
Arabic	Semitic	4134 / 140003	3181	811	96	809	831	54.64	90.89	31.61
Armenian	Indo-European	7033 / 338461	4657	907	99	875	902	22.81	94.27	1.78
Basque	Isolate	26 / 11889	26	26	22	26	22	97.63	92.07	12.87
Bengali†	Indo-Aryan	136 / 4443	136	134	65	65	68	0.04	94.98	17.59
Bulgarian	Slavic	2468 / 55730	2133	716	98	742	744	15.65	92.09	4.28
Catalan	Romance	1547 / 81576	1545	742	96	744	733	0.41	98.04	6.89
Czech	Slavic	5125 / 134527	3862	836	98	852	850	8.73	87.07	0.99
Danish	Germanic	3193 / 25503	3148	875	100	869	865	0.17	81.52	1.28
Dutch	Germanic	4993 / 55467	4146	895	99	899	899	3.06	80.61	4.30
English	Germanic	22765 / 115523	8377	989	100	985	983	0.06	79.00	0.79
Estonian	Uralic	886 / 38215	886	587	94	553	577	25.94	95.70	10.18
Faroese	Germanic	3077 / 45474	2967	842	100	839	880	0.66	80.52	12.93
Finnish	Uralic	57642 / 2490377	8668	981	100	984	986	31.47	94.47	10.57
French	Romance	7535 / 367732	5588	941	98	940	943	2.79	97.78	3.95
Georgian	Kartvelian	3782 / 74412	3537	861	100	872	874	3.28	94.70	0.42
German	Germanic	15060 / 179339	6767	959	100	964	964	5.03	65.83	5.01
Haida†	Isolate	41 / 7040	41	41	40	34	38	0.26	98.96	0.49
Hebrew	Semitic	510 / 13818	510	470	95	431	453	43.58	78.96	2.40
Hindi	Indo-Aryan	258 / 54438	258	252	85	254	255	8.16	98.65	11.14
Hungarian	Uralic	13989 / 490394	7097	966	100	967	964	0.52	97.00	0.52
Icelandic	Germanic	4775 / 76915	4108	899	100	906	899	0.56	84.54	9.28
Irish	Celtic	7464 / 107298	5040	906	99	913	893	55.09	61.60	4.47
Italian	Romance	10009 / 509574	6365	953	100	940	936	18.81	92.38	20.92
Khaling	Sino-Tibetan	591 / 156097	584	426	92	411	422	76.39	99.04	24.87
Kurmanji Kurdish	Iranian	15083 / 216370	7046	945	100	949	958	9.62	91.43	0.90
Latin	Romance	17214 / 509182	6517	943	100	939	945	4.12	90.04	47.74
Latvian	Baltic	7548 / 136998	5293	923	100	920	924	3.69	91.50	2.91
Lithuanian	Baltic	1458 / 34130	1443	632	96	664	639	3.64	90.58	35.32
Lower Sorbian	Germanic	994 / 20121	994	626	96	625	630	0.24	93.33	0.48
Macedonian	Slavic	10313 / 168057	6079	958	100	939	946	1.15	90.56	0.53
Navajo	Athabaskan	674 / 12354	674	496	91	491	491	79.03	35.08	21.49
Northern Sami	Uralic	2103 / 62677	1964	745	93	738	744	4.62	90.39	18.12
Norwegian Bokmål	Germanic	5527 / 19238	5041	925	100	928	930	0.19	92.77	2.08
Norwegian Nynorsk	Germanic	4689 / 15319	4413	915	98	914	919	0.35	88.59	1.98
Persian	Iranian	273 / 37128	273	269	82	268	267	27.1	95.28	15.70
Polish	Slavic	10185 / 201024	5926	929	99	934	942	5.24	91.68	1.79
Portuguese	Romance	4001 / 303996	3668	902	100	872	865	0.01	93.26	3.19
Quechua	Quechuan	1006 / 180004	963	521	93	495	526	1.25	98.92	0.05
Romanian	Romance	4405 / 80266	3351	858	99	854	828	22.40	87.65	4.78
Russian	Slavic	28068 / 473481	8186	974	100	980	980	5.20	79.88	11.33
Scottish Gaelic†	Celtic	73 / 781	—	73	58	36	40	38.03	42.73	4.85
Serbo-Croatian	Slavic	24419 / 840799	6746	964	100	971	954	16.75	89.84	9.64
Slovak	Slavic	1046 / 14796	1046	631	93	622	622	0.48	88.21	1.55
Slovene	Slavic	2535 / 60110	2007	769	100	746	762	1.19	88.90	4.95
Sorani Kurdish	Iranian	274 / 22990	263	197	74	198	199	67.89	94.76	15.21
Spanish	Romance	5460 / 382955	4621	906	99	902	922	11.34	98.43	5.13
Swedish	Germanic	10553 / 78411	6511	962	99	956	962	0.36	81.82	0.79
Turkish	Turkic	3579 / 275460	2934	834	99	852	840	0.22	98.30	0.99
Ukrainian	Slavic	1493 / 20904	1490	722	98	744	729	1.89	84.75	5.19
Urdu	Indo-Aryan	182 / 12572	182	111	55	101	106	8.01	95.93	8.10
Welsh	Celtic	183 / 10641	183	183	76	80	78	1.98	96.90	7.31

Table 3: Total number of lemmata and forms available for sampling, and number of distinct lemmata present in each data condition in Task 1. For almost all languages, these were spread across 10000, 1000, and 100 forms in the High, Medium, and Low conditions, respectively, and 1000 forms in each Dev and Test set. For †-marked languages, there was not enough total data to support these numbers. Bengali had 4423 forms in the High condition, and Dev and Test sets of 100 forms each. Haida had 6840 forms in the High condition and Dev and Test sets of 100 forms. Scottish Gaelic had no High condition, a Medium condition of 681 forms, and Dev and Test sets of 50 forms each. The three last columns indicate how many inflected forms have undergone changes in a prefix (Pr), a change in a suffix (Su), or a stem-internal change (Ap) versus the given lemma form.

Language Name	ADJ	N	V
Albanian	–	10-20	123
Arabic	40-48	12-36	61-115
Armenian	17-34	17-34	154-155
Basque	–	–	112-810
Bengali	–	9-12	51
Bulgarian	30	4-8	–
Catalan	–	–	50-53
Czech	25-35	14	30
Danish	–	6	8
Dutch	3-9	–	16
English	–	–	7
Estonian	–	30	79
Faroese	17	8-16	12
Finnish	28	13-28	141
French	–	–	49
Georgian	19	19	–
German	–	4-8	29
Haida	–	–	41-176
Hebrew	–	30	23-28
Hindi	–	–	219
Hungarian	–	17-34	–
Icelandic	–	8-16	28
Irish	13	7-13	65
Italian	–	–	47-51
Khaling	–	–	45-382
Kurmanji Kurdish	1-2	1-14	83
Latin	18-31	8-12	99
Latvian	20-24	7-14	49-50
Lithuanian	28-76	7-14	63
Lower Sorbian	33	18	21
Macedonian	16	5-11	20-29
Navajo	–	8	6-50
Northern Sami	13	13	45-54
Norwegian Bokmål	2-5	1-3	3-9
Norwegian Nynorsk	1-5	1-3	8
Persian	–	–	140
Polish	28	7-14	47
Portuguese	–	–	74-76
Quechua	256	256	41
Romanian	8-16	5-6	37
Russian	26-30	6-14	15-16
Scottish Gaelic	12	–	8
Serbo-Croatian	1-43	2-14	63
Slovak	27	6-12	–
Slovene	53	6-18	22
Sorani Kurdish	1-15	1-28	95-186
Spanish	–	–	70
Swedish	5-15	4-8	11
Turkish	72	12-108	120
Ukrainian	26	7-14	17-24
Urdu	–	6	219
Welsh	–	–	20-65

Table 4: Quantity of data available in sub-task 2. For each possible part of speech in each language, we present the range in the number of forms that comprise a paradigm as an indication of the difficulty of the task of forming a full paradigm. These ranges were computed using the data in the Train Medium condition.

shared task.

5.1 Alignment

For each (lemma, feature bundle, inflected form) triple in training data, the system initially aligns the lemma with the inflected form by finding the minimum-cost edit path. Costs are computed with a weighted scheme such that substitutions have a slightly higher cost (1.1) than insertions or deletions (1.0). For example, the German training data pair `schielen-geschielt` 'to squint' (going from the lemma to the past participle) is aligned as:

```
--schielen
geschielt-
```

The system now assumes that each aligned pair can be broken up into a prefix, stem and a suffix, based on where the inputs or outputs have initial or trailing blanks after alignment. We assume that initial or trailing blanks in either input or output reflect boundaries between a prefix and a stem, or a stem and a suffix. This allows us to divide each training example into three parts. Using the example above, the pairs would be aligned as follows, after padding the edges with \$-symbols:

prefix	stem	suffix
\$	schiele	n\$
\$ge	schielt	\$

5.2 Inflection Rules

From this alignment, the system extracts a prefix-changing rule based on the prefix pairing, as well as a set of suffix-changing rules based on suffixes of the stem+suffix pairing. The example alignment above yields the eight extracted suffix-modifying rules

```
n$ → $            ielen$ → ielt$
en$ → t$          hielen$ → hielt$
len$ → lt$        chielen$ → chielt$
elen$ → elt$      schielen$ → schielt$
```

as well as the prefix-modifying rule \$ → \$ge.

Since these rules were obtained from the triple (`schielen`, **V;V.PTCP;PST**, `geschielt`), they are associated with a token of the feature bundle **V;V.PTCP;PST**.

5.3 Generation

At test time, to inflect a lemma with features, the baseline system applies rules associated with

Team	Institute(s)	System Description Paper
CLUZH	University of Zurich	Makarov et al. (2017)
CMU	Carnegie Mellon University	Zhou and Neubig (2017a)
CU	University of Colorado Boulder	Silfverberg et al. (2017)
EHU	University of the Basque Country	Alegria and Etxeberria (2016)*
IIT (BHU)	Birla Institute of Technology and Science / Indian Institute of Technology (BHU) Varanasi	Sudhakar and Singh (2017)
ISI	Indian Statistical Institute	Chakrabarty and Garain (2017)
LMU	Ludwig-Maximilian University of Munich	Kann and Schütze (2017)
SU-RUG	Stockholm University / University of Groningen	Östling and Bjerva (2017)
UA	University of Alberta	Nicolai et al. (2017)
UE-LMU	University of Edinburgh / Ludwig-Maximilian University of Munich	Bergmanis et al. (2017)
UF	University of Florida	Zhu et al. (2017)
UTNII	National Institute of Informatics / University of Tokyo	Senuma and Aizawa (2017)

Table 5: The teams' abbreviations as well as their members' institutes and the accompanying system description paper are listed here. Note that in the main text the abbreviations are used with a integer index, indicating the specific submission. One team (marked ∗), did not submit a system description.

training tokens of the precise feature bundle. There is no generalization across bundles that share features.

Specifically, the longest-matching suffix rule associated with the feature bundle is consulted and applied to the input form. Ties are broken by frequency, in favor of the rule that has occurred most often with this feature bundle. After this, the prefix rule that occurred most often with the bundle is likewise applied. That is, the prefix-matching rule has no longest-match preference, while the suffix-matching rule does.

For example, to inflect `kaufen` 'to buy' with the features V;V.PTCP;PST, using the single example above as training data, we would find that the longest matching stored suffix-rule is `en$` → `t$`, which would transform `kaufen` into an intermediate form `kauft`, after which the most frequent prefix-rule, `$` → `$ge` would produce the final output `gekauft`. If no rules have been associated with a particular feature bundle (as often happens in the low data condition), the inflected form is simply taken to be a copy of the lemma.

In sub-task 2, paradigm completion, the baseline system simply repeats the sub-task 1 method and generates all the missing forms independently from the lemma. It does not take advantage of the other forms that are presented in the partially filled paradigm.

In addition to the above, the baseline system uses a heuristic to place a language into one of two categories: largely prefixing or largely suffixing. Some languages, such as Navajo, are largely prefixing and have more complex changes in the left periphery of the input rather than at the right. However, in the method described above, the operation of the prefix rules is more restricted than that of the suffix rules: prefix rules tend to perform no change at all, or insert or delete a prefix. For largely prefixing languages, the method performs better when operating with reversed strings. Classifying a language into prefixing or suffixing is done by simply counting how often there is a prefix change vs. suffix change in going from the lemma form to the inflected form in the training data. Whenever a language is found to be largely prefixing, the system works with reversed strings throughout to allow more expressive changes in the left edge of the input.

6 System Descriptions

The CoNLL-SIGMORPHON 2017 shared task received submissions from 11 teams with members from 15 universities and institutes (Table 5). Many of the teams submitted more than one system, yielding a total of 25 unique systems entered including the baseline system.

In contrast to the 2016 shared task, all but one of the submitted systems included a neural component. Despite the relative uniformity of the sub-

	Neural	Hard	Rerank	Data+
baseline	✗	✓	✗	✗
CLUZH	✓	✓	✗	✗
CMU	✓	✗	✗	✓
CU	✓	✗	✗	✓
EHU	✗	✓	✗	✗
IIT (BHU)	✓	✗	✗	✓
ISI	✓	✗	✓	✗
LMU	✓	✗	✗	✓
SU-RUG	✓	✗	✗	✗
UA	✓	✓	✓	✓
UE-LMU	✓	✗	✗	✓
UF	✓	✗	✗	✗
UTNII	✓	✗	✗	✗

Table 6: Features of the various submitted systems.

mitted architectures, we still observed large differences in the individual performances. Rather than differences in architecture, a major difference this year was the various methods for supplying the neural network with auxiliary training data. For ease of presentation, we break down the systems into the features of their system (see Table 6) and discuss the systems that had those features. In all cases, further details of the methods can be found in the system description papers, which are cited in Table 5.

Neural Parameterization. All systems except for the EHU team employed some form of a neural network. Moreover, all teams except for SU-RUG, which employed a convolutional neural network, made use of some form of gated recurrent network—either a gated recurrent network (GRU) (Chung et al., 2014) or long short-term memory (LSTM) (Hochreiter and Schmidhuber, 1997). In these neural models, a common strategy was to feed in the morphological tag of the form to be predicted along with the input into the network, where each subtag was its own symbol.

Hard Alignment versus Soft Attention. Another axis, along which the systems differ is the use of hard alignment, over soft attention. The neural attention mechanism was introduced in Bahdanau et al. (2015) for neural machine translation (NMT). In short, these mechanisms avoid the necessity of encoding the input word into a fixed length vector, by allowing the decoder to attend to different parts of the inputs. Just as in NMT, the attention mechanism has led to large gains in mor-

phological inflection. The CMU, CU, IIT (BHU), LMU, UE-LMU, UF and UTNII systems all employed such mechanisms.

An alternative to soft attention is hard, monotonic alignment, i.e., a neural parameterization of a traditional finite-state transduction system. These systems enforce a monotonic alignment between source and target forms. In the 2016 shared task (see Cotterell et al., 2016a, Table 6) such a system placed second (Aharoni et al., 2016), and this year's winning system—CLUZH—was an extension of that one. (See, also, Aharoni and Goldberg (2017) for a further explication of the technique and Rastogi et al. (2016) for discussion of a related neural parameterization of a weighted finite-state machine.) Their system allows for explicit biasing towards a copy action that appears useful in the low-resource setting. Despite its neural parameterization, the CLUZH system is most closely related to the systems of UA and EHU, which train weighted finite-state transducers, albeit with a log-linear parameterization.

Reranking. Reranking the output of a weaker system was a tack taken by two systems: ISI and UA. The ISI system started with a heuristically induced candidate set, using the edit tree approach described by Chrupała et al. (2008), and then chose the best edit tree. This approach is effectively a neuralized version of the lemmatizer proposed in Müller et al. (2015) and, indeed, was originally intended for that task (Chakrabarty et al., 2017). The UA team, following their 2016 submission, proposed a linear reranking on top of the k-best output of their transduction system.

Data Augmentation. Many teams made use of auxiliary training data—unlabeled or synthetic forms. Some teams leveraged the provided Wikipedia corpora (see §3). The UE-LMU team used these unlabeled corpora to bias their methods towards copying by transducing an unlabeled word to itself. The same team also explored a similar setup that instead learned to transduce *random* strings to themselves, and found that using random strings worked almost as well as words that appeared in unlabeled corpora. CMU used a variational autoencoder and treated the tags of unannotated words in the Wikipedia corpus as latent variables (see Zhou and Neubig (2017b) for more details). Other teams attempted to get silver-standard labels for the unlabeled corpora. For example,

	High	Medium	Low
UE-LMU-1	**95.32/0.10**	81.02/0.41	—/—
CLUZH-7	95.12/0.10	**82.80/0.34**	**50.61/1.29**
CLUZH-6	95.12/0.10	**82.80/0.34**	**50.61/1.29**
CLUZH-2	94.95/0.10	81.80/0.37	46.82/1.38
LMU-2	94.70/0.11	82.64/0.35	46.59/1.56
LMU-1	94.70/0.11	82.64/0.35	45.29/1.62
CLUZH-5	94.69/0.11	81.00/0.39	48.24/1.48
CLUZH-1	94.47/0.12	80.88/0.39	45.99/1.43
SU-RUG-1	93.56/0.14	—/—	—/—
CU-1	92.97/0.17	77.60/0.50	45.74/1.62
UTNII-1	91.46/0.17	65.06/0.73	1.28/5.71
CLUZH-4	89.53/0.23	80.33/0.41	48.53/1.52
IIT(BHU)-1	89.38/0.22	50.73/1.69	13.88/4.54
CLUZH-3	89.10/0.24	79.57/0.44	47.95/1.55
UF-1	87.33/0.27	68.82/0.78	27.46/2.70
CMU-1†	86.56/0.28	68.00/0.86‡	—/—
ISI-1	74.01/0.78	54.47/1.39	26.00/2.43
EHU-1	64.38/0.72‡	38.50/1.70‡	3.50/3.23‡
UE-LMU-2†	—/—	82.37/0.39	—/—
IIT(BHU)-2	—/—	55.46/1.78	14.27/4.33
UA-3†	—/—	—/—	57.70/1.34‡
UA-4†	—/—	—/—	57.52/1.36‡
UA-1	—/—	—/—	54.22/1.66‡
UA-2	—/—	—/—	42.85/2.23‡
baseline	77.81/0.50	64.70/0.90	37.90/2.15
oracle-fc	99.99/*	97.76/*	70.84/*
oracle-e	98.25/*	92.10/*	64.56/*

Table 7: Sub-task 1 results: Per-form accuracy (in %age points) and average Levenshtein distance from the correct form (in characters), averaged across the 52 languages with all languages weighted equally. The columns represent the different training size conditions. Systems marked with † used external resources. Accuracies marked with ‡ indicate that the submission did not include all 52 languages and should not be compared to the other accuracies.

	High	Medium	Low
LMU-2	**88.52/0.22**	**82.02/0.38**	**67.76/0.75**
LMU-1	87.40/0.24	77.02/0.47	54.74/1.22
CU-1	67.77/0.75	60.94/1.03	47.89/1.67
baseline	76.87/0.51	65.84/0.83	50.14/1.28
oracle-e	94.11/*	88.70/*	75.84/*

Table 8: Sub-task 2 results: Per-form accuracy (in %age points) and average Levenshtein distance from the correct form (in characters).

the UA team trained a tagger on the given training examples, and then tagged the corpus with the goal to obtain additional instances, while the UE-LMU team used a series of unsupervised heuristics. The CU team—which did not make use of external resources—hallucinated more training data by identifying suffix and prefix changes in the given training pairs and then using that information to create new artificial training pairs. The LMU submission also experimented with handwritten rules to artificially generate more data. It seems likely that the primary difference in the performance of the various neural systems lay in these strategies for the creation of new data to train the parameters, rather than in the neural architectures themselves.

7 Performance of the Systems

Relative system performance is described in Tables 7 and 8, which show the average per-language accuracy of each system by resource condition, for each of the sub-tasks. The table reflects the fact that some teams submitted more than one system (e.g. LMU-1 & LMU-2 in the table). Learning curves for each language across conditions are shown in Table 9, which indicates the best per-form accuracy achieved by a submitted system. Full results can be found in Appendix A, including full-paradigm accuracy.

Three teams exploited external resources in some form: UA, CMU, and UE-LMU. In general, any relative performance gained was minimal. The CMU system was outranked by several systems that avoided external resource use in the High and Medium conditions in which it competed. UE-LMU only submitted a system that used additional resources in the Medium condition, and saw gains of ~%1 compared to their basic system, while it was still outranked overall by CLUZH. In the Low condition, UA saw gains of ~%3 using external data. However, all UA submissions were limited to a small handful of languages.

All but one of the systems submitted were neural. As expected given the results from SIGMORPHON 2016, these systems perform very well when in the High training condition where data is relatively plentiful. In the Low and Medium conditions, however, standard encoder-decoder architectures perform worse than the baseline using only the training data provided. Teams that beat the baseline succeeded by biasing networks towards the correct solutions through pre-training on synthetic data designed to capture the overall inflectional patterns in a language. As seen in Table 9, these techniques worked better for some languages than for others. Languages with smaller, more regular paradigms were handled well (e.g., English sub-task 1 low-resource accuracy was at

	Sub-task 1			Sub-task 2		
	High	Medium	Low	High	Medium	Low
Albanian	99.00(UE-LMU)	89.40(CU-1)	31.00(CU-1)	98.35(LMU-2)	88.81(LMU-1)	66.63(LMU-2)
Arabic	94.50(CLUZH-7)	79.70(LMU-2)	37.00(CLUZH-7)	95.48(LMU-2)	90.21(LMU-2)	80.43(LMU-2)
Armenian	97.50(UE-LMU)	91.50(LMU-2)	58.70(CLUZH-7)	98.78(LMU-2)	97.77(LMU-2)	93.92(LMU-2)
Basque	100.00(UTNII-1)	89.00(UE-LMU)	20.00(LMU-2)	—	94.14(LMU-2)	93.02(LMU-2)
Bengali	100.00(UE-LMU)	99.00(CLUZH-1)	68.00(CLUZH-3)	92.61(LMU-1)	91.72(LMU-2)	90.19(LMU-2)
Bulgarian	98.10(UE-LMU)	82.50(LMU-2)	57.10(CU-1)	85.93(LMU-2)	55.95(LMU-2)	49.58(LMU-2)
Catalan	98.40(CLUZH-1)	92.60(CLUZH-7)	66.40(CU-1)	99.35(LMU-2)	97.06(LMU-2)	94.16(baseline)
Czech	94.10(UE-LMU)	86.30(CU-1)	44.00(CLUZH-7)	86.00(LMU-1)	58.61(LMU-2)	34.96(LMU-2)
Danish	94.50(UE-LMU)	83.60(LMU-2)	75.50(CLUZH-7)	75.74(LMU-2)	71.15(baseline)	53.11(CU-1)
Dutch	96.90(UE-LMU)	86.50(LMU-2)	53.60(baseline)	89.30(LMU-2)	86.53(LMU-2)	56.64(LMU-2)
English	97.20(UE-LMU)	94.70(LMU-2)	90.60(UA-1)	91.60(baseline)	84.00(baseline)	84.40(CU-1)
Estonian	98.90(UE-LMU)	82.40(UE-LMU)	32.90(LMU-2)	97.90(LMU-2)	92.43(LMU-2)	77.42(LMU-2)
Faroese	87.80(CLUZH-7)	68.10(CLUZH-7)	42.40(CLUZH-7)	71.90(LMU-2)	68.31(LMU-2)	57.55(LMU-2)
Finnish	95.10(UE-LMU)	78.40(UE-LMU)	19.70(CLUZH-7)	93.67(LMU-2)	89.48(LMU-2)	76.30(LMU-2)
French	89.50(UE-LMU)	80.30(CLUZH-7)	66.00(CLUZH-7)	98.83(LMU-2)	95.38(LMU-2)	87.45(LMU-2)
Georgian	99.40(LMU-2)	93.40(CLUZH-7)	85.60(LMU-2)	96.20(LMU-2)	89.67(LMU-2)	86.82(LMU-2)
German	93.00(UE-LMU)	80.00(CLUZH-4)	68.10(CLUZH-4)	85.88(LMU-2)	77.56(LMU-2)	74.66(LMU-2)
Haida	99.00(UTNII-1)	95.00(LMU-2)	46.00(LMU-2)	—	96.40(LMU-2)	95.24(LMU-2)
Hebrew	99.50(LMU-2)	83.80(LMU-2)	35.40(CU-1)	93.42(LMU-2)	85.59(LMU-2)	68.06(LMU-2)
Hindi	100.00(UTNII-1)	97.40(CLUZH-3)	75.50(LMU-2)	99.95(LMU-2)	95.01(LMU-2)	93.84(LMU-2)
Hungarian	86.80(CLUZH-7)	75.10(CLUZH-4)	38.10(CLUZH-7)	89.04(LMU-2)	79.97(LMU-2)	54.50(LMU-2)
Icelandic	92.10(CLUZH-7)	74.70(CLUZH-7)	40.80(CU-1)	74.30(LMU-1)	67.21(LMU-2)	56.57(LMU-2)
Irish	92.10(CLUZH-7)	72.60(CLUZH-7)	37.80(CLUZH-7)	69.53(LMU-2)	52.92(LMU-2)	43.43(LMU-2)
Italian	97.90(UE-LMU)	93.30(UE-LMU)	56.40(CU-1)	97.05(LMU-2)	90.67(LMU-2)	72.00(LMU-2)
Khaling	99.50(UE-LMU)	87.10(LMU-2)	18.00(LMU-2)	99.73(LMU-2)	98.62(LMU-2)	97.15(LMU-2)
Kurmanji	94.80(UE-LMU)	92.80(CLUZH-7)	86.60(CLUZH-2)	94.26(LMU-2)	88.87(LMU-2)	80.17(LMU-2)
Latin	81.30(UE-LMU)	51.80(CLUZH-7)	19.30(CU-1)	87.70(LMU-2)	84.63(LMU-2)	51.98(LMU-2)
Latvian	97.30(UE-LMU)	88.60(CLUZH-4)	68.10(CLUZH-4)	96.69(LMU-2)	89.19(LMU-2)	75.79(LMU-2)
Lithuanian	95.80(UE-LMU)	62.60(UE-LMU)	23.30(baseline)	85.82(LMU-2)	82.87(LMU-2)	49.51(LMU-2)
Lower Sorbian	97.50(UE-LMU)	84.10(UE-LMU)	52.30(CU-1)	87.39(LMU-2)	84.02(LMU-2)	56.43(LMU-2)
Macedonian	97.30(UE-LMU)	91.80(CLUZH-1)	65.50(CLUZH-7)	97.14(LMU-2)	88.98(LMU-2)	60.23(LMU-2)
Navajo	92.30(UE-LMU)	50.80(CLUZH-7)	20.40(CLUZH-7)	58.22(LMU-2)	47.12(LMU-2)	35.48(LMU-2)
Northern Sami	98.60(UE-LMU)	74.00(UE-LMU)	18.70(CU-1)	91.56(LMU-2)	83.51(LMU-2)	39.86(LMU-2)
Norwegian Bokmål	92.60(CLUZH-2)	84.40(UE-LMU)	78.00(CLUZH-7)	70.44(CU-1)	57.23(CU-1)	49.06(CU-1)
Norwegian Nynorsk	92.80(CLUZH-1)	65.60(LMU-2)	54.60(CLUZH-7)	64.42(baseline)	60.74(baseline)	42.33(baseline)
Persian	99.90(LMU-2)	91.90(UE-LMU)	51.00(CLUZH-7)	100.00(LMU-2)	99.56(LMU-2)	99.20(LMU-2)
Polish	92.80(UE-LMU)	79.90(CLUZH-7)	47.90(CLUZH-7)	90.27(baseline)	82.71(LMU-2)	64.53(LMU-2)
Portuguese	99.30(LMU-2)	95.00(LMU-2)	73.30(CLUZH-7)	98.84(LMU-1)	98.58(LMU-2)	96.94(LMU-2)
Quechua	100.00(CLUZH-4)	98.30(CLUZH-7)	61.10(CLUZH-7)	99.84(LMU-2)	99.60(LMU-2)	99.98(LMU-2)
Romanian	89.10(UE-LMU)	77.40(CU-1)	46.30(CLUZH-7)	78.99(baseline)	76.63(LMU-2)	25.00(LMU-2)
Russian	92.80(CLUZH-2)	84.10(CLUZH-2)	52.30(CLUZH-7)	87.42(CU-1)	85.74(LMU-2)	46.17(LMU-2)
Scottish Gaelic	—	90.00(UE-LMU)	64.00(CLUZH-3)	—	51.82(LMU-1)	50.61(LMU-2)
Serbo-Croatian	93.80(CLUZH-2)	83.30(CU-1)	39.20(CU-1)	88.29(LMU-2)	59.18(LMU-2)	40.46(LMU-2)
Slovak	95.30(CLUZH-2)	80.50(CLUZH-7)	53.60(CLUZH-7)	71.84(LMU-2)	66.67(LMU-2)	53.65(LMU-2)
Slovene	97.10(CLUZH-5)	88.80(LMU-2)	63.00(LMU-2)	93.71(LMU-1)	85.10(LMU-2)	79.28(LMU-2)
Sorani	89.40(CLUZH-7)	82.90(LMU-2)	27.10(CU-1)	86.39(LMU-2)	86.05(LMU-2)	57.65(LMU-2)
Spanish	97.50(CLUZH-7)	91.70(UE-LMU)	66.40(CLUZH-7)	98.53(LMU-2)	97.89(LMU-2)	91.05(LMU-2)
Swedish	93.10(UE-LMU)	79.70(UE-LMU)	64.20(CLUZH-3)	84.71(LMU-2)	70.88(LMU-2)	51.18(LMU-2)
Turkish	98.40(UE-LMU)	89.70(UE-LMU)	42.00(CLUZH-7)	99.41(LMU-2)	98.65(LMU-2)	87.65(LMU-2)
Ukrainian	95.00(UE-LMU)	82.50(CLUZH-7)	50.40(CU-1)	74.76(LMU-1)	67.14(baseline)	49.21(LMU-2)
Urdu	99.70(UE-LMU)	98.00(CLUZH-4)	74.10(CLUZH-7)	98.44(LMU-1)	94.29(LMU-2)	88.53(LMU-2)
Welsh	99.00(CLUZH-1)	93.00(LMU-2)	56.00(CLUZH-7)	97.96(LMU-2)	97.80(LMU-2)	89.89(LMU-2)

Table 9: Best per-form accuracy (and corresponding system) by language.

90%). Languages with more complex systems, like Latin, proved more challenging (the best system achieved only 19% accuracy in the low condition). For these languages, it is possible that the relevant variation required to learn a best per-form inflectional pattern was simply not present in the limited training data, and that a language-specific learning bias was required.

Even though the top-ranked systems do well on their own, different systems may contain some amount of complementary information, so that an ensemble over multiple approaches has a chance to improve accuracy. We present an upper bound on the possible performance of such an ensemble. Table 7 and Table 8 include an "Ensemble Oracle" system (oracle-e) that gives the correct answer if *any* of the submitted systems is correct. The oracle performs significantly better than any one system in both the Medium ($\sim$10%) and Low ($\sim$15%) conditions. This suggests that the different strategies used by teams to "bias" their systems in an effort to make up for sparse data lead to substantially different generalization patterns.

For sub-task 1, we also present a second "Feature Combination" Oracle (oracle-fc) that gives the correct answer for a given test triple iff its feature bundle appeared in training (with any lemma). Thus, oracle-fc provides an upper bound on the performance of systems that treat a feature bundle such as V;SBJV;FUT;3;PL as atomic. In the low-data condition, this upper bound was only 71%, meaning that 29% of the test bundles had never been seen in training data. Nonetheless, systems should be able to make some accurate predictions on this 29% by decomposing each test bundle into individual morphological features such as FUT (future) and PL (plural), and generalizing from training examples that involve those features. For example, a particular feature or sub-bundle might be realized as a particular affix. Several of the systems treated each individual feature as a separate input to the recurrent network, in order to enable this type of generalization. In the medium data condition for some languages, these systems sometimes far surpassed oracle-fc. The most notable example of this is Basque, where oracle-fc produced a 47% accuracy while six of the submitted systems produced an accuracy of 85% or above. Basque is an extreme example with very large paradigms for the verbs that inflect in the language (only a few dozen common ones do). This result demonstrates the ability of the neural systems to generalize and correctly inflect according to unseen feature combinations.

8 Future Directions

As regards morphological inflection, there is a plethora of future directions to consider. First, one might consider morphological transductions over pronunciations, rather than spellings. This is more challenging in the many languages (including English) where the orthography does not reflect the phonological changes that accompany morphological processes such as affixation. Orthography usually also does not reflect predictable allophonic distinctions in pronunciation (Sampson, 1985), which one might attempt to predict, such as the difference in aspiration of /t/ in English [tʰɑp] (top) vs. [stɑp] (stop).

A second future direction involves the effective incorporation of external unannotated monolingual corpora into the state-of-the-art inflection or reinflection systems. The best systems in our competition *did not* make use of external data and those that did make heavy use of such data, e.g., the CMU team, did not see much gain. The best way to use external corpora remains an open question; we surmise that they can be useful, especially in the lower-resource cases. A related line of inquiry is the incorporation of cross-lingual information, which Kann et al. (2017b) did find to be helpful.

A third direction revolves around the efficient elicitation of morphological information (i.e., active learning). In the low-resource section, we asked our participants to find the best approach to generate new forms given existing morphological annotation. However, it remains an open question, which of the cells in a paradigm are best to collect annotation for in the first place. Likely, it is better to collect *diagnostic* forms that are closer to principal parts of the paradigm (Finkel and Stump, 2007; Ackerman et al., 2009; Montermini and Bonami, 2013; Cotterell et al., 2017) as these will contain enough information such that the remaining transformations are largely deterministic. Experimental studies however suggest that speakers also strongly rely on pattern frequencies for inferring unknown forms (Seyfarth et al., 2014). Another interesting direction would therefore also include the organization of data according to plausible real frequency distributions (especially in spoken data) and exploring possibly varying learning strategies associated with lexical items of various frequencies.

Finally, there is a wide variety of other tasks involving morphology. While some of these have had a shared task, e.g., the parsing of morphologically-rich languages (Tsarfaty et al., 2010) and unsupervised morphological segmentation (Kurimo et al., 2010), many have not, e.g., supervised morphological segmentation and morphological tagging. A key purpose of shared tasks in the NLP community is the preparation and release of standardized data sets for fair comparison among methods. Future shared tasks in other areas of computational morphology would seem in order, giving the overall effectiveness of shared tasks in unifying research objectives in subfields of NLP, and as a starting point for possible cross-over with cognitively-grounded theoretical and quantitative linguistics.

9 Conclusion

The CoNLL-SIGMORPHON shared task provided an evaluation on 52 languages, with large and small datasets, of systems for inflection and paradigm completion—two core tasks in computational morphological learning. On sub-task 1 (inflection), 24 systems were submitted, while on sub-task 2 (paradigm completion), 3 systems were submitted. All but one of the systems used rather similar neural network models, popularized by the SIGMORPHON shared task in 2016.

The results reinforce the conclusions of the 2016 shared task that encoder-decoder architectures perform strongly when training data is plentiful, with exact-match accuracy on held-out forms surpassing 90% on many languages; we note there was a shortage of non-neural systems this year to compare with. In addition, and contrary to common expectation, many participants showed that neural systems can do reasonably well even with small training datasets. A baseline sequence-to-sequence model achieves close to zero accuracy: e.g., Silfverberg et al. (2017) reported that all the team's neural models on the low data condition delivered accuracies in the 0-1% range without data augmentation, and other teams reported similar findings. However, with judicious application of biasing and data augmentation techniques, the best neural systems achieved over 50% exact-match prediction of inflected form strings on 100

examples, and 80% on 1,000 examples, as compared to 38% for a baseline system that learns simple inflectional rules. It is hard to say whether these are "good" results in an absolute sense. An interesting experiment would be to pit the small-data systems against human linguists who do not know the languages, to see whether the systems are able to identify the predictive patterns that humans discover (or miss).

An oracle ensembling of all systems shows that there is still much room for improvement, in particular in low-resource settings. We have released the training, development, and test sets, and expect these datasets to provide a useful benchmark for future research into learning of inflectional morphology and string-to-string transduction.

Acknowledgements

The first author would like to acknowledge the support of an NDSEG fellowship. Google provided support for the shared task in the form of an award. Several authors (CK, DY, JSG, MH) were supported in part by the Defense Advanced Research Projects Agency (DARPA) in the program Low Resource Languages for Emergent Incidents (LORELEI) under contract No. HR0011-15-C-0113. Any opinions, findings and conclusions or recommendations expressed in this material are those of the authors and do not necessarily reflect the views of the Defense Advanced Research Projects Agency (DARPA).

References

Farrell Ackerman, James P. Blevins, and Robert Malouf. 2009. Parts and wholes: Patterns of relatedness in complex mophological systems and why they matter. In James P. Blevins and Juliette Blevins, editors, *Analogy in grammar: Form and acquisition*, pages 54–82. Oxford University Press, Oxford.

Farrell Ackerman and Robert Malouf. 2013. Morphological organization: The low conditional entropy conjecture. *Language*, 89:429–464.

Roee Aharoni and Yoav Goldberg. 2017. Morphological inflection generation with hard monotonic attention. In *Proceedings of the 55th Annual Meeting of the Association for Computational Linguistics (Volume 1: Long Papers)*, Vancouver, Canada. Association for Computational Linguistics.

Roee Aharoni, Yoav Goldberg, and Yonatan Belinkov. 2016. Improving sequence to sequence learning for morphological inflection generation: The BIU-MIT systems for the SIGMORPHON 2016 shared task for morphological reinflection. In *Proceedings of the 14th SIGMORPHON Workshop on Computational Research in Phonetics, Phonology, and Morphology*, pages 41–48, Berlin, Germany. Association for Computational Linguistics.

Malin Ahlberg, Markus Forsberg, and Mans Hulden. 2014. Semi-supervised learning of morphological paradigms and lexicons. In *Proceedings of the 14th Conference of the European Chapter of the Association for Computational Linguistics*, pages 569–578, Gothenburg, Sweden. Association for Computational Linguistics.

Malin Ahlberg, Markus Forsberg, and Mans Hulden. 2015. Paradigm classification in supervised learning of morphology. In *Human Language Technologies: The 2015 Annual Conference of the North American Chapter of the ACL*, pages 1024–1029, Denver, CO. Association for Computational Linguistics.

Iñaki Alegria, Izaskun Etxeberria, Mans Hulden, and Montserrat Maritxalar. 2009. Porting Basque morphological grammars to *foma*, an open-source tool. In *International Workshop on Finite-State Methods and Natural Language Processing*, pages 105–113. Springer.

Iñaki Alegria and Izaskun Etxeberria. 2016. EHU at the SIGMORPHON 2016 shared task. A simple proposal: Grapheme-to-phoneme for inflection. In *Proceedings of the 2016 Meeting of SIGMORPHON*, Berlin, Germany. Association for Computational Linguistics.

Inbal Arnon and Michael Ramscar. 2012. Granularity and the acquisition of grammatical gender: How order-of-acquisition affects what gets learned. *Cognition*, 122:292–305.

R. Harald Baayen, Peter Hendrix, and Michael Ramscar. 2013. Sidestepping the combinatorial explosion: Towards a processing model based on discriminative learning. *Language and Speech*, 56(3):329–34.

Dzmitry Bahdanau, Kyunghyun Cho, and Yoshua Bengio. 2015. Neural machine translation by jointly learning to align and translate. In *Internationoal Conference on Learning Representations*, volume abs/1409.0473.

Toms Bergmanis, Katharina Kann, Hinrich Schütze, and Sharon Goldwater. 2017. Training data augmentation for low-resource morphological inflection. In *Proceedings of the CoNLL SIGMORPHON 2017 Shared Task: Universal Morphological Reinflection*, pages 31–39, Vancouver. Association for Computational Linguistics.

James Peter Blevins. 2013. The information-theoretic turn. *Psihologija*, 46(3):355–375.

James Peter Blevins. 2016. *Word and Paradigm Morphology*. Oxford University Press, Oxford.

Abhisek Chakrabarty and Utpal Garain. 2017. ISI at the SIGMORPHON 2017 shared task on morphological reinflection. In *Proceedings of the CoNLL SIGMORPHON 2017 Shared Task: Universal Morphological Reinflection*, pages 66–70, Vancouver. Association for Computational Linguistics.

Abhisek Chakrabarty, Arun Onkar Pandit, and Utpal Garain. 2017. Context sensitive lemmatization using two successive bidirectional gated recurrent networks. In *Proceedings of the 55th Annual Meeting of the Association for Computational Linguistics (Volume 1: Long Papers)*, Vancouver, Canada. Association for Computational Linguistics.

Grzegorz Chrupała, Georgiana Dinu, and Josef van Genabith. 2008. Learning morphology with Morfette. In *Proceedings of the Sixth International Conference on Language Resources and Evaluation (LREC 2008)*, Marrakech, Morocco.

Junyoung Chung, Çaglar Gülçehre, Kyunghyun Cho, and Yoshua Bengio. 2014. Empirical evaluation of gated recurrent neural networks on sequence modeling. *CoRR*, abs/1412.3555.

Ryan Cotterell, Christo Kirov, John Sylak-Glassman, David Yarowsky, Jason Eisner, and Mans Hulden. 2016a. The SIGMORPHON 2016 shared task— morphological reinflection. In *Proceedings of the 2016 Meeting of SIGMORPHON*, Berlin, Germany. Association for Computational Linguistics.

Ryan Cotterell, Nanyun Peng, and Jason Eisner. 2014. Stochastic contextual edit distance and probabilistic FSTs. In *Proceedings of the 52nd Annual Meeting of the Association for Computational Linguistics (Volume 2: Short Papers)*, pages 625–630, Baltimore, Maryland. Association for Computational Linguistics.

Ryan Cotterell, Nanyun Peng, and Jason Eisner. 2015. Modeling word forms using latent underlying morphs and phonology. *Transactions of the Association for Computational Linguistics*, 3:433–447.

Ryan Cotterell, Hinrich Schütze, and Jason Eisner. 2016b. Morphological smoothing and extrapolation of word embeddings. In *Proceedings of the 54th Annual Meeting of the Association for Computational Linguistics (Volume 1: Long Papers)*, pages 1651–1660, Berlin, Germany. Association for Computational Linguistics.

Ryan Cotterell, John Sylak-Glassman, and Christo Kirov. 2017. Neural graphical models over strings for principal parts morphological paradigm completion. In *Proceedings of the 15th Conference of the European Chapter of the Association for Computational Linguistics (Volume 2: Short Papers)*, pages 759–765, Valencia, Spain. Association for Computational Linguistics.

Mathias Creutz, Teemu Hirsimäki, Mikko Kurimo, Antti Puurula, Janne Pylkkönen, Vesa Siivola, Matti

Varjokallio, Ebru Arisoy, Murat Saraclar, and Andreas Stolcke. 2007. Analysis of morph-based speech recognition and the modeling of out-of-vocabulary words across languages. In *Human Language Technologies 2007: The Conference of the North American Chapter of the Association for Computational Linguistics; Proceedings of the Main Conference*, pages 380–387. Association for Computational Linguistics.

Markus Dreyer and Jason Eisner. 2009. Graphical models over multiple strings. In *Proceedings of the 2009 Conference on Empirical Methods in Natural Language Processing*, pages 101–110, Singapore. Association for Computational Linguistics.

Markus Dreyer, Jason Smith, and Jason Eisner. 2008. Latent-variable modeling of string transductions with finite-state methods. In *Proceedings of the 2008 Conference on Empirical Methods in Natural Language Processing*, pages 1080–1089, Honolulu, Hawaii. Association for Computational Linguistics.

Greg Durrett and John DeNero. 2013. Supervised learning of complete morphological paradigms. In *Proceedings of the 2013 Conference of the North American Chapter of the Association for Computational Linguistics: Human Language Technologies*, pages 1185–1195, Atlanta, Georgia. Association for Computational Linguistics.

Christopher Dyer, Smaranda Muresan, and Philip Resnik. 2008. Generalizing word lattice translation. In *Proceedings of the 46th Annual Meeting of the Association for Computational Linguistics*, pages 1012–1020, Columbus, Ohio. Association for Computational Linguistics.

Manaal Faruqui, Yulia Tsvetkov, Graham Neubig, and Chris Dyer. 2016. Morphological inflection generation using character sequence to sequence learning. In *Proceedings of the 2016 Conference of the North American Chapter of the Association for Computational Linguistics: Human Language Technologies*, pages 634–643, San Diego, California. Association for Computational Linguistics.

Raphael Finkel and Gregory Stump. 2007. Principal parts and morphological typology. *Morphology*, 17(1):39–75.

Martin Haspelmath, Matthew Dryer, David Gil, and Bernard Comrie. 2005. The world atlas of language structures (WALS).

Sepp Hochreiter and Jürgen Schmidhuber. 1997. Long short-term memory. *Neural Computation*, 9(8):1735–1780.

Sittichai Jiampojamarn, Colin Cherry, and Grzegorz Kondrak. 2008. Joint processing and discriminative training for letter-to-phoneme conversion. In *Proceedings of the 46th Annual Meeting of the Association for Computational Linguistics*, pages 905–913, Columbus, Ohio. Association for Computational Linguistics.

Katharina Kann, Ryan Cotterell, and Hinrich Schütze. 2017a. Neural multi-source morphological reinflection. In *Proceedings of the 15th Conference of the European Chapter of the Association for Computational Linguistics (Volume 1: Long Papers)*, pages 514–524, Valencia, Spain. Association for Computational Linguistics.

Katharina Kann, Ryan Cotterell, and Hinrich Schütze. 2017b. One-shot neural cross-lingual transfer for paradigm completion. In *Proceedings of the 55th Annual Meeting of the Association for Computational Linguistics (Volume 1: Long Papers)*, Vancouver, Canada. Association for Computational Linguistics.

Katharina Kann and Hinrich Schütze. 2016. Single-model encoder-decoder with explicit morphological representation for reinflection. In *Proceedings of the 54th Annual Meeting of the Association for Computational Linguistics (Volume 2: Short Papers)*, pages 555–560, Berlin, Germany. Association for Computational Linguistics.

Katharina Kann and Hinrich Schütze. 2017. The LMU system for the CoNLL-SIGMORPHON 2017 shared task on universal morphological reinflection. In *Proceedings of the CoNLL SIGMORPHON 2017 Shared Task: Universal Morphological Reinflection*, pages 40–48, Vancouver. Association for Computational Linguistics.

Christo Kirov, John Sylak-Glassman, Roger Que, and David Yarowsky. 2016. Very-large scale parsing and normalization of Wiktionary morphological paradigms. In *Proceedings of the Tenth International Conference on Language Resources and Evaluation (LREC 2016)*, pages 3121–3126. European Language Resources Association (ELRA).

Mikko Kurimo, Sami Virpioja, Ville Turunen, and Krista Lagus. 2010. Morpho challenge competition 2005–2010: Evaluations and results. In *Proceedings of the 11th Meeting of the ACL Special Interest Group on Computational Morphology and Phonology*, pages 87–95. Association for Computational Linguistics.

Ling Liu and Lingshuang Jack Mao. 2016. Morphological reinflection with conditional random fields and unsupervised features. In *Proceedings of the 2016 Meeting of SIGMORPHON*, Berlin, Germany. Association for Computational Linguistics.

Peter Makarov, Tatiana Ruzsics, and Simon Clematide. 2017. Align and copy: UZH at SIGMORPHON 2017 shared task for morphological reinflection. In *Proceedings of the CoNLL SIGMORPHON 2017 Shared Task: Universal Morphological Reinflection*, pages 49–57, Vancouver. Association for Computational Linguistics.

Robert Malouf. 2016. Generating morphological paradigms with a recurrent neural network. *San Diego Linguistic Papers*, pages 122–129.

Petar Milin, Victor Kuperman, Aleksandar Kostić, and R. Harald Baayen. 2009. Words and paradigms bit by bit: An information-theoretic approach to the processing of inflection and derivation. pages 214–253. Oxford University Press, Oxford.

Fabio Montermini and Olivier Bonami. 2013. Stem spaces and predictibility in verbal inflection. *Lingue e Linguaggio*, 12:171–190.

Thomas Müller, Ryan Cotterell, Alexander Fraser, and Hinrich Schütze. 2015. Joint lemmatization and morphological tagging with Lemming. In *Proceedings of the 2015 Conference on Empirical Methods in Natural Language Processing*, pages 2268–2274, Lisbon, Portugal. Association for Computational Linguistics.

Karthik Narasimhan, Damianos Karakos, Richard Schwartz, Stavros Tsakalidis, and Regina Barzilay. 2014. Morphological segmentation for keyword spotting. In *Proceedings of the 2014 Conference on Empirical Methods in Natural Language Processing (EMNLP)*, pages 880–885, Doha, Qatar. Association for Computational Linguistics.

Garrett Nicolai, Colin Cherry, and Grzegorz Kondrak. 2015. Inflection generation as discriminative string transduction. In *Proceedings of the 2015 Conference of the North American Chapter of the Association for Computational Linguistics: Human Language Technologies*, pages 922–931, Denver, Colorado. Association for Computational Linguistics.

Garrett Nicolai, Bradley Hauer, Mohammad Motallebi, Saeed Najafi, and Grzegorz Kondrak. 2017. If you can't beat them, join them: The university of Alberta system description. In *Proceedings of the CoNLL SIGMORPHON 2017 Shared Task: Universal Morphological Reinflection*, pages 79–84, Vancouver. Association for Computational Linguistics.

Robert Östling and Johannes Bjerva. 2017. SU-RUG at the CoNLL-SIGMORPHON 2017 shared task: Morphological inflection with attentional sequence-to-sequence models. In *Proceedings of the CoNLL SIGMORPHON 2017 Shared Task: Universal Morphological Reinflection*, pages 110–113, Vancouver. Association for Computational Linguistics.

Vito Pirrelli, Marcello Ferro, and Claudia Marzi. 2015. Computational complexity of abstractive morphology. pages 141–166. Oxford University Press, Oxford.

Fermin Moscoso del Prado Martín, Aleksandar Kostić, and R. Harald Baayen. 2004. Putting the bits together: An information-theoretical perspective on morphological processing. *Cognition*, 94:1–18.

Pushpendre Rastogi, Ryan Cotterell, and Jason Eisner. 2016. Weighting finite-state transductions with neural context. In *Proceedings of the 2016 Conference of the North American Chapter of the Association for Computational Linguistics: Human Language*

Technologies, pages 623–633, San Diego, California. Association for Computational Linguistics.

Benoît Sagot and Géraldine Walther. 2011. Non-canonical inflection : data, formalisation and complexity measures. In *Systems and Frameworks in Computational Morphology*, volume 100, pages 23–45, Zurich, Switzerland. Springer.

Geoffrey Sampson. 1985. *Writing Systems: A Linguistic Introduction*. Stanford University Press.

Sunita Sarawagi and William W. Cohen. 2004. Semi-Markov conditional random fields for information extraction. In *Advances in Neural Information Processing Systems*, pages 1185–1192.

Wolfgang Seeker and Özlem Çetinoğlu. 2015. A graph-based lattice dependency parser for joint morphological segmentation and syntactic analysis. *Transactions of the Association for Computational Linguistics*, 3:359–373.

Hajime Senuma and Akiko Aizawa. 2017. Seq2seq for morphological reinflection: When deep learning fails. In *Proceedings of the CoNLL SIGMORPHON 2017 Shared Task: Universal Morphological Reinflection*, pages 100–109, Vancouver. Association for Computational Linguistics.

Scott Seyfarth, Farrell Ackerman, and Robert Malouf. 2014. Implicative organization facilitates morphological learning. In *Proceedings of the Fortieth Annual Meeting of the Berkeley Linguistics Society*, pages 480–494.

Miikka Silfverberg, Adam Wiemerslage, Ling Liu, and Lingshuang Jack Mao. 2017. Data augmentation for morphological reinflection. In *Proceedings of the CoNLL SIGMORPHON 2017 Shared Task: Universal Morphological Reinflection*, pages 90–99, Vancouver. Association for Computational Linguistics.

Akhilesh Sudhakar and Anil Kumar Singh. 2017. Experiments on morphological reinflection: CoNLL-2017 shared task. In *Proceedings of the CoNLL SIGMORPHON 2017 Shared Task: Universal Morphological Reinflection*, pages 71–78, Vancouver. Association for Computational Linguistics.

Ilya Sutskever, Oriol Vinyals, and Quoc V. Le. 2014. Sequence to sequence learning with neural networks. In *Advances in Neural Information Processing Systems*, pages 3104–3112, Montreal, Quebec, Canada.

John Sylak-Glassman, Christo Kirov, Matt Post, Roger Que, and David Yarowsky. 2015a. A universal feature schema for rich morphological annotation and fine-grained cross-lingual part-of-speech tagging. In Cerstin Mahlow and Michael Piotrowski, editors, *Proceedings of the 4th Workshop on Systems and Frameworks for Computational Morphology (SFCM)*, Communications in Computer and Information Science, pages 72–93. Springer, Berlin.

John Sylak-Glassman, Christo Kirov, and David Yarowsky. 2016. Remote elicitation of inflectional paradigms to seed morphological analysis in low-resource languages. In *Proceedings of the Tenth International Conference on Language Resources and Evaluation (LREC 2016)*. European Language Resources Association (ELRA).

John Sylak-Glassman, Christo Kirov, David Yarowsky, and Roger Que. 2015b. A language-independent feature schema for inflectional morphology. In *Proceedings of the 53rd Annual Meeting of the Association for Computational Linguistics and the 7th International Joint Conference on Natural Language Processing (Volume 2: Short Papers)*, pages 674–680, Beijing, China. Association for Computational Linguistics.

Reut Tsarfaty, Djamé Seddah, Yoav Goldberg, Marie Candito, Jennifer Foster, Yannick Versley, Ines Rehbein, and Lamia Tounsi. 2010. Statistical parsing of morphologically rich languages (SPMRL) what, how and whither. In *Proceedings of the NAACL HLT 2010 First Workshop on Statistical Parsing of Morphologically-Rich Languages*, pages 1–12. Association for Computational Linguistics.

Géraldine Walther, Guillaume Jacques, and Benoît Sagot. 2013. Uncovering the inner architecture of Khaling verbal morphology. Presentation at the 3rd Workshop on Sino-Tibetan Languages of Sichuan, Paris, September 2013.

Géraldine Walther and Benoît Sagot. 2010. Developing a large-scale lexicon for a less-resourced language: General methodology and preliminary experiments on Sorani Kurdish. In *Proceedings of the SaLTMiL Workshop on Creation and Use of Basic Lexical Resources for Less-Resourced Languages (at LREC)*, Valetta, Malta. European Language Resources Association (ELRA).

Géraldine Walther, Benoît Sagot, and Karën Fort. 2010. Fast development of basic NLP tools: Towards a lexicon and a POS tagger for Kurmanji Kurdish. In *Proceedings of the 29th International Conference on Lexis and Grammar*, Belgrade.

Chunting Zhou and Graham Neubig. 2017a. Morphological inflection generation with multi-space variational encoder-decoders. In *Proceedings of the CoNLL SIGMORPHON 2017 Shared Task: Universal Morphological Reinflection*, pages 58–65, Vancouver. Association for Computational Linguistics.

Chunting Zhou and Graham Neubig. 2017b. Multi-space variational encoder-decoders for semi-supervised labeled sequence transduction. In *Proceedings of the 55th Annual Meeting of the Association for Computational Linguistics (Volume 1: Long Papers)*, Vancouver, Canada. Association for Computational Linguistics.

Qile Zhu, Yanjun Li, and Xiaolin Li. 2017. Character sequence-to-sequence model with global attention for universal morphological reinflection. In *Proceedings of the CoNLL SIGMORPHON 2017 Shared Task: Universal Morphological Reinflection*, pages 85–89, Vancouver. Association for Computational Linguistics.

A Detailed Results

This section contains detailed results for each submitted system on each language. Systems are ordered by average per-form accuracy for each sub-task and data condition. Three metrics are presented for each system/language combination.

1. Per-Form Accuracy: Percentage of test forms inflected correctly.

2. Levenshtein Distance: Average Levenshtein distance of system-predicted form from gold inflected form.

3. Per-Paradigm Accuracy: Percentage of unique lemmata (paradigms) for which every form was inflected correctly.

Scores in bold include the highest scoring non-oracle system for each language as well as any other systems that did not differ significantly in terms of per-form accuracy according to a sign test ($p >= 0.05$). Scores marked with a † indicate submissions that were significantly better than the feature combination oracle ($p < 0.05$), showing per-feature generalization. Scores marked with ‡ did not differ significantly from the ensemble oracle, suggesting minimal complementary information across systems.

	oracle-fc	oracle-e	UE-LMU-1	CLUZH-7	CLUZH-6	CLUZH-2	LMU-2	LMU-1
Albanian	100.00/*/100.00	99.80/*/99.46	**99.00/0.01/98.37**	97.40/0.08/94.31	97.40/0.08/94.31	96.80/0.10/92.95	**97.10/0.09/92.95**	97.10/0.09/92.95
Arabic	100.00/*/100.00	97.40/*/97.11	**94.40/0.21/93.50**	**94.50/0.22/93.62**	**94.50/0.22/93.62**	93.60/0.26/92.66	**93.50/0.22/92.42**	93.50/0.22/92.42
Armenian	100.00/*/100.00	98.70/*/98.56	**97.50/0.04/97.23**	**97.30/0.06/97.01**	**97.30/0.06/97.01**	96.70/0.07/96.34	**97.20/0.06/96.90**	97.20/0.06/96.90
Basque	100.00/*/100.00	100.00/*/100.00	**100.00/0.00/100.00‡**	**100.00/0.00/100.00‡**	**100.00/0.00/100.00‡**	**100.00/0.00/100.00‡**	**100.00/0.00/100.00‡**	100.00/0.00/100.00‡
Bengali	100.00/*/100.00	100.00/*/100.00	**100.00/0.00/100.00‡**	**99.00/0.05/98.53‡**	**99.00/0.05/98.53‡**	**99.00/0.05/98.53‡**	**99.00/0.05/98.53‡**	99.00/0.05/98.53‡
Bulgarian	100.00/*/100.00	99.50/*/99.33	**98.10/0.04/97.45**	97.50/0.05/96.64	97.50/0.05/96.64	97.40/0.05/96.51	97.40/0.05/96.51	97.40/0.05/96.51
Catalan	100.00/*/100.00	99.00/*/98.64	**98.20/0.05/97.68**	**98.30/0.04/97.82**	**98.30/0.04/97.82**	**98.30/0.04/97.82**	**98.30/0.05/97.68**	98.30/0.05/97.68
Czech	100.00/*/100.00	97.60/*/97.18	**94.10/0.10/93.18**	93.40/0.11/92.59	93.40/0.11/92.59	93.70/0.11/92.82	93.40/0.12/92.59	93.40/0.12/92.59
Danish	100.00/*/100.00	97.70/*/97.46	**94.50/0.08/93.99**	93.80/0.10/93.29	93.80/0.10/93.29	93.20/0.10/92.72	**93.80/0.10/93.18**	93.80/0.10/93.18
Dutch	100.00/*/100.00	98.60/*/98.44	**96.90/0.06/96.66**	96.80/0.07/96.55	96.80/0.07/96.55	96.70/0.06/96.44	96.50/0.07/96.11	96.50/0.07/96.11
English	100.00/*/100.00	98.60/*/98.58	**97.20/0.06/97.15**	96.80/0.06/96.74	96.80/0.06/96.74	96.70/0.06/96.64	96.90/0.06/96.85	96.90/0.06/96.85
Estonian	100.00/*/100.00	99.40/*/98.96	**98.90/0.04/98.09‡**	98.00/0.06/96.88	98.00/0.06/96.88	97.60/0.07/96.19	98.10/0.06/97.05	98.10/0.06/97.05
Faroese	100.00/*/100.00	95.70/*/95.11	86.90/0.28/85.91	**87.80/0.25/86.93**	**87.80/0.25/86.93**	87.30/0.26/86.36	85.30/0.31/83.98	85.30/0.31/83.98
Finnish	100.00/*/100.00	99.10/*/99.09	**95.10/0.12/95.03**	93.50/0.11/93.41	93.50/0.11/93.41	93.20/0.12/93.10	**94.80/0.10/94.73**	94.80/0.10/94.73
French	100.00/*/100.00	95.20/*/95.33	**89.50/0.20/89.29**	**88.90/0.20/88.65**	**88.90/0.20/88.65**	**88.90/0.20/88.65**	**88.20/0.23/87.91**	88.20/0.23/87.91
Georgian	100.00/*/100.00	99.70/*/99.66	**99.10/0.01/99.08**	98.80/0.01/98.74	98.80/0.01/98.74	99.10/0.01/98.97	**99.40/0.01/99.31†**	99.40/0.01/99.31†
German	100.00/*/100.00	97.40/*/97.30	**93.00/0.12/92.74**	91.20/0.20/90.98	91.20/0.20/90.98	91.00/0.21/90.77	**92.00/0.14/91.70**	92.00/0.14/91.70
Haida	100.00/*/100.00	100.00/*/100.00	**98.00/0.03/94.74‡**	**99.00/0.02/97.37‡**	**99.00/0.02/97.37‡**	**99.00/0.02/97.37‡**	**99.00/0.01/97.37‡**	99.00/0.01/97.37‡
Hebrew	100.00/*/100.00	99.80/*/99.78	**99.30/0.01/98.68‡**	**99.40/0.01/98.90‡**	**99.40/0.01/98.90‡**	**99.50/0.01/99.12‡**	**99.50/0.01/99.12‡**	99.50/0.01/99.12‡
Hindi	100.00/*/100.00	100.00/*/100.00	**100.00/0.00/100.00‡**	**100.00/0.00/100.00‡**	**100.00/0.00/100.00‡**	**100.00/0.00/100.00‡**	**100.00/0.00/100.00‡**	100.00/0.00/100.00‡
Hungarian	100.00/*/100.00	93.70/*/93.57	86.40/0.32/86.10	**86.80/0.30/86.51**	**86.80/0.30/86.51**	86.50/0.30/86.20	**86.30/0.31/86.10**	86.30/0.31/86.10
Icelandic	100.00/*/100.00	96.10/*/95.88	90.20/0.21/89.32	**92.10/0.17/91.43**	**92.10/0.17/91.43**	91.50/0.19/90.88	89.50/0.23/88.54	89.50/0.23/88.54
Irish	100.00/*/100.00	96.80/*/96.64	90.90/0.26/90.03	**92.10/0.26/91.49**	**92.10/0.26/91.49**	91.10/0.28/90.37	**91.40/0.27/90.71**	91.40/0.27/90.71
Italian	100.00/*/100.00	98.80/*/98.72	**97.90/0.06/97.76**	97.60/0.06/97.44	97.60/0.06/97.44	96.90/0.08/96.69	97.60/0.07/97.44	97.60/0.07/97.44
Khaling	100.00/*/100.00	99.90/*/99.76	**99.50/0.01/98.82‡**	99.30/0.01/98.34	99.30/0.01/98.34	99.20/0.01/98.10	**99.40/0.01/98.58‡**	99.40/0.01/98.58‡
Kurmanji	100.00/*/100.00	98.20/*/98.12	**94.80/0.06/94.68**	94.50/0.10/94.36	94.50/0.10/94.36	94.20/0.11/94.05	94.50/0.07/94.47	94.50/0.07/94.47
Latin	100.00/*/100.00	94.80/*/94.71	**81.30/0.42/80.74**	**81.00/0.28/80.63**	**81.00/0.28/80.63**	**81.10/0.27/80.63**	77.60/0.34/77.14	77.60/0.34/77.14
Latvian	100.00/*/100.00	98.90/*/98.81	**97.30/0.04/97.19**	96.50/0.05/96.65	96.50/0.05/96.65	96.40/0.05/96.54	**96.80/0.04/96.65**	96.80/0.04/96.65
Lithuanian	100.00/*/100.00	98.50/*/97.65	**95.80/0.07/93.43**	94.10/0.09/91.08	94.10/0.09/91.08	93.40/0.10/89.98	91.90/0.13/87.95	91.90/0.13/87.95
Lower Sorbian	100.00/*/100.00	99.50/*/99.21	**97.50/0.04/96.35**	97.00/0.06/95.87	97.00/0.06/95.87	96.80/0.06/95.56	96.90/0.06/95.71	96.90/0.06/95.71
Macedonian	100.00/*/100.00	98.80/*/98.73	**97.30/0.05/97.15**	96.90/0.05/96.83	96.90/0.05/96.83	96.80/0.05/96.72	96.70/0.05/96.51	96.70/0.05/96.51
Navajo	100.00/*/100.00	97.20/*/95.52	**92.30/0.20/89.41**	**92.20/0.19/89.82**	**92.20/0.19/89.82**	91.10/0.23/88.39	90.10/0.21/84.73	90.10/0.21/84.73
Northern Sami	100.00/*/100.00	99.20/*/98.92	**98.60/0.04/98.25**	97.90/0.05/97.45	97.90/0.05/97.45	98.00/0.05/97.58	97.60/0.06/97.04	97.60/0.06/97.04
Norwegian Bokmal	99.90/*/99.89	97.80/*/97.74	**92.40/0.13/92.04**	**92.60/0.12/92.26**	**92.60/0.12/92.26**	**92.60/0.12/92.37**	**92.30/0.13/92.04**	92.30/0.13/92.04
Norwegian Nynorsk	100.00/*/100.00	97.30/*/97.39	90.80/0.16/90.75	**92.50/0.14/92.60**	**92.50/0.14/92.60**	92.40/0.13/92.49	88.80/0.19/88.57	88.80/0.19/88.57
Persian	100.00/*/100.00	100.00/*/100.00	**99.80/0.00/99.25‡**	**99.70/0.01/98.88‡**	**99.70/0.01/98.88‡**	99.40/0.01/97.75	**99.90/0.00/99.63‡**	99.90/0.00/99.63‡
Polish	100.00/*/100.00	96.10/*/95.97	**92.80/0.15/92.46**	92.10/0.16/91.83	92.10/0.16/91.83	92.00/0.18/91.72	91.60/0.22/91.30	91.60/0.22/91.30
Portuguese	100.00/*/100.00	99.40/*/99.42	**99.10/0.02/99.08‡**	**99.00/0.02/98.96‡**	**99.00/0.02/98.96‡**	**99.00/0.02/98.96‡**	**99.30/0.02/99.31‡**	99.30/0.02/99.31‡
Quechua	100.00/*/100.00	100.00/*/100.00	**99.90/0.00/99.81‡**	**99.90/0.00/99.81‡**	**99.90/0.00/99.81‡**	**99.90/0.00/99.81‡**	**99.90/0.00/99.81‡**	99.90/0.00/99.81‡
Romanian	100.00/*/100.00	94.50/*/93.60	**89.10/0.33/87.32**	87.80/0.36/85.75	87.80/0.36/85.75	87.90/0.33/85.87	88.00/0.39/85.99	88.00/0.39/85.99
Russian	100.00/*/100.00	96.50/*/96.53	91.60/0.21/91.53	92.10/0.23/92.04	92.10/0.23/92.04	92.80/0.19/92.76	92.10/0.20/92.04	92.10/0.20/92.04
Scottish Gaelic	—	—	—	—	—	—	—	—
Serbo-Croatian	100.00/*/100.00	96.50/*/96.33	**93.50/0.13/93.19**	93.30/0.13/93.08	93.30/0.13/93.08	93.80/0.13/93.50	92.10/0.16/91.72	92.10/0.16/91.72
Slovak	100.00/*/100.00	98.50/*/97.59	94.20/0.10/91.32	**95.30/0.08/93.41**	**95.30/0.08/93.41**	**95.30/0.08/93.41**	94.40/0.09/91.64	94.40/0.09/91.64
Slovene	100.00/*/100.00	98.50/*/98.16	**97.00/0.05/96.72**	96.90/0.06/96.72	96.90/0.06/96.72	96.80/0.06/96.59	**97.00/0.06/96.85**	97.00/0.06/96.85
Sorani	100.00/*/100.00	98.10/*/92.46	89.30/0.12/65.33	**89.40/0.12/64.32**	**89.40/0.12/64.32**	89.00/0.13/63.82	88.80/0.13/62.31	88.80/0.13/62.31
Spanish	100.00/*/100.00	98.80/*/98.70	97.30/0.05/97.07	**97.50/0.05/97.29**	**97.50/0.05/97.29**	97.20/0.06/96.96	97.20/0.05/96.96	97.20/0.05/96.96
Swedish	100.00/*/100.00	98.40/*/98.34	**93.10/0.14/93.04**	92.60/0.13/92.41	92.60/0.13/92.41	92.80/0.13/92.62	92.00/0.13/91.79	92.00/0.13/91.79
Turkish	99.70/*/99.64	99.40/*/99.29	**98.40/0.04/98.21**	97.70/0.06/97.62	97.70/0.06/97.62	97.60/0.06/97.38	97.60/0.05/97.38	97.60/0.05/97.38
Ukrainian	100.00/*/100.00	98.60/*/98.08	**95.00/0.09/93.55**	94.60/0.09/93.28	94.60/0.09/93.28	94.40/0.09/93.14	94.30/0.09/93.00	94.30/0.09/93.00
Urdu	100.00/*/100.00	99.90/*/99.06	**99.70/0.01/97.17‡**	**99.60/0.01/96.23‡**	**99.60/0.01/96.23‡**	**99.60/0.01/96.23‡**	**99.60/0.01/96.23‡**	99.60/0.01/96.23‡
Welsh	100.00/*/100.00	99.00/*/98.72	**99.00/0.03/98.72‡**	**99.00/0.03/98.72‡**	**99.00/0.03/98.72‡**	**99.00/0.03/98.72‡**	**99.00/0.03/98.72‡**	99.00/0.03/98.72‡

Table 10: Sub-task 1 High Condition Part 1.

	CLUZH-5	CLUZH-1	SURUG-1	CU-1	UTNII-1	CLUZH-4	IIT(BHU)-1	CLUZH-3
Albanian	**98.80/0.04/97.02**	97.00/0.09/93.22	97.90/0.07/94.58	97.60/0.06/95.12	98.30/0.03/96.48	92.80/0.33/86.18	95.40/0.13/89.16	92.30/0.34/85.09
Arabic	92.50/0.36/91.34	91.40/0.35/90.01	89.80/0.39/88.21	90.40/0.46/88.81	90.20/0.42/88.69	86.50/0.50/84.60	88.20/0.40/86.28	86.70/0.47/84.48
Armenian	96.00/0.07/95.57	96.50/0.07/96.12	95.60/0.08/95.12	96.30/0.08/95.90	94.10/0.11/93.46	96.00/0.08/95.57	94.00/0.12/93.46	95.30/0.09/94.79
Basque	**100.00/0.00/100.00**‡	**100.00/0.00/100.00**‡	**100.00/0.00/100.00**‡	**100.00/0.00/100.00**‡	**100.00/0.00/100.00**‡	93.00/0.17/77.27	**100.00/0.00/100.00**‡	94.00/0.15/77.27
Bengali	**99.00/0.03/98.53**‡	**99.00/0.03/98.53**‡	**99.00/0.05/98.53**‡	**99.00/0.05/98.53**‡	**99.00/0.05/98.53**‡	**99.00/0.05/98.53**‡	**98.00/0.05/97.06**‡	**99.00/0.05/98.53**‡
Bulgarian	96.20/0.06/95.03	96.70/0.06/95.56	96.70/0.07/95.56	**97.40/0.06/96.64**	96.40/0.06/95.56	95.40/0.09/94.09	94.30/0.10/92.47	95.70/0.07/94.35
Catalan	**98.30/0.05/97.82**	**98.40/0.04/97.95**	**97.80/0.06/97.27**	97.60/0.07/96.86	96.40/0.09/95.50	97.10/0.07/96.32	97.20/0.07/96.32	97.10/0.07/96.32
Czech	92.70/0.13/91.76	92.70/0.13/91.76	92.00/0.15/90.94	92.40/0.15/91.53	90.60/0.16/89.18	91.40/0.16/90.47	89.60/0.19/87.88	90.60/0.18/89.53
Danish	**93.90/0.10/93.29**	**93.90/0.10/93.29**	**93.80/0.09/93.64**	90.50/0.15/89.60	88.40/0.18/87.28	83.30/0.25/81.97	89.20/0.17/88.09	82.60/0.26/81.04
Dutch	95.30/0.10/95.11	**96.50/0.07/96.22**	**95.90/0.07/95.44**	95.60/0.10/95.22	94.30/0.10/93.66	92.10/0.15/91.77	92.10/0.16/91.32	91.50/0.15/91.10
English	**96.80/0.06/96.74**	**96.80/0.06/96.74**	**96.60/0.07/96.64**	95.60/0.09/95.52	94.20/0.09/94.10	95.60/0.09/95.52	94.30/0.10/94.20	95.50/0.09/95.42
Estonian	97.90/0.07/97.23	96.60/0.08/94.45	96.80/0.08/94.97	97.10/0.09/95.67	96.30/0.07/94.80	93.10/0.18/90.12	94.80/0.11/92.37	92.20/0.20/88.73
Faroese	**86.90/0.27/85.91**	**86.90/0.27/85.91**	84.60/0.31/83.64	85.40/0.32/84.32	81.40/0.34/80.11	72.40/0.60/71.02	77.80/0.45/76.48	71.10/0.62/69.55
Finnish	93.10/0.13/93.00	91.70/0.14/91.58	91.00/0.17/90.87	**93.80/0.14/93.71**	84.10/0.26/83.98	87.90/0.22/87.73	80.50/0.40/80.43	86.10/0.24/85.90
French	**88.40/0.22/88.12**	**88.40/0.22/88.12**	87.50/0.24/87.17	**88.20/0.23/87.91**	81.10/0.34/80.49	80.50/0.37/80.06	80.30/0.38/79.75	80.10/0.40/79.75
Georgian	**98.80/0.01/98.63**	**98.80/0.01/98.63**	97.60/0.05/97.71	95.40/0.13/96.00	97.40/0.04/97.25	98.10/0.05/98.05	97.50/0.04/97.25	98.00/0.04/97.94
German	**91.50/0.20/91.18**	90.20/0.23/90.04	89.50/0.21/89.11	89.70/0.31/89.42	85.70/0.37/85.37	84.60/0.49/84.23	83.10/0.35/82.57	83.90/0.50/83.51
Haida	**99.00/0.02/97.37**‡	**99.00/0.02/97.37**‡	**95.00/0.10/89.47**‡	80.00/0.63/57.89	**99.00/0.01/97.37**‡	**99.00/0.02/97.37**‡	**96.00/0.09/89.47**‡	**98.00/0.03/94.74**‡
Hebrew	**99.40/0.01/98.90**‡	**99.40/0.01/98.90**‡	**99.00/0.01/98.23**	98.50/0.02/97.35	**99.00/0.01/98.23**	95.40/0.07/91.61	96.70/0.05/94.26	97.00/0.04/94.70
Hindi	**100.00/0.00/100.00**‡	**100.00/0.00/100.00**‡	**99.80/0.00/99.22**‡	**100.00/0.00/100.00**‡	**100.00/0.00/100.00**‡	**100.00/0.00/100.00**‡	99.30/0.02/97.25	**99.80/0.01/99.22**‡
Hungarian	**86.30/0.30/86.10**	**86.70/0.30/86.41**	84.80/0.35/84.54	**86.40/0.30/86.10**	79.10/0.44/78.73	82.60/0.36/82.37	80.20/0.41/79.77	81.90/0.38/81.54
Icelandic	**91.20/0.18/90.55**	**91.20/0.18/90.55**	86.30/0.25/85.32	89.10/0.24/88.21	81.30/0.33/80.31	83.50/0.33/82.42	79.70/0.40/78.09	81.40/0.38/80.31
Irish	**91.30/0.28/90.71**	**91.30/0.28/90.71**	87.60/0.35/86.45	88.70/0.37/87.79	83.10/0.43/82.08	86.60/0.45/86.00	67.90/1.05/65.85	86.90/0.41/86.23
Italian	**97.60/0.06/97.44**	**97.00/0.08/96.79**	96.80/0.09/96.58	**97.00/0.09/96.79**	96.00/0.11/95.73	95.40/0.13/95.09	95.30/0.10/95.09	95.70/0.12/95.41
Khaling	**99.00/0.01/97.63**	**98.80/0.02/97.39**	98.30/0.03/95.97	**98.90/0.01/97.39**	**98.90/0.01/97.39**	87.80/0.19/77.01	97.40/0.04/94.31	88.80/0.17/78.44
Kurmanji	**94.00/0.08/93.95**	**93.70/0.11/93.53**	**93.80/0.10/93.63**	**94.40/0.18/94.26**	92.00/0.19/91.75	**94.10/0.08/94.05**	93.50/0.09/93.74	**94.00/0.08/93.95**
Latin	80.30/0.29/79.79	80.30/0.29/79.79	75.30/0.39/74.81	80.50/0.31/80.21	70.90/0.43/70.05	59.70/0.65/59.15	54.50/0.71/53.65	57.00/0.69/56.30
Latvian	96.10/0.06/96.21	96.10/0.06/96.21	95.40/0.08/95.24	94.60/0.13/94.37	92.20/0.13/91.88	94.90/0.08/94.91	92.10/0.17/91.99	94.70/0.09/94.70
Lithuanian	93.40/0.12/90.30	90.80/0.13/86.38	91.00/0.15/86.85	92.90/0.12/89.83	86.00/0.22/80.59	85.20/0.23/79.34	83.10/0.27/75.90	84.30/0.26/78.72
Lower Sorbian	**96.60/0.06/95.40**	**96.60/0.06/95.40**	**96.90/0.06/95.56**	95.40/0.11/93.81	95.30/0.08/93.81	96.30/0.09/95.24	93.10/0.12/90.32	96.40/0.07/95.40
Macedonian	96.50/0.06/96.41	96.50/0.06/96.41	**96.60/0.06/96.41**	95.20/0.11/94.93	93.40/0.10/93.13	94.60/0.10/94.29	94.60/0.12/94.29	94.40/0.11/94.08
Navajo	89.80/0.28/85.95	88.40/0.28/84.73	88.90/0.28/83.91	83.10/0.46/76.37	85.10/0.30/78.00	59.80/1.24/49.49	85.60/0.33/77.19	59.80/1.24/49.90
Northern Sami	97.60/0.06/96.91	97.50/0.07/96.91	94.50/0.12/92.74	96.10/0.10/95.16	92.60/0.14/90.46	87.40/0.22/84.68	93.60/0.12/91.53	84.50/0.27/81.85
Norwegian Bokmal	91.20/0.14/90.86	91.20/0.14/90.86	**92.40/0.13/92.15**	**91.50/0.15/91.29**	89.60/0.17/89.35	86.80/0.21/86.24	84.10/0.24/83.23	86.50/0.21/85.91
Norwegian Nynorsk	**92.80/0.13/92.93**	**92.80/0.13/92.93**	89.40/0.18/89.34	87.50/0.23/87.49	81.70/0.30/81.28	69.30/0.53/68.44	73.30/0.45/72.80	67.60/0.58/66.38
Persian	**99.50/0.02/98.50**‡	98.40/0.03/95.51	99.30/0.01/97.75	**99.50/0.01/98.13**‡	**99.60/0.01/98.50**‡	92.40/0.18/81.65	98.90/0.02/96.25	92.20/0.19/80.52
Polish	**91.90/0.18/91.61**	**91.90/0.18/91.61**	90.60/0.22/90.23	90.90/0.27/90.66	88.10/0.27/87.69	90.30/0.21/89.92	82.00/0.50/81.21	89.70/0.20/89.28
Portuguese	**99.00/0.02/98.96**‡	**99.00/0.02/98.96**‡	**98.80/0.02/98.73**	**99.30/0.02/99.31**‡	97.90/0.03/97.69	98.50/0.03/98.38	98.50/0.03/98.38	98.50/0.03/98.38
Quechua	99.10/0.02/98.48	98.90/0.03/97.91	**100.00/0.00/100.00**‡	90.30/0.19/83.08	**99.60/0.00/99.43**‡	**100.00/0.00/100.00**‡	98.50/0.05/97.15	99.10/0.02/98.48
Romanian	**87.70/0.34/85.63**	**87.70/0.34/85.63**	86.40/0.42/84.06	85.50/0.48/83.82	82.80/0.47/80.31	80.10/0.58/77.42	76.00/0.70/73.31	79.70/0.60/77.05
Russian	**92.60/0.21/92.55**	**92.60/0.21/92.55**	89.30/0.31/89.18	90.80/0.28/90.71	86.10/0.31/86.02	90.40/0.28/90.31	82.80/0.47/82.55	90.30/0.29/90.20
Scottish Gaelic	—	—	—	—	—	—	—	—
Serbo-Croatian	**93.30/0.14/92.98**	**93.30/0.14/92.98**	90.10/0.24/89.62	92.10/0.24/91.72	88.80/0.25/88.26	90.80/0.19/90.57	81.00/0.43/80.08	90.10/0.20/89.83
Slovak	**94.50/0.10/92.12**	**94.50/0.10/92.12**	93.10/0.13/90.03	89.30/0.19/84.41	91.70/0.12/87.62	90.10/0.18/85.69	89.50/0.18/85.21	89.10/0.20/84.89
Slovene	**97.10/0.05/96.72**	96.90/0.07/96.59	**96.60/0.07/96.19**	95.80/0.12/95.01	95.20/0.09/94.75	95.80/0.07/95.01	94.30/0.11/93.31	94.80/0.10/93.70
Sorani	**88.70/0.14/62.81**	**88.70/0.14/62.81**	**88.60/0.14/60.80**	**89.10/0.14/61.81**	87.30/0.15/59.80	80.10/0.44/54.77	87.30/0.17/62.31	79.00/0.47/52.76
Spanish	**97.30/0.05/97.07**	**97.10/0.07/96.85**	93.50/0.15/92.95	**96.80/0.07/96.53**	95.00/0.10/94.69	94.80/0.09/94.47	94.00/0.13/93.49	95.00/0.09/94.69
Swedish	91.20/0.15/91.06	91.20/0.15/91.06	**91.80/0.13/91.58**	87.60/0.21/87.21	87.50/0.21/87.01	81.80/0.29/81.08	86.70/0.23/86.49	81.60/0.30/80.87
Turkish	97.30/0.07/97.02	97.30/0.07/97.02	96.60/0.11/96.19	96.40/0.09/96.07	93.50/0.27/93.21	96.30/0.07/95.95	96.40/0.07/95.83	97.20/0.07/96.90
Ukrainian	93.10/0.12/91.36	93.10/0.12/91.36	**94.20/0.11/92.73**	90.20/0.21/88.07	90.80/0.15/88.61	90.60/0.16/88.34	87.60/0.22/84.36	89.70/0.17/87.38
Urdu	**99.60/0.01/96.23**‡	**99.60/0.01/96.23**‡	**99.70/0.01/97.17**‡	98.30/0.03/86.79	**99.60/0.01/96.23**‡	**99.60/0.01/96.23**‡	**99.40/0.01/95.28**‡	**99.50/0.01/95.28**‡
Welsh	**99.00/0.04/98.72**‡	**99.00/0.03/98.72**‡	**99.00/0.03/98.72**‡	**98.00/0.04/97.44**‡	**98.00/0.04/97.44**‡	**97.00/0.05/96.15**‡	**99.00/0.03/98.72**‡	**98.00/0.04/97.44**‡

Table 11: Sub-task 1 High Condition Part 2.

	UF-1	CMU-1	baseline	ISI-1	EHU-1
Albanian	92.90/0.17/87.53	91.30/0.13/78.59	78.90/0.66/68.83	79.10/0.95/70.46	—
Arabic	84.90/0.68/82.79	85.90/0.49/83.87	50.70/1.45/50.18	60.20/1.33/59.57	—
Armenian	93.50/0.11/92.90	82.30/0.34/80.93	87.20/0.27/86.14	89.50/0.25/88.91	—
Basque	**96.00/0.12/86.36**‡	**97.00/0.11/90.91**‡	5.00/3.38/4.55	0.00/6.13/0.00	31.00/1.66/9.09
Bengali	96.00/0.08/94.12‡	**99.00/0.05/98.53**‡	81.00/0.26/83.82	76.00/0.63/76.47	—
Bulgarian	92.70/0.12/90.46	86.70/0.24/83.20	88.80/0.18/86.83	80.90/0.40/78.49	—
Catalan	93.40/0.14/92.22	96.50/0.09/95.50	95.50/0.11/94.68	92.00/0.21/90.31	—
Czech	87.20/0.23/85.53	81.90/0.32/79.65	89.60/0.22/88.71	83.00/0.34/81.41	—
Danish	88.60/0.23/87.63	85.40/0.23/85.09	87.80/0.21/86.59	82.30/0.26/80.58	—
Dutch	90.80/0.20/90.10	88.90/0.22/88.21	87.00/0.22/86.10	90.20/0.21/89.43	—
English	93.90/0.10/93.79	94.60/0.10/94.51	94.70/0.09/94.61	93.30/0.11/93.18	—
Estonian	94.80/0.12/92.72	93.70/0.15/90.81	78.00/0.39/71.40	75.50/0.78/69.67	—
Faroese	77.00/0.48/75.45	74.50/0.51/72.84	74.10/0.57/73.30	64.30/0.74/62.39	—
Finnish	74.40/0.46/74.24	74.90/0.57/74.54	78.20/0.35/77.99	52.40/2.00/51.93	—
French	79.10/0.41/78.69	82.40/0.33/82.08	81.50/0.36/81.12	80.80/0.43/80.49	—
Georgian	81.60/0.24/80.66	92.30/0.13/91.99	93.80/0.11/93.59	94.40/0.13/95.08	—
German	81.40/0.55/81.02	78.70/0.44/78.22	82.40/0.59/81.95	79.40/0.42/78.84	—
Haida	**97.00/0.06/92.11**‡	**97.00/0.12/92.11**‡	67.00/0.77/50.00	57.00/1.36/39.47	—
Hebrew	93.10/0.09/88.74	97.50/0.03/95.36	54.00/0.56/39.96	71.10/0.53/60.26	77.60/0.28/63.36
Hindi	99.10/0.01/96.47	**99.60/0.01/98.43**‡	93.50/0.09/82.35	99.10/0.01/98.43	—
Hungarian	78.70/0.41/78.42	73.60/0.58/73.34	68.50/0.66/67.95	77.50/0.46/77.07	—
Icelandic	78.00/0.42/76.53	68.10/0.63/66.41	76.30/0.50/75.19	78.20/0.45/77.20	—
Irish	73.10/0.87/70.66	71.90/0.80/69.88	53.00/1.13/52.97	60.60/1.60/60.69	—
Italian	92.40/0.19/92.09	92.60/0.14/92.09	76.90/0.72/76.39	91.10/0.23/90.60	—
Khaling	96.60/0.05/93.36	94.80/0.10/88.63	53.70/0.87/33.18	56.00/1.55/33.89	—
Kurmanji	93.60/0.08/93.32	83.80/0.34/83.40	93.00/0.08/93.01	93.00/0.09/93.11	—
Latin	54.70/0.72/54.39	66.20/0.60/65.71	47.60/0.81/48.25	21.10/2.49/21.90	70.10/0.69/69.42
Latvian	87.40/0.26/86.69	87.50/0.25/86.90	92.10/0.20/91.88	77.90/0.50/76.95	—
Lithuanian	79.20/0.35/70.42	81.60/0.33/73.40	64.20/0.48/53.83	43.50/1.33/31.14	—
Lower Sorbian	94.00/0.12/92.06	91.30/0.14/86.83	86.40/0.25/83.97	85.00/0.29/80.63	—
Macedonian	89.90/0.20/89.43	86.10/0.25/85.41	92.10/0.17/91.75	90.80/0.14/90.49	—
Navajo	68.50/0.85/57.64	84.20/0.34/78.00	37.80/2.12/31.16	23.30/2.68/18.33	—
Northern Sami	88.40/0.22/85.35	85.80/0.33/82.12	64.00/0.73/58.47	28.50/2.26/23.79	76.30/0.56/71.91
Norwegian Bokmal	87.60/0.22/87.10	82.00/0.29/81.40	**91.00/0.17/90.54**	83.60/0.26/83.01	—
Norwegian Nynorsk	80.30/0.34/80.09	73.80/0.49/73.34	76.90/0.41/76.50	66.40/0.57/65.51	73.30/0.48/72.03
Persian	96.30/0.08/89.14	98.70/0.02/95.13	79.00/0.56/61.80	71.30/0.96/51.69	—
Polish	79.50/0.50/78.77	78.10/0.50/77.28	88.00/0.28/87.47	83.40/0.43/82.80	—
Portuguese	92.50/0.11/91.56	96.40/0.06/96.07	98.10/0.04/97.92	96.10/0.07/95.84	—
Quechua	97.10/0.05/94.49	95.50/0.11/92.02	95.40/0.09/94.68	93.10/0.16/92.78	—
Romanian	77.30/0.63/73.91	78.60/0.51/75.48	79.80/0.54/77.17	77.30/0.71/75.00	—
Russian	79.90/0.62/79.59	76.40/0.65/76.33	85.70/0.47/85.51	86.10/0.43/85.92	—
Scottish Gaelic	—	—	—	—	—
Serbo-Croatian	78.60/0.46/77.67	79.60/0.41/78.93	84.60/0.32/84.17	77.40/0.63/76.73	—
Slovak	90.60/0.15/86.33	87.90/0.18/81.83	83.30/0.30/78.14	82.40/0.34/76.53	—
Slovene	92.90/0.13/91.86	87.80/0.20/85.17	88.90/0.19/86.48	85.70/0.24/83.20	—
Sorani	85.80/0.20/54.77	**87.80/0.16/59.80**	63.60/0.68/43.72	54.90/1.13/41.71	—
Spanish	86.80/0.26/86.01	92.80/0.12/92.19	90.70/0.21/90.24	88.40/0.36/87.53	—
Swedish	85.50/0.25/85.14	80.60/0.39/80.25	85.40/0.24/84.93	82.70/0.30/82.02	—
Turkish	94.80/0.11/94.17	90.30/0.32/89.40	72.60/0.75/69.29	73.50/0.87/70.48	—
Ukrainian	88.80/0.20/86.15	84.00/0.24/80.66	85.40/0.28/82.44	84.90/0.30/81.34	—
Urdu	**99.40/0.01/94.34**‡	97.90/0.03/81.13	96.50/0.05/84.91	98.20/0.03/84.91	—
Welsh	**98.00/0.04/97.44**‡	**99.00/0.03/98.72**‡	69.00/0.52/65.38	62.00/0.88/57.60	58.00/0.66/52.56

Table 12: Sub-task 1 High Condition Part 3.

	oracle-fc	oracle-e	CLUZH-7	CLUZH-6	LMU-2	LMU-1	UE-LMU-2	CLUZH-2
Albanian	100.00/*/100.00	94.60/*/90.79	88.00/0.33/77.78	88.00/0.33/77.78	88.70/0.28/79.13	88.70/0.28/79.13	86.10/0.31/74.53	87.00/0.36/76.15
Arabic	99.40/*/99.28	87.90/*/86.28	79.30/0.64/77.26	79.30/0.64/77.26	79.70/0.66/76.77	79.70/0.66/76.77	78.00/0.67/75.33	78.00/0.67/75.21
Armenian	97.90/*/97.78	96.50/*/96.23	91.20/0.16/90.69	91.20/0.16/90.69	91.50/0.15/90.80	91.50/0.15/90.80	90.70/0.22/89.80	90.90/0.17/90.02
Basque	47.00/*/18.18	95.00/*/81.82	85.00/0.29/54.55†	85.00/0.29/54.55†	87.00/0.28/63.64†	87.00/0.28/63.64†	88.00/0.28/68.18†	83.00/0.38/54.55†
Bengali	100.00/*/100.00	99.00/*/98.53	99.00/0.05/98.53‡	99.00/0.05/98.53‡	98.00/0.08/97.06‡	98.00/0.08/97.06‡	98.00/0.06/97.06‡	99.00/0.05/98.53‡
Bulgarian	100.00/*/100.00	93.30/*/91.67	82.50/0.28/79.84	82.50/0.28/79.84	82.50/0.28/80.51	82.50/0.28/80.51	80.90/0.31/78.09	81.60/0.28/78.49
Catalan	100.00/*/100.00	96.80/*/95.91	92.60/0.17/91.27	92.60/0.17/91.27	91.00/0.21/88.81	91.00/0.21/88.81	91.20/0.19/89.50	92.30/0.19/90.86
Czech	98.30/*/98.12	91.90/*/91.18	85.00/0.30/83.18	85.00/0.30/83.18	82.40/0.32/80.35	82.40/0.32/80.35	81.90/0.38/79.65	83.90/0.32/81.88
Danish	100.00/*/100.00	92.80/*/92.14	83.00/0.25/81.27	83.00/0.25/81.27	83.60/0.25/81.85	83.60/0.25/81.85	82.80/0.27/81.16	82.50/0.26/80.58
Dutch	100.00/*/100.00	94.50/*/93.99	85.20/0.23/84.20	85.20/0.23/84.20	86.50/0.21/85.76	86.50/0.21/85.76	85.20/0.31/83.98	84.50/0.24/83.31
English	100.00/*/100.00	97.80/*/97.76	94.10/0.11/94.00	94.10/0.11/94.00	94.70/0.09/94.61	94.70/0.09/94.61	93.50/0.18/93.39	94.40/0.10/94.30
Estonian	100.00/*/100.00	91.70/*/89.08	79.10/0.34/74.00	79.10/0.34/74.00	82.20/0.29/77.30	82.20/0.29/77.30	82.40/0.30/77.12	77.00/0.38/71.23
Faroese	100.00/*/100.00	83.10/*/81.93	68.10/0.64/66.25	68.10/0.64/66.25	67.50/0.61/65.34	67.50/0.61/65.34	66.30/0.66/64.77	67.20/0.67/65.00
Finnish	98.80/*/98.78	91.90/*/91.78	75.50/0.40/75.25	75.50/0.40/75.25	75.60/0.40/75.35	75.60/0.40/75.35	78.40/0.41/78.19	72.70/0.44/72.41
French	100.00/*/100.00	86.80/*/86.53	80.30/0.37/79.85	80.30/0.37/79.85	78.60/0.38/78.37	78.60/0.38/78.37	78.00/0.40/77.52	80.10/0.38/79.64
Georgian	95.60/*/95.77	95.70/*/96.00	93.40/0.15/94.05	93.40/0.15/94.05	92.90/0.16/93.02	92.90/0.16/93.02	93.40/0.22/94.05	93.10/0.16/93.71
German	100.00/*/100.00	88.30/*/87.97	79.10/0.58/78.53	79.10/0.58/78.53	78.40/0.54/78.01	78.40/0.54/78.01	79.10/0.51/78.53	78.50/0.58/77.90
Haida	100.00/*/100.00	99.00/*/97.37	93.00/0.14/81.58	93.00/0.14/81.58	95.00/0.06/86.84‡	95.00/0.06/86.84‡	93.00/0.13/81.58	89.00/0.20/73.68
Hebrew	100.00/*/100.00	95.20/*/90.95	82.30/0.23/70.86	82.30/0.23/70.86	83.80/0.21/71.52	83.80/0.21/71.52	79.90/0.27/66.23	81.50/0.24/70.20
Hindi	99.70/*/98.82	99.20/*/97.65	97.30/0.03/92.55	97.30/0.03/92.55	97.00/0.04/90.59	97.00/0.04/90.59	96.20/0.05/89.02	96.40/0.04/89.41
Hungarian	98.60/*/98.55	87.30/*/87.03	74.70/0.47/74.27	74.70/0.47/74.27	74.90/0.49/74.38	74.90/0.49/74.38	73.50/0.59/73.03	73.70/0.50/73.13
Icelandic	100.00/*/100.00	87.80/*/86.99	74.70/0.51/73.08	74.70/0.51/73.08	71.90/0.55/70.19	71.90/0.55/70.19	72.20/0.57/70.52	73.70/0.52/72.19
Irish	99.10/*/98.99	86.30/*/85.44	72.60/0.77/71.56	72.60/0.77/71.56	68.30/0.88/66.74	68.30/0.88/66.74	68.10/0.95/66.63	69.30/0.92/68.53
Italian	100.00/*/100.00	96.00/*/95.73	92.00/0.17/91.77	92.00/0.17/91.77	92.50/0.17/92.41	92.50/0.17/92.41	93.30/0.17/93.16	91.70/0.18/91.45
Khaling	90.90/*/80.33	94.40/*/87.91	78.50/0.41/60.90	78.50/0.41/60.90	87.10/0.19/74.88	87.10/0.19/74.88	84.00/0.29/71.09	77.70/0.42/60.90
Kurmanji	97.20/*/97.08	96.50/*/96.35	92.80/0.10/92.69	92.80/0.10/92.69	90.90/0.13/91.34	90.90/0.13/91.34	89.80/0.22/90.19	91.50/0.16/91.65
Latin	100.00/*/100.00	77.70/*/77.67	51.80/0.80/51.22	51.80/0.80/51.22	49.30/0.86/48.47	49.30/0.86/48.47	48.90/1.09/47.94	50.40/0.82/50.16
Latvian	99.30/*/99.24	93.10/*/92.86	88.60/0.19/88.20	88.60/0.19/88.20	85.40/0.28/84.74	85.40/0.28/84.74	86.70/0.39/86.26	88.10/0.21/87.77
Lithuanian	98.90/*/98.44	79.80/*/73.87	62.10/0.54/50.55	62.10/0.54/50.55	61.90/0.58/50.55	61.90/0.58/50.55	62.60/0.58/52.27	60.80/0.57/48.98
Lower Sorbian	100.00/*/100.00	92.90/*/90.79	83.90/0.31/79.21	83.90/0.31/79.21	83.50/0.30/78.73	83.50/0.30/78.73	84.10/0.30/79.52	83.10/0.33/78.10
Macedonian	98.70/*/98.63	96.20/*/96.09	91.70/0.15/91.44	91.70/0.15/91.44	91.80/0.13/91.44	91.80/0.13/91.44	89.60/0.21/89.32	91.80/0.16/91.54
Navajo	99.00/*/98.78	67.70/*/57.64	50.80/1.45/38.90	50.80/1.45/38.90	48.00/1.68/36.05	48.00/1.68/36.05	49.30/1.60/36.66	49.60/1.48/38.09
Northern Sami	100.00/*/100.00	88.10/*/85.35	70.70/0.56/65.32	70.70/0.56/65.32	70.70/0.57/64.92	70.70/0.57/64.92	74.00/0.54/68.01	67.90/0.61/61.96
Norwegian Bokmal	99.30/*/99.25	93.40/*/93.01	83.70/0.26/82.90	83.70/0.26/82.90	83.90/0.27/83.01	83.90/0.27/83.01	84.40/0.27/83.55	83.50/0.26/82.69
Norwegian Nynorsk	99.70/*/99.67	86.10/*/85.31	65.40/0.56/64.20	65.40/0.56/64.20	65.60/0.56/64.31	65.60/0.56/64.31	64.00/0.62/63.00	64.40/0.59/63.22
Persian	100.00/*/100.00	96.30/*/90.26	87.10/0.23/70.41	87.10/0.23/70.41	90.70/0.14/77.90	90.70/0.14/77.90	91.90/0.14/81.65	85.90/0.27/69.66
Polish	99.70/*/99.68	89.80/*/89.38	79.90/0.45/79.09	79.90/0.45/79.09	77.30/0.54/76.11	77.30/0.54/76.11	76.40/0.64/75.48	79.00/0.46/78.13
Portuguese	100.00/*/100.00	96.90/*/96.53	94.50/0.08/93.99	94.50/0.08/93.99	95.00/0.08/94.45	95.00/0.08/94.45	94.10/0.10/93.41	94.50/0.08/94.10
Quechua	86.20/*/79.09	99.80/*/99.62	98.30/0.04/97.91†	98.30/0.04/97.91†	96.60/0.08/94.11†	96.60/0.08/94.11†	97.20/0.06/95.25†	97.10/0.10/95.63†
Romanian	100.00/*/100.00	87.10/*/85.39	76.60/0.59/73.67	76.60/0.59/73.67	73.00/0.68/69.57	73.00/0.68/69.57	75.00/0.66/72.10	76.40/0.60/73.31
Russian	99.30/*/99.39	92.10/*/92.04	83.80/0.39/83.57	83.80/0.39/83.57	79.80/0.56/79.49	79.80/0.56/79.49	79.30/0.60/78.98	84.10/0.39/83.88
Scottish Gaelic	100.00/*/100.00	94.00/*/95.00	80.00/0.42/77.50	80.00/0.42/77.50	88.00/0.32/87.50‡	88.00/0.32/87.50‡	90.00/0.32/90.00‡	82.00/0.42/80.00
Serbo-Croatian	92.10/*/91.93	92.30/*/91.93	82.40/0.33/82.08	82.40/0.33/82.08	81.80/0.35/81.03	81.80/0.35/81.03	80.40/0.45/79.56	81.10/0.38/80.50
Slovak	100.00/*/100.00	91.10/*/86.98	80.50/0.32/73.15	80.50/0.32/73.15	77.60/0.39/69.29	77.60/0.39/69.29	78.70/0.38/69.61	79.50/0.35/71.54
Slovene	99.10/*/98.95	93.10/*/91.99	87.70/0.22/85.30	87.70/0.22/85.30	88.80/0.22/86.75	88.80/0.22/86.75	87.80/0.32/86.09	87.00/0.24/84.51
Sorani	97.40/*/87.44	91.30/*/70.85	76.00/0.39/37.69	76.00/0.39/37.69	82.90/0.25/52.76	82.90/0.25/52.76	79.10/0.34/44.72	71.90/0.48/35.18
Spanish	100.00/*/100.00	95.60/*/95.23	90.80/0.17/90.24	90.80/0.17/90.24	90.80/0.17/90.35	90.80/0.17/90.35	91.30/0.16/90.56	90.80/0.17/90.13
Swedish	100.00/*/100.00	92.90/*/92.62	79.40/0.34/78.69	79.40/0.34/78.69	79.40/0.35/78.79	79.40/0.35/78.79	79.70/0.36/79.00	78.60/0.35/77.96
Turkish	93.80/*/93.21	94.40/*/93.57	89.00/0.27/87.38	89.00/0.27/87.38	85.00/0.32/82.98	85.00/0.32/82.98	89.70/0.33/88.69	87.70/0.31/85.95
Ukrainian	99.60/*/99.45	90.90/*/89.44	82.50/0.33/79.42	82.50/0.33/79.42	78.00/0.46/74.35	78.00/0.46/74.35	77.90/0.48/74.62	81.60/0.35/78.05
Urdu	98.90/*/90.57	99.40/*/94.34	98.00/0.03/82.08	98.00/0.03/82.08	97.30/0.03/74.53	97.30/0.03/74.53	96.00/0.07/66.04	97.70/0.04/78.30
Welsh	100.00/*/100.00	98.00/*/97.44	92.00/0.14/89.74	92.00/0.14/89.74	93.00/0.09/91.03‡	93.00/0.09/91.03‡	91.00/0.15/88.46	89.00/0.19/85.90

Table 13: Sub-task 1 Medium Condition Part 1.

	UE-LMU-1	CLUZH-5	CLUZH-1	CLUZH-4	CLUZH-3	CU-1	UF-1	UTNII-1
Albanian	86.40/0.33/74.53	85.30/0.42/72.63	85.30/0.42/72.63	83.70/0.47/73.17	83.90/0.47/72.90	**89.40/0.28/79.95**	64.20/1.18/48.78	61.20/0.88/36.31
Arabic	76.00/0.74/72.92	77.60/0.68/74.85	77.60/0.68/74.85	77.10/0.71/75.33	76.50/0.73/74.85	73.60/0.99/71.24	55.80/1.53/53.19	53.60/1.33/50.06
Armenian	89.70/0.24/88.91	**90.30/0.19/89.69**	89.80/0.18/88.91	**90.30/0.19/89.80**	**90.30/0.19/89.69**	87.50/0.23/86.47	73.50/0.66/72.95	73.20/0.47/71.73
Basque	**89.00/0.28/68.18†**	69.00/0.66/22.73†	69.00/0.66/22.73†	72.00/0.80/36.36†	72.00/0.78/36.36†	66.00/0.87/22.73†	80.00/0.44/31.82†	**81.00/0.32/54.55†**
Bengali	**98.00/0.06/97.06‡**	**97.00/0.07/95.59‡**	**99.00/0.05/98.53‡**	**98.00/0.06/97.06‡**	**97.00/0.07/95.59‡**	**95.00/0.17/92.65‡**	93.00/0.12/89.71	**95.00/0.12/92.65‡**
Bulgarian	**80.80/0.32/78.36**	**81.30/0.28/78.36**	**81.30/0.28/78.36**	80.70/0.31/78.36	80.70/0.30/78.09	79.90/0.33/77.82	63.60/0.89/60.62	65.50/0.60/60.62
Catalan	**91.20/0.19/89.36**	**92.20/0.19/90.72**	**92.20/0.19/90.72**	90.00/0.23/87.86	89.20/0.25/86.90	89.50/0.21/87.45	80.60/0.38/76.94	77.20/0.43/72.71
Czech	81.60/0.36/79.53	84.10/0.32/82.12	84.10/0.32/82.12	84.00/0.30/82.12	82.90/0.32/81.06	**86.30/0.26/85.18**	68.10/0.94/65.53	60.30/0.73/57.53
Danish	81.40/0.29/79.77	81.50/0.28/79.42	81.50/0.28/79.42	81.20/0.28/79.19	80.80/0.30/78.73	76.70/0.35/74.80	79.30/0.34/77.23	75.00/0.37/72.95
Dutch	**85.00/0.30/83.98**	83.10/0.31/81.76	83.10/0.31/81.76	80.80/0.28/80.09	80.40/0.28/79.64	74.70/0.42/73.08	69.70/0.72/68.19	73.10/0.43/71.52
English	92.80/0.18/92.68	**94.40/0.10/94.30**	**94.40/0.10/94.30**	**93.60/0.11/93.49**	**93.60/0.11/93.49**	91.60/0.14/91.45	88.30/0.25/88.10	90.40/0.16/90.34
Estonian	80.30/0.33/74.18	77.00/0.39/70.88	77.00/0.39/70.88	78.70/0.40/74.00	77.40/0.42/72.27	74.00/0.40/67.94	64.60/0.71/59.27	65.80/0.60/59.62
Faroese	**65.90/0.68/64.20**	66.10/0.71/64.55	66.70/0.69/64.43	**67.10/0.67/65.45**	66.10/0.71/64.55	64.60/0.74/62.95	52.00/0.97/49.89	39.00/1.23/36.70
Finnish	**76.80/0.44/76.47**	71.60/0.46/71.30	71.60/0.46/71.30	71.60/0.50/71.30	70.20/0.55/69.88	67.20/0.72/67.04	37.30/1.98/37.42	51.20/0.94/50.71
French	77.90/0.42/77.31	78.50/0.47/77.84	78.50/0.47/77.84	77.90/0.40/77.73	76.90/0.41/76.67	77.80/0.40/77.52	67.50/0.72/67.13	68.00/0.56/67.66
Georgian	**93.00/0.21/93.48**	**93.10/0.16/93.59**	**93.10/0.16/93.59**	**93.00/0.19/93.48**	**92.90/0.19/93.36**	**92.50/0.24/93.14**	78.60/0.47/77.57	88.50/0.36/88.90
German	77.50/0.57/76.97	77.30/0.60/76.76	77.30/0.60/76.76	**80.00/0.55/79.46**	78.80/0.56/78.22	74.60/0.75/74.07	72.80/0.76/72.10	60.90/0.92/60.37
Haida	**94.00/0.13/84.21‡**	88.00/0.24/71.05	88.00/0.24/71.05	**93.00/0.16/81.58**	**92.00/0.18/78.95**	68.00/0.80/50.00	81.00/0.66/52.63	**88.00/0.24/73.68**
Hebrew	80.90/0.26/67.77	80.60/0.25/68.87	80.60/0.25/68.87	75.10/0.34/61.15	75.00/0.34/61.15	77.80/0.28/64.90	67.70/0.48/52.32	67.30/0.45/50.55
Hindi	**96.20/0.04/88.63**	**97.40/0.04/92.16**	96.10/0.04/87.84	**97.30/0.04/92.16**	**97.40/0.04/92.16**	93.30/0.14/82.35	86.80/0.35/61.18	81.90/0.41/55.29
Hungarian	70.20/0.60/69.71	**74.80/0.48/74.38**	**73.60/0.49/73.13**	**75.10/0.46/74.69**	**74.80/0.48/74.38**	56.20/0.86/55.60	66.50/0.65/66.29	52.80/0.94/52.59
Icelandic	67.50/0.66/65.29	**73.40/0.52/71.97**	**73.40/0.52/71.97**	73.00/0.55/71.19	72.50/0.56/70.86	67.10/0.67/65.29	57.90/0.85/56.17	41.20/1.20/38.71
Irish	65.40/1.03/64.39	**71.20/0.85/70.21**	68.50/0.96/67.75	**71.20/0.85/70.21**	**71.20/0.85/70.21**	57.00/1.14/55.99	35.40/2.47/34.71	31.90/1.92/30.46
Italian	92.10/0.18/91.88	91.60/0.19/91.35	91.60/0.19/91.35	91.00/0.19/90.81	90.80/0.20/90.60	85.90/0.26/85.47	69.10/0.99/68.38	86.10/0.27/85.47
Khaling	82.90/0.35/68.48	75.80/0.45/58.53	75.80/0.45/58.53	68.10/0.56/48.34	67.80/0.57/47.87	82.90/0.30/68.25	79.20/0.35/65.64	69.30/0.53/49.05
Kurmanji	89.00/0.22/89.25	91.60/0.14/91.65	90.50/0.17/90.61	**92.50/0.12/92.59**	91.60/0.14/91.65	91.10/0.20/91.23	86.30/0.45/87.68	76.20/0.58/76.72
Latin	43.00/1.20/42.12	49.30/0.84/48.89	49.30/0.84/48.89	48.90/0.85/48.25	47.60/0.92/46.98	46.10/0.97/46.24	30.90/1.30/30.79	30.70/1.44/29.74
Latvian	86.30/0.43/86.04	**87.60/0.22/87.23**	**87.60/0.22/87.23**	87.40/0.24/86.90	87.30/0.24/86.80	86.00/0.56/85.71	73.10/0.78/72.51	61.90/0.85/61.47
Lithuanian	**61.40/0.65/49.61**	**60.30/0.60/48.36**	**60.30/0.60/48.36**	59.40/0.64/48.04	57.10/0.68/44.91	58.40/0.67/45.85	49.20/0.94/35.99	38.70/1.25/27.70
Lower Sorbian	82.00/0.32/75.71	**82.50/0.34/76.98**	**82.90/0.33/77.94**	**82.80/0.34/77.46**	**82.50/0.34/76.98**	**83.60/0.31/78.25**	73.50/0.48/66.83	59.10/0.69/47.78
Macedonian	89.10/0.20/88.79	**91.80/0.17/91.54**	**91.80/0.17/91.54**	90.90/0.17/90.59	**90.70/0.17/90.38**	90.40/0.18/90.06	78.30/0.39/77.59	76.20/0.39/75.26
Navajo	46.40/1.71/33.60	48.80/1.49/37.47	48.80/1.49/37.47	39.90/2.02/29.33	39.90/2.01/29.33	40.50/2.16/30.14	28.90/2.46/17.31	31.80/2.05/23.22
Northern Sami	68.90/0.61/62.50	64.50/0.67/58.33	64.50/0.67/58.33	63.30/0.74/56.45	60.60/0.80/53.23	57.00/0.91/50.94	50.40/1.01/43.68	34.40/1.56/28.23
Norwegian Bokmal	**84.10/0.28/83.33**	**83.70/0.25/82.90**	**83.50/0.26/82.69**	**83.10/0.27/82.26**	**83.70/0.25/82.90**	80.80/0.32/80.00	80.60/0.37/79.78	76.70/0.38/75.59
Norwegian Nynorsk	61.50/0.65/59.96	**64.00/0.59/62.79**	**64.00/0.59/62.79**	**64.40/0.58/63.33**	**63.30/0.61/62.35**	62.50/0.65/61.92	58.80/0.70/57.34	55.70/0.77/54.95
Persian	90.30/0.19/76.78	85.80/0.28/69.66	85.80/0.28/69.66	81.80/0.43/61.05	81.20/0.45/59.93	86.10/0.33/71.54	66.20/1.01/32.96	71.70/0.53/46.82
Polish	73.30/0.72/72.51	**79.20/0.46/78.34**	**79.20/0.46/78.34**	77.20/0.53/76.22	77.50/0.52/76.54	**78.00/0.52/77.18**	64.20/1.09/63.06	49.60/1.23/48.73
Portuguese	**94.80/0.09/94.22**	**94.50/0.09/94.10**	**94.50/0.09/94.10**	**94.30/0.10/93.64**	**94.10/0.10/93.41**	**94.70/0.08/94.22**	84.30/0.29/83.24	85.50/0.22/84.28
Quechua	96.80/0.07/94.68†	96.50/0.36/94.11†	96.10/0.16/93.73†	**97.90/0.11/96.77†**	96.50/0.36/94.11†	88.20/0.25/80.42	90.70/0.29/83.65†	90.20/0.26/83.27†
Romanian	71.50/0.71/68.36	**75.70/0.62/72.58**	**75.70/0.62/72.58**	74.80/0.62/71.98	74.80/0.64/72.10	**77.40/0.58/74.64**	57.50/1.37/53.02	46.00/1.26/40.94
Russian	78.10/0.65/77.76	**83.50/0.40/83.27**	**83.50/0.40/83.27**	82.00/0.47/81.73	82.10/0.46/81.84	81.90/0.51/81.63	67.70/0.89/67.14	53.10/1.25/52.55
Scottish Gaelic	**86.00/0.38/85.00‡**	**80.00/0.44/77.50**	**80.00/0.44/77.50**	78.00/0.48/77.50	66.00/1.18/65.00	74.00/0.66/72.50	78.00/0.54/75.00	**80.00/0.54/77.50**
Serbo-Croatian	79.40/0.46/78.72	**82.30/0.35/81.97**	80.80/0.38/80.19	**82.80/0.34/82.49**	**82.30/0.35/81.97**	**83.30/0.32/82.91**	59.00/1.41/57.65	41.80/1.17/40.46
Slovak	77.50/0.40/68.49	**79.50/0.37/71.86**	**79.50/0.37/71.86**	77.30/0.40/69.45	77.60/0.40/69.94	78.00/0.38/70.42	69.20/0.53/60.77	61.40/0.63/50.48
Slovene	85.30/0.36/83.46	86.70/0.24/83.99	86.70/0.24/83.99	86.70/0.25/84.25	85.50/0.26/83.07	86.30/0.29/83.73	78.80/0.45/75.72	65.80/0.55/59.58
Sorani	76.80/0.38/41.21	70.20/0.51/34.67	70.20/0.51/34.67	65.80/0.70/35.68	65.00/0.70/34.67	71.50/0.52/39.70	60.00/0.75/20.60	58.10/0.85/10.55
Spanish	**91.70/0.15/91.11**	**90.60/0.17/89.91**	**90.60/0.17/89.91**	87.90/0.25/87.20	88.20/0.24/87.53	89.50/0.24/88.83	71.20/0.81/69.96	80.30/0.40/79.39
Swedish	**79.30/0.36/78.59**	**77.40/0.37/76.61**	76.90/0.38/76.20	**79.10/0.34/78.27**	**77.40/0.37/76.61**	76.30/0.51/75.68	74.40/0.46/73.70	68.00/0.55/67.57
Turkish	**88.20/0.31/86.67**	87.80/0.30/86.07	87.80/0.30/86.07	**88.80/0.30/87.74**	**88.40/0.29/87.26**	66.60/0.98/64.29	83.20/0.54/81.79	60.70/1.06/58.57
Ukrainian	76.60/0.49/72.70	**81.50/0.35/78.33**	**81.50/0.35/78.33**	79.80/0.40/75.86	80.10/0.39/76.27	79.70/0.48/76.27	62.80/0.76/57.48	57.20/0.79/51.03
Urdu	95.30/0.10/63.21	**97.60/0.03/81.13**	97.40/0.04/78.30	**98.00/0.03/83.02**	**97.60/0.03/81.13**	96.10/0.05/71.70	90.80/0.23/41.51	89.10/0.29/20.75
Welsh	**88.00/0.19/84.62**	**87.00/0.21/85.90**	**87.00/0.21/85.90**	**89.00/0.23/87.18**	**88.00/0.24/85.90**	82.00/0.27/80.77	78.00/0.35/73.08	**86.00/0.21/82.05**

Table 14: Sub-task 1 Medium Condition Part 2.

	baseline	IIT(BHU)-2	ISI-1	IIT(BHU)-1	CMU-1	EHU-1
Albanian	66.30/1.12/55.01	41.50/1.88/26.29	53.90/2.29/35.23	32.20/2.44/18.16	—	—
Arabic	42.10/1.77/41.88	37.60/2.20/33.94	34.60/2.36/33.81	37.60/2.20/33.94	—	—
Armenian	72.70/0.53/70.95	68.10/0.78/67.96	58.20/1.16/57.54	58.40/1.14/58.43	—	—
Basque	2.00/5.57/0.00	66.00/0.75/31.82†	1.00/2.95/0.00	66.00/0.75/31.82†	—	6.00/5.10/0.00
Bengali	76.00/0.33/77.94	91.00/0.19/86.76	53.00/1.28/48.53	91.00/0.19/86.76	—	—
Bulgarian	72.80/0.47/69.22	55.50/0.98/52.02	62.30/0.86/58.06	54.80/1.13/50.27	—	—
Catalan	84.30/0.37/81.31	79.70/0.38/75.85	78.10/0.57/74.35	79.70/0.38/75.85	—	—
Czech	81.50/0.41/79.53	52.90/1.41/50.35	67.60/0.74/64.12	38.60/1.74/35.65	—	—
Danish	78.10/0.35/76.07	0.50/5.53/0.58	76.80/0.35/74.91	69.20/0.47/66.71	—	—
Dutch	73.20/0.41/71.30	74.60/0.44/73.30	60.50/0.64/57.95	66.50/0.62/64.74	—	—
English	90.90/0.16/90.74	0.00/8.74/0.00	91.10/0.13/90.95	87.90/0.20/87.69	—	—
Estonian	62.90/0.77/51.65	45.70/1.63/43.33	34.80/2.05/24.96	39.90/1.68/34.84	—	—
Faroese	60.60/0.85/58.86	40.40/1.20/37.61	52.00/1.00/49.77	0.00/8.13/0.00	—	—
Finnish	43.70/1.24/43.20	21.50/2.75/21.40	20.50/3.59/20.18	15.00/3.21/14.91	—	—
French	72.50/0.51/71.79	69.70/0.61/69.03	73.90/0.65/73.70	63.60/0.77/63.10	—	—
Georgian	92.00/0.20/92.11	87.70/0.32/87.41	91.10/0.24/91.30	87.70/0.32/87.41	—	—
German	72.10/0.72/71.37	57.30/0.93/56.74	62.50/0.81/61.83	30.10/1.49/29.88	—	—
Haida	56.00/1.31/26.32	0.00/17.48/0.00	28.00/4.09/13.16	83.00/0.47/63.16	—	—
Hebrew	37.50/0.98/23.62	65.80/0.51/50.33	46.60/1.13/31.35	55.90/0.69/38.19	—	48.40/0.76/35.76
Hindi	85.90/0.21/55.29	87.40/0.42/60.78	80.60/0.54/50.20	85.20/0.56/57.25	—	—
Hungarian	42.30/1.54/41.29	62.80/0.68/62.24	40.60/1.33/39.73	47.70/1.05/47.51	—	—
Icelandic	60.40/0.85/58.29	41.60/1.16/39.71	53.90/1.01/51.72	0.00/8.09/0.00	—	—
Irish	44.00/1.57/43.45	26.10/3.11/25.42	39.50/2.19/39.08	20.10/3.71/19.26	—	—
Italian	71.60/0.84/70.94	70.30/0.80/69.44	75.70/0.57/75.00	58.50/1.26/57.48	—	—
Khaling	17.90/2.01/8.06	58.20/0.81/35.55	16.40/3.17/7.35	52.20/0.97/29.86	—	—
Kurmanji	89.10/0.19/89.46	19.20/1.72/19.42	88.00/0.26/88.73	81.60/0.62/82.78	—	—
Latin	37.60/1.17/37.99	22.10/1.72/21.90	14.50/2.90/14.92	22.10/1.72/21.90	—	39.70/1.29/39.58
Latvian	85.70/0.25/85.17	60.20/0.88/58.01	62.70/0.83/61.47	57.70/0.95/56.06	—	—
Lithuanian	52.20/0.70/40.06	37.60/1.34/25.20	20.70/2.24/13.15	33.70/1.34/22.54	—	—
Lower Sorbian	70.80/0.57/63.33	69.00/0.52/60.00	69.90/0.66/61.75	0.00/7.01/0.00	—	—
Macedonian	83.60/0.31/82.98	79.10/0.32/78.44	76.00/0.36/74.95	69.30/0.50/68.39	—	—
Navajo	33.50/2.37/25.46	19.30/2.78/11.81	14.40/3.60/9.98	19.90/2.82/12.63	—	—
Northern Sami	37.00/1.42/29.70	40.80/1.26/35.75	11.80/3.29/9.54	34.00/1.64/28.63	—	38.90/1.43/32.80
Norwegian Bokmal	80.70/0.31/79.78	78.30/0.33/77.20	78.00/0.32/76.77	48.70/0.74/47.20	—	—
Norwegian Nynorsk	61.10/0.67/59.74	56.40/0.71/55.06	59.60/0.70/58.22	0.00/8.68/0.00	—	54.00/0.80/52.67
Persian	62.30/1.18/36.33	57.00/1.46/25.84	41.20/2.69/16.85	57.10/1.27/24.34	—	—
Polish	74.00/0.58/73.04	48.40/1.33/46.82	59.70/1.29/58.49	19.60/2.01/18.58	—	—
Portuguese	93.40/0.10/92.72	89.60/0.16/88.67	87.70/0.26/86.47	86.00/0.21/85.09	—	—
Quechua	70.30/1.52/59.89	93.00/0.28/87.83†	36.20/2.35/26.62	93.00/0.28/87.83†	—	—
Romanian	69.40/0.75/65.70	49.00/1.57/44.32	60.90/1.09/57.25	36.90/1.95/32.85	—	—
Russian	75.90/0.62/75.61	66.60/0.83/66.12	69.40/0.77/68.98	39.40/1.37/38.67	—	—
Scottish Gaelic	48.00/0.98/42.50	76.00/0.68/75.00	62.00/0.94/60.00	66.00/1.04/62.50	68.00/0.86/65.00	—
Serbo-Croatian	64.50/0.85/64.15	49.50/1.52/48.53	55.50/1.52/54.61	38.70/1.83/37.32	—	—
Slovak	72.30/0.50/63.83	63.70/0.60/52.41	69.90/0.57/59.00	52.80/0.82/40.68	—	—
Slovene	82.20/0.32/78.35	73.50/0.45/68.50	69.20/0.52/62.07	32.30/1.13/24.54	—	—
Sorani	51.70/1.06/31.66	57.50/0.95/18.09	23.00/2.38/16.58	46.50/1.31/8.54	—	—
Spanish	84.70/0.35/83.84	73.90/0.68/72.23	71.40/0.78/70.17	66.70/0.89/65.62	—	—
Swedish	75.70/0.43/74.95	70.00/0.49/69.13	73.00/0.44/71.93	47.70/1.00/46.78	—	—
Turkish	32.90/2.90/30.00	0.00/12.97/0.00	27.10/2.56/23.69	74.50/0.65/71.67	—	—
Ukrainian	72.80/0.48/68.59	61.50/0.70/55.83	65.20/0.69/59.40	30.80/1.47/23.73	—	—
Urdu	87.50/0.21/36.79	88.00/0.47/33.02	80.20/0.46/27.36	88.00/0.47/33.02	—	—
Welsh	56.00/1.11/50.00	83.00/0.29/80.77	32.00/1.97/29.49	74.00/0.40/69.23	—	44.00/0.80/38.46

Table 15: Sub-task 1 Medium Condition Part 3.

	oracle-fc	oracle-e	CLUZH-7	CLUZH-6	CLUZH-4	CLUZH-5	CLUZH-3	CLUZH-2
Albanian	49.40/*/31.98	41.40/*/27.37	29.50/2.35/14.09	29.50/2.35/14.09	26.30/2.96/13.55	25.40/2.89/12.20	25.40/2.89/12.20	27.10/2.38/14.09
Arabic	49.40/*/49.22	51.10/*/49.58	37.00/2.03/34.66	37.00/2.03/34.66	36.70/2.08/35.14	36.60/2.07/35.02	36.60/2.07/35.02	34.00/2.05/32.25
Armenian	53.60/*/53.99	71.60/*/72.06	58.70/1.21/59.20†	58.70/1.21/59.20†	54.60/1.94/55.88	53.40/2.05/55.10	53.40/2.05/55.10	55.10/1.19/55.65
Basque	8.00/*/0.00	25.00/*/9.09	10.00/4.06/4.55	10.00/4.06/4.55	7.00/4.67/0.00	11.00/4.02/4.55	7.00/4.67/0.00	11.00/4.11/4.55
Bengali	83.00/*/75.00	82.00/*/75.00	66.00/0.61/61.76	66.00/0.61/61.76	67.00/0.65/63.24	68.00/0.64/64.71	68.00/0.64/64.71	65.00/0.69/52.94
Bulgarian	60.70/*/54.84	70.70/*/66.67	54.60/0.82/50.13	54.60/0.82/50.13	52.90/0.87/48.52	51.70/0.93/47.31	51.70/0.93/47.31	45.80/0.99/40.99
Catalan	87.40/*/83.90	75.90/*/70.67	65.30/0.71/58.66	65.30/0.71/58.66	63.10/0.83/56.21	63.10/0.82/56.34	63.10/0.82/56.34	61.70/0.82/54.71
Czech	57.10/*/56.82	62.00/*/59.76	44.00/1.47/41.06	44.00/1.47/41.06	43.60/1.43/40.94	42.90/1.49/40.71	42.90/1.49/40.71	35.70/1.63/33.53
Danish	97.80/*/97.57	84.00/*/82.43	75.50/0.37/73.18	75.50/0.37/73.18	73.80/0.39/71.45	74.00/0.40/71.79	74.00/0.40/71.79	73.20/0.43/70.64
Dutch	87.30/*/85.87	69.00/*/67.19	51.80/0.72/48.83	51.80/0.72/48.83	51.70/0.71/48.61	51.50/0.72/48.61	51.50/0.72/48.61	50.80/0.77/47.94
English	100.00/*/100.00	92.20/*/92.07	89.70/0.15/89.52	89.70/0.15/89.52	89.10/0.16/88.91	90.40/0.15/90.23	89.00/0.16/88.81	90.20/0.15/90.03
Estonian	70.30/*/64.82	54.70/*/44.71	32.90/1.59/23.05	32.90/1.59/23.05	30.00/3.04/20.28	28.80/3.10/19.76	28.80/3.10/19.76	28.30/1.80/20.28
Faroese	81.50/*/79.66	57.90/*/55.11	42.40/1.15/40.00	42.40/1.15/40.00	39.80/1.21/37.50	38.20/1.26/35.57	38.20/1.26/35.57	39.30/1.19/36.70
Finnish	50.60/*/50.81	32.30/*/32.25	19.70/2.13/19.47	19.70/2.13/19.47	16.40/5.17/16.43	16.10/2.37/15.82	14.20/6.07/14.30	17.50/2.31/17.24
French	96.60/*/96.50	73.70/*/73.06	66.00/0.65/65.43	66.00/0.65/65.43	65.30/0.68/64.69	64.00/0.81/63.52	64.20/0.70/63.52	65.50/0.70/65.01
Georgian	88.80/*/89.02	90.90/*/91.08	83.60/0.37/83.07	83.60/0.37/83.07	81.50/0.50/80.66	80.80/0.52/80.09	80.80/0.52/80.09	79.60/0.41/79.18
German	94.40/*/94.19	81.00/*/80.39	67.10/0.81/66.18	67.10/0.81/66.18	68.10/0.84/67.12	67.30/0.89/66.49	67.30/0.89/66.49	64.30/0.84/63.49
Haida	41.00/*/18.42	60.00/*/34.21	44.00/2.61/18.42	44.00/2.61/18.42	37.00/2.57/18.42	39.00/2.96/15.79	37.00/2.57/18.42	40.00/2.87/15.79
Hebrew	82.40/*/67.55	55.30/*/37.75	31.90/1.16/18.76	31.90/1.16/18.76	28.30/1.25/16.34	27.50/1.27/15.23	27.50/1.27/15.23	30.30/1.21/15.67
Hindi	37.20/*/8.24	84.00/*/52.16	73.70/0.96/34.12†	73.70/0.96/34.12†	68.60/1.18/27.45†	69.00/1.04/32.55†	68.60/1.19/27.45†	68.90/1.04/32.55†
Hungarian	86.00/*/86.10	54.50/*/54.15	38.10/1.28/37.45	38.10/1.28/37.45	35.20/1.38/34.65	37.20/1.41/36.41	34.20/1.45/33.51	36.90/1.39/36.10
Icelandic	85.30/*/85.54	59.70/*/58.18	39.40/1.33/37.93	39.40/1.33/37.93	39.60/1.36/38.26	38.80/1.40/37.37	38.80/1.40/37.37	37.50/1.38/35.82
Irish	82.70/*/84.88	50.10/*/50.84	37.80/2.20/38.07	37.80/2.20/38.07	35.20/2.49/35.61	34.90/2.51/35.27	34.90/2.51/35.27	31.20/2.51/31.24
Italian	81.80/*/80.66	64.00/*/62.61	53.80/1.02/52.35	53.80/1.02/52.35	54.50/1.04/53.31	53.00/1.07/51.82	53.00/1.07/51.82	48.40/1.13/47.01
Khaling	22.00/*/6.87	33.80/*/15.17	17.10/2.41/7.11	17.10/2.41/7.11	12.30/2.59/3.79	15.50/2.52/5.45	12.60/2.49/3.55	15.80/2.53/5.69
Kurmanji	90.20/*/91.34	88.00/*/89.25	86.50/0.64/88.10	86.50/0.64/88.10	86.30/0.74/88.00	86.30/0.76/88.00	86.30/0.76/88.00	86.60/0.57/87.79
Latin	52.30/*/51.53	29.10/*/30.05	18.40/2.30/19.15	18.40/2.30/19.15	16.90/2.48/17.78	16.20/2.37/16.83	16.20/2.37/16.83	15.30/2.51/15.98
Latvian	83.90/*/83.12	76.40/*/75.65	67.60/0.77/66.88	67.60/0.77/66.88	68.10/0.80/67.21	66.40/0.84/65.48	66.40/0.84/65.48	60.10/0.89/59.09
Lithuanian	65.40/*/66.35	32.70/*/24.10	21.50/1.79/13.46	21.50/1.79/13.46	19.70/2.01/11.42	19.20/2.10/12.21	19.30/2.08/11.27	19.80/2.02/12.52
Lower Sorbian	76.80/*/70.48	69.00/*/57.94	51.40/0.89/39.37	51.40/0.89/39.37	50.30/0.94/37.78	49.60/0.97/37.62	49.60/0.97/37.62	46.30/0.97/33.81
Macedonian	80.20/*/79.49	82.80/*/82.14	65.50/0.54/64.48	65.50/0.54/64.48	60.50/0.60/59.20	59.70/0.62/58.46	59.70/0.62/58.46	61.40/0.64/60.47
Navajo	92.60/*/88.39	28.00/*/21.38	20.40/3.28/11.81	20.40/3.28/11.81	19.30/3.33/11.41	19.40/3.33/11.41	19.40/3.33/11.41	17.50/3.20/10.39
Northern Sami	69.10/*/61.42	29.90/*/24.33	17.30/2.34/13.58	17.30/2.34/13.58	14.50/2.68/11.02	14.80/2.66/11.42	15.00/2.64/11.42	16.30/2.59/12.90
Norwegian Bokmal	99.30/*/99.25	88.90/*/88.49	78.00/0.33/77.20	78.00/0.33/77.20	77.50/0.35/76.56	77.10/0.35/76.24	77.30/0.35/76.45	77.10/0.35/76.24
Norwegian Nynorsk	98.60/*/98.48	76.30/*/74.97	54.60/0.78/53.86	54.60/0.78/53.86	52.80/0.87/52.23	52.80/0.90/52.34	52.80/0.90/52.34	51.20/0.89/49.95
Persian	51.50/*/17.23	65.00/*/35.58	51.00/1.21/19.85	51.00/1.21/19.85	47.50/1.59/16.48	45.30/1.67/14.23	45.30/1.67/14.23	46.00/1.30/16.10
Polish	74.70/*/74.52	62.60/*/61.36	47.90/1.49/47.03	47.90/1.49/47.03	46.70/2.04/45.86	46.30/2.33/45.75	46.30/2.33/45.75	40.80/1.49/39.92
Portuguese	75.90/*/72.72	78.30/*/75.95	73.30/0.44/70.40	73.30/0.44/70.40	71.70/0.49/68.67	70.50/0.48/67.28	70.50/0.48/67.28	70.20/0.51/67.17
Quechua	23.60/*/16.54	78.40/*/65.78	61.10/1.38/43.35†	61.10/1.38/43.35†	60.00/1.62/41.83†	60.10/1.61/42.02†	60.10/1.61/42.02†	49.90/1.73/31.94†
Romanian	79.40/*/75.97	60.70/*/55.80	46.30/1.47/40.10	46.30/1.47/40.10	43.40/1.70/36.96	41.90/1.52/36.84	41.30/1.75/35.02	42.30/1.50/36.96
Russian	77.00/*/76.73	72.60/*/72.24	52.30/1.05/51.84	52.30/1.05/51.84	47.90/1.17/47.35	48.30/1.16/47.86	48.30/1.16/47.86	48.60/1.15/47.96
Scottish Gaelic	92.00/*/90.00	72.00/*/70.00	64.00/1.00/60.00‡	64.00/1.00/60.00‡	64.00/0.98/60.00‡	64.00/1.06/60.00‡	64.00/1.06/60.00‡	52.00/1.34/52.50
Serbo Croatian	31.90/*/31.76	53.60/*/52.62	34.90/1.77/33.96	34.90/1.77/33.96	28.60/2.10/28.30	28.60/2.13/28.41	28.60/2.13/28.41	33.00/1.79/31.97
Slovak	85.90/*/79.74	74.50/*/64.63	53.60/0.75/41.00	53.60/0.75/41.00	52.20/0.81/39.07	49.60/0.86/35.53	49.60/0.86/35.53	45.90/0.85/35.37
Slovene	77.00/*/73.88	77.20/*/72.18	63.00/0.60/55.38	63.00/0.60/55.38	62.10/0.63/54.46	62.40/0.63/54.86	62.40/0.63/54.86	58.10/0.70/50.00
Sorani	38.20/*/18.09	43.20/*/18.59	23.80/2.19/12.56	23.80/2.19/12.56	21.90/2.41/13.07	21.10/2.33/11.06	21.10/2.33/11.06	18.80/2.16/5.53
Spanish	76.90/*/75.49	75.60/*/74.19	66.40/0.71/65.08	66.40/0.71/65.08	60.40/0.86/59.00	60.00/1.27/58.24	60.50/0.86/58.89	62.60/0.86/61.06
Swedish	97.00/*/96.88	79.60/*/78.79	63.90/0.59/62.58	63.90/0.59/62.58	63.70/0.57/62.37	64.20/0.56/62.89	64.20/0.56/62.89	61.80/0.63/60.29
Turkish	41.20/*/38.81	54.30/*/51.90	42.00/1.75/39.52	42.00/1.75/39.52	37.10/1.99/35.00	37.50/1.99/35.60	37.50/1.99/35.60	35.80/1.78/33.33
Ukrainian	91.90/*/92.04	68.00/*/62.55	47.10/1.00/39.92	47.10/1.00/39.92	46.10/1.18/38.55	44.10/1.27/37.59	44.10/1.27/37.59	43.40/1.10/36.63
Urdu	39.00/*/39.62	83.40/*/33.96	74.10/0.75/28.30†	74.10/0.75/28.30†	72.80/0.82/27.36†	73.00/0.85/29.25†	73.00/0.85/29.25†	70.90/0.80/17.92†
Welsh	88.00/*/84.62	80.00/*/76.92	56.00/0.94/50.00	56.00/0.94/50.00	54.00/1.04/48.15	52.00/1.10/44.87	52.00/1.10/44.87	50.00/1.07/47.44

Table 16: Sub-task 1 Low Condition Part 1.

	LMU-2	CLUZH-1	CU-1	LMU-1	baseline	UF-1	ISI-1	IIT(BHU)-2
Albanian	21.10/4.46/15.18	26.70/2.38/13.82	**31.00/2.33/18.70**	10.20/4.63/7.32	21.10/4.46/15.18	4.50/6.66/4.88	21.60/4.20/12.74	1.40/6.36/2.44
Arabic	27.80/2.56/27.44	33.40/2.06/31.65	29.50/2.38/28.64	27.80/2.56/27.44	21.80/2.97/22.38	1.50/5.41/1.20	12.40/3.38/12.64	0.00/9.76/0.00
Armenian	49.40/1.64/50.22	49.30/1.85/50.67	51.30/1.15/50.89	49.40/1.64/50.22	35.80/2.22/34.92	22.10/2.84/22.28	16.40/2.49/15.63	22.00/2.82/21.95
Basque	**20.00/3.11/4.55**†‡	11.00/4.02/4.55	4.00/5.89/0.00	**20.00/3.11/4.55**†‡	2.00/6.60/0.00	1.00/4.81/0.00	0.00/4.80/0.00	6.00/3.73/0.00
Bengali	**66.00/0.69/58.82**	**63.00/0.76/50.00**	**60.00/0.89/54.41**	**66.00/0.69/58.82**	50.00/1.24/42.65	23.00/1.98/16.18	23.00/2.22/16.18	28.00/1.72/20.59
Bulgarian	49.20/1.22/43.41	43.80/1.03/38.84	**57.10/0.89/51.75**	49.20/1.22/43.41	30.20/1.74/26.08	20.60/2.89/17.47	24.80/2.03/20.83	13.50/2.78/11.29
Catalan	60.30/0.73/53.62	60.30/0.82/53.48	**66.40/0.76/60.03**	60.30/0.73/53.62	55.90/1.07/48.43	41.10/1.51/34.52	49.00/1.40/42.70	25.20/1.71/20.60
Czech	39.30/1.97/37.18	35.50/1.65/32.82	**41.90/1.61/39.18**	30.00/2.16/27.76	39.30/1.97/37.18	22.70/2.69/21.41	19.90/2.57/17.65	16.10/3.05/14.71
Danish	65.80/0.57/63.12	72.80/0.41/70.29	68.90/0.49/66.59	65.80/0.57/63.12	58.40/0.69/55.49	59.70/0.74/56.88	61.90/0.60/58.61	49.80/0.87/47.17
Dutch	**53.60/0.72/51.17**	**50.90/0.91/48.05**	**51.90/0.74/48.94**	52.40/0.80/49.17	**53.60/0.72/51.17**	37.60/1.58/35.60	35.90/1.09/32.93	33.80/1.24/31.26
English	88.40/0.19/88.20	**90.40/0.15/90.23**	87.80/0.22/87.59	88.40/0.19/88.20	80.60/0.34/80.26	74.70/0.56/74.57	73.50/0.35/73.25	0.00/8.14/0.00
Estonian	**30.10/2.48/25.30**	26.70/1.86/19.24	**32.20/1.73/21.66**	**30.10/2.48/25.30**	21.50/2.60/14.73	16.50/3.37/15.77	8.80/3.42/4.33	6.70/3.93/5.20
Faroese	38.20/1.30/35.57	37.40/1.23/34.77	**41.20/1.25/38.52**	38.20/1.30/35.57	30.00/1.53/27.16	22.10/1.73/19.43	25.70/1.70/23.86	4.50/3.56/3.75
Finnish	15.40/4.07/15.52	16.10/2.37/15.82	15.80/3.15/15.82	13.90/3.87/13.89	15.40/4.07/15.52	7.60/6.29/7.71	6.50/4.46/6.39	1.60/6.53/1.52
French	60.90/0.83/60.34	64.00/0.81/63.52	63.00/0.90/62.25	60.90/0.83/60.34	61.80/0.82/61.29	46.20/1.33/46.02	39.10/1.65/38.18	23.90/1.96/22.91
Georgian	**85.60/0.43/85.24**	81.20/0.41/81.12	81.80/0.45/82.27	**85.60/0.43/85.24**	70.50/0.58/69.34	39.10/1.82/36.73	33.90/1.56/31.69	0.00/7.96/0.00
German	56.80/1.17/56.12	63.90/0.86/62.97	56.60/1.39/55.71	56.80/1.17/56.12	54.30/1.01/53.22	31.50/2.23/30.50	37.30/1.27/36.72	0.00/8.59/0.00
Haida	**46.00/2.30/26.32**	**39.00/2.96/15.79**	24.00/4.23/7.89	**46.00/2.30/26.32**	32.00/6.62/15.79	7.00/6.31/2.63	19.00/5.63/10.53	25.00/3.10/5.26
Hebrew	**35.00/1.21/19.65**	29.00/1.23/15.23	**35.40/1.16/19.65**	**35.00/1.21/19.65**	24.70/1.32/12.14	18.10/1.73/7.95	15.30/1.99/5.96	7.50/2.15/2.65
Hindi	**75.50/1.26/37.25**†	69.00/1.04/32.55†	65.30/1.05/30.20†	**75.50/1.26/37.25**†	29.10/3.98/5.88	30.60/3.19/5.10	16.50/3.01/1.57	40.80/2.02/14.51
Hungarian	**35.90/1.36/35.37**	**37.20/1.41/36.41**	16.00/2.45/15.46	**35.90/1.36/35.37**	21.00/2.02/20.33	24.90/1.97/24.17	14.90/2.17/14.32	0.00/11.04/0.00
Icelandic	35.30/1.48/34.15	36.60/1.41/35.04	**40.80/1.37/38.71**	35.30/1.48/34.15	30.00/1.69/28.70	25.30/1.80/24.25	21.90/1.91/20.24	13.30/2.50/12.24
Irish	30.30/2.80/30.01	32.10/2.22/32.14	31.30/2.61/31.58	21.50/3.83/21.28	30.30/2.34/30.01	8.60/6.77/8.85	20.50/3.52/20.83	0.00/9.89/0.00
Italian	40.40/1.57/38.78	47.30/1.14/45.94	**56.40/1.07/54.70**	40.40/1.57/38.78	41.10/2.11/39.85	18.10/3.13/17.31	27.20/2.23/26.28	0.00/10.38/0.00
Khaling	**18.00/2.40/7.82**	**15.50/2.52/5.45**	10.20/3.08/2.84	**18.00/2.40/7.82**	3.10/4.38/0.71	3.20/3.39/1.18	6.10/3.74/1.42	2.80/3.71/0.71
Kurmanji	82.80/0.45/84.03	85.90/0.78/87.37	79.50/0.57/80.58	82.50/0.75/83.92	82.80/0.45/84.03	71.10/1.09/72.23	69.40/0.81/70.46	0.00/7.77/0.00
Latin	16.10/2.84/16.61	13.70/2.53/14.29	**19.30/2.48/20.00**	15.00/2.61/15.87	16.00/2.84/16.51	7.40/3.33/7.83	8.90/3.15/9.31	6.00/3.49/6.35
Latvian	64.20/0.76/62.88	57.80/1.06/56.93	62.60/1.01/62.01	54.40/1.18/53.03	64.20/0.76/62.88	31.90/2.24/30.30	30.80/1.65/29.00	17.60/2.02/16.99
Lithuanian	**23.00/1.89/15.81**	19.20/2.10/12.21	19.80/2.28/12.52	19.50/2.06/10.80	**23.30/1.88/16.12**	7.90/2.73/4.07	13.70/2.63/7.36	0.00/8.44/0.00
Lower Sorbian	46.00/1.03/34.44	46.50/0.97/34.29	**52.30/0.94/40.32**	46.00/1.03/34.44	33.80/1.21/23.65	33.90/1.42/24.44	26.20/1.69/18.25	19.60/1.72/14.13
Macedonian	**64.30/0.58/63.32**	62.10/0.63/61.21	59.60/0.69/58.14	**64.30/0.58/63.32**	52.10/0.99/50.74	38.40/1.68/37.32	34.90/1.29/33.40	24.40/1.52/23.68
Navajo	**20.00/3.02/14.26**	17.80/3.19/10.39	11.70/4.01/7.94	**20.00/3.02/14.26**	**19.00/3.38/12.02**	0.30/5.72/0.20	7.90/4.04/4.89	1.20/5.16/0.61
Northern Sami	16.10/2.53/11.83	14.80/2.66/11.42	**18.70/2.58/14.25**	16.10/2.53/11.83	16.20/2.34/12.63	4.90/3.59/3.49	6.00/4.13/4.57	4.00/3.92/2.96
Norwegian Bokmal	72.70/0.43/71.29	77.10/0.35/76.24	73.80/0.42/72.58	72.70/0.43/71.29	67.80/0.50/66.34	73.60/0.53/72.80	56.60/0.69/55.05	62.70/0.55/61.08
Norwegian Nynorsk	50.90/0.89/49.73	50.60/0.89/49.08	50.50/0.94/48.31	50.90/0.89/49.73	49.60/0.95/47.55	45.80/1.02/45.16	43.50/1.06/42.66	32.10/1.23/31.12
Persian	45.30/2.18/14.23	43.10/1.41/12.36	38.30/2.35/11.61	45.30/2.18/14.23	24.50/3.56/3.00	15.90/3.95/2.25	11.30/4.55/1.87	14.10/3.90/2.62
Polish	43.10/1.79/42.25	39.70/1.61/38.96	43.70/1.63/42.57	43.10/1.79/42.25	41.30/1.58/40.23	29.80/2.06/28.98	18.90/2.43/18.26	17.10/2.29/16.45
Portuguese	67.90/0.52/64.74	71.10/0.49/68.09	68.40/0.59/65.20	67.90/0.52/64.74	63.60/0.81/59.88	44.50/1.03/41.62	32.20/1.62/28.21	32.80/1.35/29.71
Quechua	**58.10/1.17/41.25**†	50.00/1.72/32.13†	30.60/2.53/20.53†	**58.10/1.17/41.25**†	16.40/6.55/12.74	26.60/2.71/14.83	11.00/4.25/9.13	22.70/2.84/13.69
Romanian	**44.70/1.52/38.89**	41.90/1.52/36.84	43.10/1.73/37.08	37.10/1.98/32.00	**44.80/1.51/39.01**	24.80/2.98/20.17	21.70/2.73/18.24	1.60/4.15/1.57
Russian	45.60/1.18/44.90	43.70/1.23/43.16	45.90/1.37/45.51	38.60/1.60/38.27	45.60/1.18/44.90	29.30/2.07/29.08	23.80/2.06/23.57	17.30/2.46/17.14
Scottish Gaelic	52.00/1.58/47.50	**54.00/1.24/55.00**	**56.00/1.30/50.00**	52.00/1.58/47.50	44.00/1.10/37.50	44.00/2.14/37.50	42.00/1.52/37.50	0.00/8.32/0.00
Serbo-Croatian	29.90/2.87/29.14	31.40/1.82/30.61	**39.20/1.73/38.16**†	29.90/2.87/29.14	18.40/2.79/18.34	10.40/3.58/10.06	24.20/2.72/24.00	9.20/3.66/9.01
Slovak	48.50/0.91/34.89	44.30/0.88/34.08	46.70/0.99/34.24	48.50/0.91/34.89	42.40/1.01/29.26	32.40/1.46/22.19	23.60/1.57/14.15	0.00/6.32/0.00
Slovene	52.50/0.83/43.44	58.70/0.69/50.52	60.20/0.83/53.41	52.50/0.83/43.44	49.00/0.83/40.68	39.40/1.36/32.15	32.90/1.30/25.98	0.00/7.60/0.00
Sorani	19.80/2.25/6.53	18.60/2.15/6.03	**27.10/1.96/5.53**	19.80/2.25/6.53	19.30/3.37/14.57	0.10/5.44/0.50	8.60/3.79/7.04	1.40/4.64/0.50
Spanish	57.10/1.28/55.53	60.00/1.27/58.24	63.60/0.86/61.93	55.20/1.01/53.04	57.10/1.28/55.53	37.40/1.94/36.01	35.80/1.99/34.49	22.50/2.51/21.48
Swedish	59.20/0.92/57.90	**62.40/0.60/60.91**	60.40/0.80/59.46	59.20/0.92/57.90	54.20/0.86/52.70	51.70/1.04/50.21	45.50/0.96/44.59	39.40/1.09/38.05
Turkish	31.90/2.44/29.52	35.80/1.77/33.21	19.70/3.31/18.33	31.90/2.44/29.52	14.10/4.54/12.62	18.80/3.22/17.98	7.30/4.04/6.55	0.00/12.65/0.00
Ukrainian	43.60/0.95/37.17	41.00/1.17/34.02	**50.40/1.21/44.17**	39.00/1.38/32.37	43.90/0.95/37.59	25.20/1.81/19.48	31.50/1.44/24.83	13.70/1.87/9.33
Urdu	**73.00/0.88/28.30**†	69.00/0.92/16.04†	64.60/0.89/16.98†	**73.00/0.88/28.30**†	31.70/4.06/23.58	46.90/1.45/7.55†	30.50/2.53/17.92	43.70/1.63/7.55†
Welsh	**50.00/1.10/47.44**	**49.00/1.12/47.44**	**53.00/0.99/48.72**	**50.00/1.10/47.44**	22.00/1.65/21.79	28.00/1.83/24.36	22.00/2.30/19.23	17.00/2.47/15.38

Table 17: Sub-task 1 Low Condition Part 2.

	IIT(BHU)-1	UTNII-1	UA-3	UA-4	UA-1	UA-2	EHU-1
Albanian	0.00/10.23/0.00	0.30/7.21/0.54	—	—	—	—	—
Arabic	0.80/5.66/0.96	0.20/6.59/0.12	—	—	—	—	—
Armenian	0.00/9.17/0.00	0.00/6.39/0.00	—	—	—	—	—
Basque	1.00/4.91/0.00	5.00/4.34/0.00	—	—	—	—	—
Bengali	20.00/2.05/11.76	1.00/4.19/0.00	—	—	—	—	—
Bulgarian	11.00/3.05/9.41	0.40/5.69/0.13	—	—	—	—	—
Catalan	24.70/1.76/20.19	0.40/5.54/0.27	—	—	—	—	—
Czech	15.60/3.27/14.24	0.00/7.07/0.00	—	—	—	—	—
Danish	46.10/0.95/42.77	1.20/5.25/0.81	—	—	—	—	—
Dutch	28.20/1.42/26.25	0.50/5.01/0.44	—	—	—	—	—
English	73.00/0.46/72.63	1.10/3.98/1.12	**90.60/0.14/90.44**	**90.30/0.14/90.13**	**90.60/0.14/90.44**	—	—
Estonian	3.50/4.58/2.60	0.10/6.41/0.00	—	—	—	—	—
Faroese	9.30/2.62/7.95	0.20/5.27/0.11	—	—	—	—	—
Finnish	0.70/7.41/0.71	0.00/9.98/0.00	—	—	—	—	—
French	0.00/8.80/0.00	0.10/5.76/0.11	—	—	—	—	—
Georgian	0.00/8.82/0.00	1.20/4.23/1.26	—	—	—	—	—
German	25.60/1.75/25.52	0.30/6.42/0.31	**66.80/0.73/65.87**	**66.20/0.75/65.46**	**66.00/0.72/64.94**	—	—
Haida	7.00/4.89/0.00	1.00/6.76/0.00	—	—	—	—	—
Hebrew	7.00/2.36/1.99	0.60/3.68/0.44	—	—	—	—	1.00/3.15/0.44
Hindi	33.40/2.34/9.02	1.20/5.26/0.00	—	—	—	—	—
Hungarian	0.00/10.07/0.00	0.00/7.62/0.00	—	—	—	—	—
Icelandic	13.00/2.53/12.01	0.60/5.52/0.67	—	—	—	—	—
Irish	0.60/7.26/0.67	0.00/7.95/0.00	—	—	—	—	—
Italian	0.00/10.02/0.00	0.00/7.06/0.00	—	—	—	—	—
Khaling	0.00/7.32/0.00	0.90/4.38/0.24	—	—	—	—	—
Kurmanji	50.20/1.27/50.84	0.20/5.23/0.10	—	—	—	—	—
Latin	0.00/9.44/0.00	0.00/7.29/0.00	—	—	—	—	—
Latvian	16.60/2.18/16.02	0.00/6.57/0.00	—	—	—	—	—
Lithuanian	3.00/3.46/1.56	0.50/6.06/0.31	—	—	—	—	—
Lower Sorbian	17.60/1.82/12.86	1.20/4.48/0.63	—	—	—	—	—
Macedonian	0.00/8.68/0.00	0.20/4.98/0.21	—	—	—	—	—
Navajo	0.40/5.61/0.20	0.70/5.82/0.41	—	—	—	—	—
Northern Sami	2.50/4.12/2.15	0.50/5.86/0.27	—	—	—	—	—
Norwegian Bokmal	52.60/0.71/51.08	0.30/4.91/0.22	—	—	—	—	—
Norwegian Nynorsk	23.90/1.41/22.52	0.70/4.25/0.44	—	—	—	—	—
Persian	10.50/4.17/1.50	0.50/5.84/0.00	29.40/3.59/8.24	29.00/3.63/7.49	4.70/5.26/1.12	28.90/3.61/7.87	—
Polish	12.10/2.59/11.68	0.20/6.47/0.21	45.30/1.42/44.27	**45.90/1.42/44.90**	45.20/1.44/44.16	—	—
Portuguese	0.00/9.31/0.00	1.00/4.53/0.92	—	—	—	—	—
Quechua	0.70/5.34/0.38	0.60/5.56/0.19	—	—	—	—	—
Romanian	5.80/3.85/4.71	0.00/6.37/0.00	—	—	—	—	—
Russian	15.70/2.61/15.71	0.00/7.27/0.00	—	—	—	—	—
Scottish Gaelic	48.00/1.54/42.50	32.00/2.38/25.00	—	—	—	—	—
Serbo-Croatian	4.10/4.55/3.98	0.10/7.04/0.10	—	—	—	—	—
Slovak	12.50/1.75/7.56	0.60/4.65/0.16	—	—	—	—	—
Slovene	21.00/1.54/14.30	2.00/5.03/1.05	—	—	—	—	—
Sorani	0.00/7.64/0.00	0.90/4.72/0.00	—	—	—	—	—
Spanish	20.10/2.72/19.52	0.20/5.71/0.22	56.40/0.84/55.31	56.20/0.85/55.10	**64.60/0.75/62.91**	56.80/0.84/55.75	—
Swedish	40.60/1.08/39.19	0.20/6.13/0.21	—	—	—	—	—
Turkish	0.00/11.45/0.00	0.10/8.44/0.00	—	—	—	—	—
Ukrainian	12.20/2.04/8.23	0.70/4.99/0.27	—	—	—	—	—
Urdu	31.20/2.48/2.83	4.70/4.38/0.04					
Welsh	0.00/8.77/0.00	2.00/4.48/1.28	—	—	—	—	6.00/3.32/5.13

Table 18: Sub-task 1 Low Condition Part 3.

	oracle-fc	oracle-e	LMU-2	LMU-1	baseline	CU-1
Albanian	100.00/*/100.00	98.95/*/92.00	**98.35/0.03/86.00**	**98.35/0.03/86.00**	89.46/0.41/70.00	86.36/0.32/66.00
Arabic	100.00/*/100.00	96.52/*/84.00	**95.48/0.14/82.00**	**95.48/0.14/82.00**	55.67/1.20/24.00	75.54/0.79/56.00
Armenian	100.00/*/100.00	99.44/*/96.00	**98.78/0.04/92.00**	**98.78/0.04/92.00**	86.11/0.33/66.00	92.04/0.11/70.00
Basque	—	—	—	—	—	—
Bengali	100.00/*/100.00	96.18/*/32.00	**92.48/0.24/24.00**	**92.61/0.21/32.00**	87.52/0.24/16.00	21.02/1.25/24.00
Bulgarian	100.00/*/100.00	96.48/*/84.00	**85.93/0.24/56.00**	**85.93/0.24/56.00**	74.37/0.40/68.00	78.39/0.33/60.00
Catalan	100.00/*/100.00	99.72/*/94.00	**99.35/0.01/88.00**	**99.35/0.01/88.00**	96.03/0.07/92.00	90.06/0.17/74.00
Czech	100.00/*/100.00	92.22/*/58.00	**85.79/0.25/52.00**	**86.00/0.27/26.00**	**85.79/0.25/52.00**	68.36/1.24/30.00
Danish	100.00/*/100.00	88.20/*/60.00	**75.74/0.37/44.00**	61.64/0.53/16.00	**75.41/0.38/42.00**	**71.48/0.35/30.00**
Dutch	100.00/*/100.00	93.54/*/80.00	**89.30/0.15/66.00**	**89.30/0.15/66.00**	78.04/0.35/60.00	73.06/0.37/52.00
English	100.00/*/100.00	95.20/*/88.00	82.00/0.30/58.00	82.00/0.30/58.00	**91.60/0.15/82.00**	84.00/0.23/68.00
Estonian	100.00/*/100.00	98.20/*/80.00	**97.90/0.05/70.00‡**	**97.90/0.05/70.00‡**	77.07/0.35/54.00	78.29/0.46/34.00
Faroese	100.00/*/100.00	84.90/*/50.00	**71.90/0.54/26.00**	**71.90/0.54/26.00**	**70.10/0.58/38.00**	65.62/0.71/22.00
Finnish	100.00/*/100.00	94.95/*/76.00	**93.67/0.11/72.00**	**93.67/0.11/72.00**	68.18/0.65/56.00	68.78/0.53/52.00
French	100.00/*/100.00	99.85/*/98.00	**98.83/0.01/90.00**	**98.83/0.01/90.00**	92.63/0.13/88.00	89.48/0.17/78.00
Georgian	100.00/*/100.00	97.98/*/98.00	**96.20/0.05/90.00**	**96.20/0.05/90.00**	90.38/0.24/90.00	89.31/0.23/86.00
German	100.00/*/100.00	90.72/*/72.00	**85.88/0.21/52.00**	**85.88/0.21/52.00**	76.40/0.96/52.00	75.82/1.07/38.00
Haida	—	—	—	—	—	—
Hebrew	100.00/*/100.00	97.06/*/82.00	**93.42/0.09/70.00**	**93.42/0.09/70.00**	54.09/0.65/12.00	70.46/0.39/26.00
Hindi	100.00/*/100.00	99.98/*/96.00	**99.95/0.00/92.00‡**	**99.95/0.00/92.00‡**	96.82/0.03/92.00	9.15/3.46/4.00
Hungarian	100.00/*/100.00	90.85/*/68.00	**89.04/0.25/60.00**	**89.04/0.25/60.00**	53.97/1.13/40.00	54.95/1.15/26.00
Icelandic	100.00/*/100.00	88.63/*/64.00	68.98/0.67/22.00	**74.30/0.51/28.00**	67.36/0.69/34.00	63.22/0.77/20.00
Irish	100.00/*/100.00	81.57/*/38.00	**69.53/0.74/12.00**	**69.53/0.74/12.00**	47.99/1.64/10.00	53.28/1.29/12.00
Italian	100.00/*/100.00	97.95/*/86.00	**97.05/0.07/70.00**	**97.05/0.07/70.00**	73.05/0.93/58.00	89.86/0.30/46.00
Khaling	100.00/*/100.00	99.98/*/96.00	**99.73/0.01/90.00**	**99.73/0.01/90.00**	79.08/0.43/58.00	89.64/0.13/58.00
Kurmanji	100.00/*/100.00	98.78/*/88.00	**94.26/0.06/50.00**	**94.26/0.06/50.00**	**93.39/0.10/66.00**	**93.74/0.07/60.00**
Latin	100.00/*/100.00	95.02/*/82.00	**87.70/0.28/64.00**	77.75/0.45/44.00	47.58/0.91/32.00	50.51/0.88/16.00
Latvian	100.00/*/100.00	97.69/*/90.00	**96.69/0.10/88.00**	93.08/0.10/70.00	86.46/0.23/80.00	88.47/0.23/80.00
Lithuanian	100.00/*/100.00	94.47/*/62.00	**85.82/0.26/38.00**	85.37/0.27/28.00	60.57/0.56/26.00	64.14/0.59/20.00
Lower Sorbian	100.00/*/100.00	96.13/*/72.00	**87.39/0.23/46.00**	85.77/0.27/30.00	82.27/0.37/60.00	80.15/0.39/46.00
Macedonian	100.00/*/100.00	99.43/*/92.00	**97.14/0.05/86.00**	96.14/0.08/80.00	89.70/0.16/78.00	92.56/0.10/70.00
Navajo	100.00/*/100.00	68.36/*/30.00	**58.22/1.10/18.00**	**58.22/1.10/18.00**	37.81/2.13/20.00	46.30/1.94/18.00
Northern Sami	100.00/*/100.00	96.12/*/70.00	**91.56/0.13/46.00**	**91.56/0.13/46.00**	45.68/1.13/28.00	54.61/0.95/20.00
Norwegian Bokmal	100.00/*/100.00	81.76/*/64.00	**67.92/0.56/50.00**	64.78/0.61/42.00	**67.92/0.56/50.00**	**70.44/0.47/46.00**
Norwegian Nynorsk	96.93/*/96.00	79.14/*/72.00	**64.42/0.61/56.00**	51.53/0.85/30.00	**64.42/0.61/56.00**	**60.74/0.83/52.00**
Persian	100.00/*/100.00	100.00/*/100.00	**100.00/0.00/100.00‡**	**100.00/0.00/100.00‡**	76.44/0.61/52.00	25.09/1.69/4.00
Polish	100.00/*/100.00	96.80/*/78.00	**89.24/0.19/56.00**	85.02/0.27/36.00	**90.27/0.15/66.00**	83.10/0.41/42.00
Portuguese	100.00/*/100.00	99.16/*/96.00	**98.61/0.02/94.00**	**98.84/0.02/90.00**	96.19/0.06/90.00	36.23/1.31/14.00
Quechua	100.00/*/100.00	99.99/*/98.00	**99.84/0.00/80.00**	**99.84/0.00/80.00**	89.13/0.22/86.00	64.45/1.14/8.00
Romanian	100.00/*/100.00	91.27/*/62.00	**78.25/0.55/36.00**	76.04/0.60/16.00	**78.99/0.61/40.00**	75.00/0.60/30.00
Russian	100.00/*/100.00	92.33/*/68.00	**85.74/0.21/44.00**	**85.74/0.21/44.00**	85.58/0.28/54.00	**87.42/0.21/56.00**
Scottish Gaelic	—	—	—	—	—	—
Serbo-Croatian	99.88/*/98.00	95.65/*/72.00	**88.29/0.18/50.00**	**88.29/0.18/50.00**	77.66/0.72/70.00	74.40/0.70/54.00
Slovak	100.00/*/100.00	86.10/*/40.00	**71.84/0.47/24.00**	68.09/0.53/8.00	**69.16/0.56/26.00**	**68.27/0.53/14.00**
Slovene	100.00/*/100.00	96.86/*/72.00	**93.02/0.11/64.00**	93.71/0.10/62.00	76.48/0.44/64.00	77.18/0.45/48.00
Sorani	99.92/*/96.00	91.80/*/56.00	**86.39/0.16/16.00**	**86.39/0.16/16.00**	72.27/0.54/48.00	8.88/2.20/4.00
Spanish	100.00/*/100.00	99.09/*/96.00	**98.53/0.04/84.00**	**98.53/0.04/84.00**	93.58/0.13/82.00	34.63/1.53/6.00
Swedish	100.00/*/100.00	92.94/*/82.00	**84.71/0.22/70.00**	76.18/0.35/46.00	78.24/0.33/66.00	70.29/0.60/52.00
Turkish	100.00/*/100.00	99.54/*/96.00	**99.41/0.02/90.00‡**	**99.41/0.02/90.00‡**	85.05/0.40/80.00	31.08/2.10/14.00
Ukrainian	100.00/*/100.00	84.76/*/56.00	**73.97/0.65/48.00**	74.76/0.54/20.00	**73.97/0.65/48.00**	**72.54/0.54/32.00**
Urdu	100.00/*/100.00	99.72/*/80.00	95.33/0.07/60.00	**98.44/0.03/48.00**	95.33/0.07/60.00	90.79/0.10/32.00
Welsh	100.00/*/100.00	99.19/*/76.00	**97.96/0.02/52.00**	**97.96/0.02/52.00**	85.25/0.22/40.00	81.66/0.27/28.00

Table 19: Sub-task 2 High Condition Part 1.

	oracle-fc	oracle-e	LMU-2	LMU-1	baseline	CU-1
Albanian	100.00/*/100.00	98.25/*/90.00	83.62/0.56/72.00	**88.81/0.24/40.00**	83.87/0.56/74.00	82.17/0.44/54.00
Arabic	100.00/*/100.00	92.59/*/60.00	**90.21/0.29/46.00**	**90.21/0.29/46.00**	54.34/1.34/24.00	63.01/1.05/30.00
Armenian	100.00/*/100.00	98.88/*/92.00	**97.77/0.05/84.00**	**97.77/0.05/84.00**	80.89/0.41/54.00	86.57/0.18/44.00
Basque	77.98/*/60.00	94.27/*/20.00	**94.14/0.10/20.00**†‡	**94.14/0.10/20.00**†‡	4.40/4.03/0.00	7.35/4.03/0.00
Bengali	100.00/*/100.00	95.92/*/32.00	**91.72/0.25/24.00**	80.76/0.48/16.00	85.86/0.27/16.00	19.75/1.31/20.00
Bulgarian	74.20/*/92.00	69.68/*/60.00	**55.95/0.91/28.00**	**55.95/0.91/28.00**	49.58/1.10/46.00	49.25/1.64/38.00
Catalan	100.00/*/100.00	98.97/*/90.00	**97.06/0.05/84.00**	**96.92/0.05/78.00**	95.33/0.09/88.00	79.69/0.30/54.00
Czech	80.08/*/94.00	66.29/*/48.00	**58.61/1.85/40.00**	**56.22/1.31/32.00**	56.12/1.89/40.00	46.68/2.58/22.00
Danish	100.00/*/100.00	82.30/*/52.00	**70.16/0.55/38.00**	34.10/1.23/0.00	**71.15/0.54/44.00**	64.92/0.47/24.00
Dutch	100.00/*/100.00	90.77/*/70.00	**86.53/0.22/62.00**	75.28/0.38/42.00	67.71/0.42/54.00	60.33/0.57/30.00
English	100.00/*/100.00	90.00/*/78.00	**84.00/0.27/68.00**	69.20/0.55/38.00	**84.00/0.27/68.00**	**81.60/0.26/64.00**
Estonian	100.00/*/100.00	94.70/*/56.00	**92.43/0.15/34.00**	**92.43/0.15/34.00**	60.71/1.03/30.00	61.76/0.78/20.00
Faroese	100.00/*/100.00	79.22/*/36.00	**68.31/0.66/32.00**	61.43/0.69/12.00	59.19/0.91/32.00	53.21/1.05/20.00
Finnish	100.00/*/100.00	94.53/*/68.00	**89.48/0.25/56.00**	**89.48/0.25/56.00**	63.30/0.69/38.00	57.14/0.76/42.00
French	100.00/*/100.00	96.70/*/84.00	**95.38/0.07/76.00**	**95.38/0.07/76.00**	85.16/0.25/76.00	85.67/0.22/68.00
Georgian	93.11/*/98.00	92.52/*/90.00	**89.67/0.34/88.00**	**89.31/0.25/78.00**	82.42/0.46/82.00	81.00/0.58/80.00
German	100.00/*/100.00	85.49/*/50.00	**77.56/0.37/26.00**	**77.56/0.37/26.00**	70.41/0.99/30.00	68.47/1.95/24.00
Haida	99.86/*/90.00	97.33/*/40.00	**96.40/0.07/20.00**	**96.40/0.07/20.00**	64.53/1.15/10.00	59.63/1.30/0.00
Hebrew	100.00/*/100.00	92.08/*/58.00	**85.59/0.18/36.00**	**85.59/0.18/36.00**	42.70/0.88/6.00	54.89/0.62/16.00
Hindi	100.00/*/100.00	97.29/*/16.00	**95.01/0.12/4.00**	**95.01/0.12/4.00**	71.11/0.53/12.00	61.79/0.96/0.00
Hungarian	92.74/*/96.00	82.62/*/50.00	**79.97/0.49/38.00**	**79.97/0.49/38.00**	45.73/1.59/30.00	39.68/2.65/14.00
Icelandic	100.00/*/100.00	84.05/*/44.00	**67.21/0.71/24.00**	56.28/0.91/8.00	54.51/1.12/28.00	56.57/0.80/16.00
Irish	100.00/*/100.00	71.53/*/16.00	**52.92/1.37/2.00**	**52.92/1.37/2.00**	40.33/1.64/0.00	44.34/1.50/0.00
Italian	100.00/*/100.00	95.90/*/72.00	**90.67/0.20/40.00**	**90.67/0.20/40.00**	71.86/1.00/52.00	77.62/0.57/32.00
Khaling	100.00/*/100.00	99.20/*/66.00	**98.62/0.02/52.00**	**98.62/0.02/52.00**	58.20/0.84/32.00	7.53/2.18/0.00
Kurmanji	99.48/*/98.00	95.65/*/82.00	**88.87/0.18/56.00**	85.91/0.22/42.00	**88.35/0.19/52.00**	**87.48/0.18/48.00**
Latin	100.00/*/100.00	92.09/*/66.00	**84.63/0.30/56.00**	57.10/0.90/6.00	39.53/1.12/22.00	38.07/1.23/10.00
Latvian	100.00/*/100.00	92.51/*/78.00	**89.19/0.21/74.00**	82.28/0.31/46.00	79.97/0.37/74.00	81.99/0.36/74.00
Lithuanian	100.00/*/100.00	90.54/*/36.00	**82.87/0.29/16.00**	78.50/0.43/8.00	65.92/0.48/24.00	61.73/0.62/14.00
Lower Sorbian	100.00/*/100.00	90.76/*/54.00	**84.02/0.30/44.00**	79.28/0.37/30.00	65.92/0.81/44.00	71.16/0.74/34.00
Macedonian	100.00/*/100.00	94.56/*/80.00	**88.98/0.15/68.00**	82.12/0.27/48.00	86.41/0.20/62.00	83.12/0.25/64.00
Navajo	100.00/*/100.00	54.25/*/30.00	**47.12/1.56/24.00**	**47.12/1.56/24.00**	33.15/2.48/22.00	32.60/2.81/20.00
Northern Sami	100.00/*/100.00	90.98/*/44.00	**83.51/0.28/34.00**	76.92/0.46/16.00	31.43/1.66/14.00	27.93/2.02/8.00
Norwegian Bokmal	100.00/*/100.00	71.07/*/46.00	50.94/0.83/28.00	25.79/1.40/0.00	**50.94/0.83/28.00**	**57.23/0.71/34.00**
Norwegian Nynorsk	96.93/*/96.00	69.94/*/60.00	60.74/0.67/52.00	49.08/0.89/38.00	**60.74/0.67/52.00**	**56.44/0.79/46.00**
Persian	100.00/*/100.00	99.85/*/96.00	**99.56/0.00/88.00**	**99.56/0.00/88.00**	78.29/0.54/60.00	94.47/0.09/68.00
Polish	100.00/*/100.00	91.55/*/54.00	**82.71/0.29/46.00**	72.73/0.52/24.00	**80.28/0.34/50.00**	79.77/0.36/42.00
Portuguese	100.00/*/100.00	99.00/*/94.00	**98.58/0.02/90.00**	95.16/0.08/56.00	95.29/0.06/84.00	92.10/0.09/54.00
Quechua	100.00/*/100.00	100.00/*/100.00	**99.60/0.02/80.00**	**99.60/0.02/80.00**	91.34/0.17/94.00	0.04/4.47/0.00
Romanian	100.00/*/100.00	84.32/*/42.00	**76.63/0.56/30.00**	60.65/1.09/10.00	61.54/0.83/30.00	60.80/0.97/24.00
Russian	98.77/*/98.00	91.56/*/62.00	**85.74/0.24/48.00**	79.29/0.42/32.00	82.98/0.28/50.00	82.21/0.36/38.00
Scottish Gaelic	100.00/*/100.00	65.59/*/8.00	48.58/1.00/4.00	**51.82/1.17/4.00**	41.30/1.09/0.00	44.53/1.23/4.00
Serbo-Croatian	42.51/*/92.00	73.55/*/68.00	**59.18/0.70/30.00**†	**59.18/0.70/30.00**†	36.84/2.38/60.00	36.59/2.41/64.00
Slovak	100.00/*/100.00	78.79/*/20.00	**66.67/0.55/12.00**	49.38/0.81/4.00	59.89/0.70/14.00	59.00/0.73/12.00
Slovene	99.88/*/98.00	92.78/*/74.00	**85.10/0.23/46.00**	81.61/0.27/42.00	67.87/0.65/44.00	69.15/0.69/42.00
Sorani	99.41/*/92.00	90.96/*/56.00	**86.05/0.16/36.00**	**86.05/0.16/36.00**	68.30/0.57/48.00	67.96/0.52/44.00
Spanish	100.00/*/100.00	98.84/*/94.00	**97.89/0.05/66.00**	**97.89/0.05/66.00**	92.18/0.16/84.00	86.53/0.21/58.00
Swedish	100.00/*/100.00	84.71/*/62.00	**70.88/0.41/48.00**	56.76/0.76/20.00	57.35/0.67/42.00	59.41/0.77/28.00
Turkish	100.00/*/100.00	99.70/*/90.00	**98.65/0.03/74.00**	**98.65/0.03/74.00**	73.26/0.88/58.00	76.05/0.57/48.00
Ukrainian	100.00/*/100.00	81.11/*/50.00	**67.14/0.71/46.00**	60.32/0.74/16.00	**67.14/0.71/46.00**	**65.71/0.66/30.00**
Urdu	100.00/*/100.00	97.54/*/60.00	**94.29/0.11/28.00**	**94.29/0.11/28.00**	81.02/0.25/40.00	67.23/0.45/32.00
Welsh	100.00/*/100.00	99.10/*/64.00	**97.80/0.03/36.00**	**97.80/0.03/36.00**	82.80/0.27/28.00	79.05/0.31/12.00

Table 20: Sub-task 2 Medium Condition Part 1.

	oracle-fc	oracle-e	LMU-2	LMU-1	baseline	CU-1
Albanian	100.00/*/100.00	72.03/*/30.00	**66.63/0.72/8.00**	2.65/5.54/0.00	12.69/1.96/20.00	12.19/2.17/20.00
Arabic	100.00/*/100.00	84.88/*/40.00	**80.43/0.54/20.00**	**80.43/0.54/20.00**	42.85/1.59/22.00	48.78/1.55/30.00
Armenian	99.95/*/98.00	97.06/*/76.00	**93.92/0.17/58.00**	**93.92/0.17/58.00**	76.18/0.37/38.00	75.47/0.37/34.00
Basque	77.03/*/60.00	93.10/*/20.00	**93.02/0.12/20.00**†‡	**93.02/0.12/20.00**†‡	0.46/4.83/0.00	1.54/3.83/0.00
Bengali	100.00/*/100.00	93.89/*/28.00	**90.19/0.26/20.00**	69.94/0.77/8.00	77.20/0.48/8.00	73.38/0.64/8.00
Bulgarian	74.20/*/92.00	63.99/*/40.00	**49.58/1.29/24.00**	43.38/1.50/12.00	33.50/1.61/24.00	35.51/3.43/28.00
Catalan	100.00/*/100.00	97.43/*/82.00	**94.07/0.11/80.00**	86.83/0.24/18.00	**94.16/0.11/80.00**	90.06/0.18/58.00
Czech	53.32/*/74.00	48.24/*/16.00	**34.96/2.20/12.00**	30.71/1.79/6.00	26.56/2.30/12.00	16.39/4.71/10.00
Danish	88.52/*/90.00	60.66/*/26.00	42.30/1.22/16.00	24.26/1.76/4.00	41.31/1.23/16.00	**53.11/1.74/20.00**
Dutch	100.00/*/100.00	68.82/*/34.00	**56.64/0.55/32.00**	46.13/1.04/4.00	50.18/0.62/24.00	45.57/0.89/16.00
English	100.00/*/100.00	90.00/*/78.00	76.40/0.33/60.00	53.60/0.70/24.00	76.40/0.33/60.00	**84.40/0.21/62.00**
Estonian	100.00/*/100.00	87.37/*/44.00	**77.42/0.49/14.00**	**77.42/0.49/14.00**	39.81/2.12/12.00	50.17/1.08/12.00
Faroese	100.00/*/100.00	64.72/*/22.00	**57.55/0.89/20.00**	17.79/1.81/0.00	49.78/1.04/20.00	46.79/1.13/12.00
Finnish	86.31/*/94.00	85.12/*/56.00	**76.30/1.06/38.00**	69.20/1.01/8.00	60.82/1.37/46.00	54.58/2.47/40.00
French	100.00/*/100.00	93.34/*/78.00	**87.45/0.27/22.00**	**87.45/0.27/22.00**	**87.09/0.22/78.00**	84.10/0.27/70.00
Georgian	91.21/*/96.00	92.16/*/88.00	**86.82/0.41/86.00**	80.64/0.38/52.00	78.86/0.53/78.00	78.86/1.10/74.00
German	100.00/*/100.00	83.56/*/42.00	**74.66/0.90/32.00**	59.77/0.70/4.00	69.83/0.96/34.00	68.28/1.25/30.00
Haida	99.86/*/90.00	96.25/*/10.00	**95.24/0.12/10.00**	9.59/5.63/0.00	47.15/1.11/0.00	45.85/1.56/0.00
Hebrew	100.00/*/100.00	75.80/*/22.00	**68.06/0.44/10.00**	**68.06/0.44/10.00**	33.27/1.01/0.00	28.83/1.18/4.00
Hindi	100.00/*/100.00	95.34/*/12.00	**93.84/0.19/0.00**	**93.84/0.19/0.00**	64.49/0.72/12.00	63.62/0.97/0.00
Hungarian	92.74/*/96.00	57.60/*/18.00	**54.50/1.12/8.00**	**54.50/1.12/8.00**	17.91/2.53/10.00	11.56/3.11/10.00
Icelandic	100.00/*/100.00	68.98/*/26.00	**56.57/0.91/18.00**	32.35/1.46/0.00	45.79/1.25/24.00	51.40/1.11/20.00
Irish	85.04/*/92.00	56.57/*/10.00	**43.43/1.68/2.00**	34.67/2.27/0.00	35.95/2.22/6.00	26.46/3.49/8.00
Italian	100.00/*/100.00	79.14/*/60.00	**72.00/1.03/38.00**	**70.81/0.66/22.00**	66.95/1.75/22.00	58.29/1.79/28.00
Khaling	100.00/*/100.00	97.79/*/44.00	**97.15/0.05/24.00**	**97.15/0.05/24.00**	42.30/1.02/16.00	39.16/1.39/8.00
Kurmanji	88.52/*/80.00	86.96/*/64.00	**80.17/0.55/26.00**	62.43/0.68/16.00	78.43/0.58/14.00	65.04/2.02/6.00
Latin	88.29/*/98.00	55.78/*/20.00	**51.98/1.27/16.00**	12.30/2.20/0.00	24.45/2.14/16.00	22.55/3.10/14.00
Latvian	99.86/*/98.00	83.00/*/64.00	**75.79/0.46/52.00**	47.26/1.51/12.00	68.88/0.54/50.00	**74.78/0.56/36.00**
Lithuanian	100.00/*/100.00	71.81/*/20.00	**49.51/0.89/10.00**	**47.99/1.32/0.00**	38.27/1.04/8.00	28.19/1.43/2.00
Lower Sorbian	100.00/*/100.00	72.28/*/22.00	**56.43/0.63/16.00**	**56.05/0.82/2.00**	38.20/0.92/18.00	27.22/1.55/14.00
Macedonian	91.99/*/86.00	66.67/*/32.00	**60.23/0.63/32.00**	41.06/1.01/6.00	42.49/0.97/20.00	14.74/2.05/12.00
Navajo	100.00/*/100.00	45.34/*/26.00	**35.48/2.54/22.00**	27.40/2.10/2.00	26.58/3.08/16.00	19.73/4.08/12.00
Northern Sami	90.40/*/74.00	43.45/*/24.00	**39.86/2.09/24.00**	19.88/2.29/0.00	15.62/2.85/2.00	15.32/3.03/2.00
Norwegian Bokmal	96.23/*/92.00	64.15/*/40.00	**41.51/1.06/24.00**	31.45/1.70/8.00	**41.51/1.06/24.00**	49.06/0.97/32.00
Norwegian Nynorsk	95.71/*/94.00	47.85/*/36.00	**42.33/1.13/34.00**	13.50/2.31/10.00	**42.33/1.13/34.00**	39.88/1.23/30.00
Persian	100.00/*/100.00	99.82/*/92.00	**99.20/0.01/68.00**	**99.20/0.01/68.00**	73.42/0.72/52.00	84.69/0.43/48.00
Polish	100.00/*/100.00	73.24/*/16.00	**64.53/0.52/16.00**	35.47/1.25/0.00	56.72/0.65/16.00	55.19/0.82/10.00
Portuguese	100.00/*/100.00	98.35/*/92.00	**96.94/0.04/76.00**	91.65/0.13/38.00	91.71/0.10/64.00	89.94/0.12/50.00
Quechua	100.00/*/100.00	100.00/*/100.00	**99.98/0.00/96.00**‡	98.09/0.06/38.00	91.33/0.17/92.00	79.84/0.58/2.00
Romanian	44.97/*/76.00	28.70/*/18.00	**25.00/2.33/18.00**	11.69/3.06/2.00	14.20/2.47/14.00	10.36/6.89/10.00
Russian	96.01/*/88.00	58.44/*/8.00	**46.17/0.75/8.00**	33.90/1.21/2.00	40.18/0.81/8.00	36.66/1.21/8.00
Scottish Gaelic	100.00/*/100.00	58.30/*/4.00	**50.61/0.87/4.00**	42.91/2.07/4.00	44.13/0.96/0.00	29.96/1.41/0.00
Serbo-Croatian	37.08/*/68.00	64.25/*/44.00	**40.46/1.49/4.00**†	**40.46/1.49/4.00**†	30.07/2.51/44.00	27.90/2.90/44.00
Slovak	100.00/*/100.00	62.92/*/8.00	**53.65/0.81/4.00**	31.55/1.40/2.00	44.39/0.90/6.00	38.86/1.29/6.00
Slovene	97.56/*/98.00	86.85/*/56.00	**79.28/0.41/32.00**	54.13/0.76/0.00	57.74/0.90/44.00	52.15/1.35/14.00
Sorani	90.36/*/56.00	74.73/*/48.00	**57.65/0.72/0.00**	**57.65/0.72/0.00**	**54.78/0.96/24.00**	43.53/1.70/24.00
Spanish	100.00/*/100.00	95.82/*/60.00	**91.05/0.18/18.00**	**91.05/0.18/18.00**	79.75/0.38/50.00	79.58/0.41/38.00
Swedish	92.06/*/94.00	57.06/*/16.00	**51.18/0.90/12.00**	20.88/2.69/0.00	43.53/1.10/12.00	31.47/1.41/6.00
Turkish	90.44/*/94.00	88.93/*/44.00	**87.65/0.43/28.00**	**87.65/0.43/28.00**	20.93/3.80/14.00	34.89/2.47/6.00
Ukrainian	99.52/*/94.00	64.44/*/24.00	**49.21/0.94/6.00**	34.44/1.14/0.00	43.97/0.98/24.00	32.38/1.31/0.00
Urdu	100.00/*/100.00	95.85/*/36.00	**88.53/0.32/4.00**	**88.53/0.32/4.00**	80.59/0.25/32.00	79.56/0.27/8.00
Welsh	100.00/*/100.00	95.03/*/32.00	**89.89/0.19/8.00**	**89.89/0.19/8.00**	51.67/1.36/16.00	82.72/0.37/24.00

Table 21: Sub-task 2 Low Condition Part 1.

Training Data Augmentation for Low-Resource Morphological Inflection

Toms Bergmanis[*]
t.bergmanis@sms.ed.ac.uk

Katharina Kann[†]
kann@cis.lmu.de

Hinrich Schütze[†]
inquiries@cislmu.org

Sharon Goldwater[*]
sgwater@inf.ed.ac.uk

[*]School of Informatics
University of Edinburgh

[†]Center for Information & Language Processing
LMU Munich

Abstract

This work describes the UoE-LMU submission for the CoNLL-SIGMORPHON 2017 Shared Task on Universal Morphological Reinflection, Subtask 1: given a lemma and target morphological tags, generate the target inflected form. We evaluate several ways to improve performance in the 1000-example setting: three methods to augment the training data with identical input-output pairs (i.e., autoencoding), a heuristic approach to identify likely pairs of inflectional variants from an unlabeled corpus, and a method for cross-lingual knowledge transfer. We find that autoencoding random strings works surprisingly well, outperformed only slightly by autoencoding words from an unlabelled corpus. The random string method also works well in the 10,000-example setting despite not being tuned for it. Among 18 submissions our system takes 1st and 6th place in the 10k and 1k settings, respectively.

1 Introduction

Morphological variation is a major contributor to the sparse data problem in NLP, especially for under-resourced languages. The SIGMORPHON 2016 Shared Task (Cotterell et al., 2016) and CoNLL-SIGMORPHON 2017 Shared Task (Cotterell et al., 2017) aimed to inspire researchers to develop better systems for morphological inflection across a wide range of languages with varying training resources. In 2016, when over 10,000 training examples were provided for each language, neural network-based systems performed considerably better than other approaches (Cotterell et al., 2016). The 2017 Shared Task therefore included settings with different amounts of

training data (100, 1000, or 10,000 examples), to examine which approaches might work best when data is even more limited.

We focus on the 1000-example setting of Subtask 1: given a lemma with its part of speech and target morphological tags, generate the target inflected form. Our baseline system is the winning system from 2016, the morphological encoder-decoder (MED) from LMU (Kann and Schütze, 2016). We explore methods for improving its performance in the face of fewer training examples, either with or without additional data from unlabeled corpora.[1]

In particular, we focus on various training data augmentation methods. One uses a heuristic approach to identify likely pairs of inflectional variants from an unlabeled corpus in an unsupervised way, and uses these as input-output pairs. Three other methods augment the training data with identical input-output pairs—i.e., simultaneously training the network to perform autoencoding. We compare three types of autoencoder inputs: either lemmas and inflected forms from the training data, words from an unlabeled corpus, or random strings.

We present detailed results and comparisons for various amounts of added training data for all 52 languages of the shared task. We find that all methods improve considerably over the MED baseline (7.2-10.7% across all languages; a 15.5% improvement over the shared task baseline). Most of the benefit comes with only 4k extra examples, but performance continues to improve up to 16k added examples.

After controlling for the amount of additional data, we see only a small benefit from autoencoding corpus words rather than random strings. Using hypothesized morphological variants works

---

[1]We did not pursue the 100-example setting because preliminary experiments yielded such low baseline performance that we felt additional work would be unlikely to help much.

Proceedings of the CoNLL SIGMORPHON 2017 Shared Task: Universal Morphological Reinflection, pages 31–39,
Vancouver, Canada, August 3–4, 2017. ©2017 Association for Computational Linguistics

as well as random strings. These results suggest that the main advantage of all these methods is providing a strong bias towards learning the identity transformation and/or working as regularizers, rather than learning language-specific phonotactics or morpho-phonological changes.[2]

Finally, following Kann et al. (2017), we test whether cross-lingual knowledge transfer can help, by multilingual training of joint models for groups of up to 10 related languages. However, we find no improvement as compared to using an equivalent amount of random-string autoencoder examples.

Our final submission to the shared task consists of two submissions for Subtask 1 (Inflection): the random string autoencoder for the medium and high data settings of the restricted (main) track and the corpus word autoencoder for the medium data setting of the bonus track (track with external monolingual corpora). All systems use 16K autoencoder examples and an ensemble of three training runs with majority voting.

In the high resource setting of the restricted track, our system outperforms all 17 other submissions, with an average test set accuracy of 95.32% over 52 languages. In the medium resource setting, among 18 submissions our system takes the 6th place with 81.02% (1.78% below the top system). In the medium resource setting of the bonus track, among 2 submissions our system comes first with 82.37%.

2 Baseline MED System

For our baseline system (henceforth **MED-baseline** or **MED**), we use the sequence encoder-decoder architecture and input/output format of the 2016 Shared Task winner (Kann and Schütze, 2016). The architecture follows Bahdanau et al. (2015): that is, the encoder is a bidirectional gated recurrent neural network (GRU) with attention, and the decoder is a uni-directional GRU. For details, see Kann and Schütze (2016) and Bahdanau et al. (2015).

The input sequence consists of space separated characters of the input lemma—the dictionary form of the word—followed by space separated morphological tags, each prepended with a

tag marker, for example:

$$\texttt{w a l k t=V t=V.PTCP t=PRS} \qquad (1)$$

The target output is a sequence of characters forming the inflected word, e.g., $\texttt{w a l k i n g}$.

3 Augmenting the Training Data

For the Shared Task, the main competition permits no additional resources beyond the labeled training examples given for each setting. However, Wikipedia dumps in each language are provided for teams who wish to explore semi-supervised methods as well. We examine two methods that use only the training data, and two that also incorporate corpus data. Finally, we explore a method that uses multilingual resources.

3.1 No Outside Resources (AE-TD, AE-RS)

Morphologically related words are typically similar in form, and in many cases, parts of the word are copied from the lemma to the inflected form. As suggested by Kann and Schütze (2017), we hypothesized that training MED to copy strings as a secondary task would help with the morphological inflection task. That is, we train the model simultaneously on the tasks of morphological re-inflection and sequence autoencoding, interspersing inflection training examples and autoencoding examples. This can be viewed as a form of multi-task learning,[3] and is equivalent to maximizing the log-likelihood for both tasks:

$$\mathcal{L}(\boldsymbol{\theta}) = \sum_{(l,t,w)\in\mathcal{D}} \log p_{\boldsymbol{\theta}}\left(w \mid e(l,t)\right) \qquad (2)$$
$$+ \sum_{s\in\mathcal{S}} \log p_{\boldsymbol{\theta}}(s \mid e(s)),$$

where $\mathcal{D}$ is the labeled training data, with each example consisting of a lemma l, a morphological tag t and an inflected form w, and $\mathcal{S}$ is a set of autoencoding examples. The function e represents the encoder, which depends on $\boldsymbol{\theta}$.

In the setting with no outside resources we experiment with two variants of the sequence autoencoder. The first of these, **AE-TD**, uses the

---

[2]Of course, the morphological variants we find may be noisy, so a better method for identifying these might still improve upon random strings.

[3]Multitask learning for NLP using encoder-decoder networks typically assumes that the separate tasks either have distinct encoders, distinct decoders, or both (e.g., Luong et al., 2016; Alonso and Plank, 2017; Bollmann et al., 2017). Here, we use the same encoder and decoder for both tasks. In preliminary experiments, we tried pre-training the autoencoder instead (see, e.g., Dai and Le, 2015; Kamper et al., 2015), but found that interspersing examples gave a clear advantage.

lemmas and target forms in the training data as inputs to the autoencoder, yielding up to twice as many autoencoder inputs as inflection training pairs (any duplicate lemmas or target forms are included only once).

Our second autoencoder variant, **AE-RS**, uses randomly generated strings as inputs, which means we can produce an arbitrary number of autoencoding examples. In this and following systems, we use the postfix XXK (e.g. 1K, 2K, 4K) to indicate the number of additional examples generated. To obtain each example, we first choose its length uniformly at random from the interval [4, 12] and then sample each character uniformly at random from the alphabet of the respective language.

Input/Output Format We generally follow the input representation outlined in §2, except that morphological tags are replaced with one special tag that stands for autoencoding. The output format does not change.

3.2 Corpus Word Autoencoder (AE-CW)

In the setting where corpus data is available we can replace randomly generated strings with corpus words (system **AE-CW**). We hypothesized that autoencoding words from the actual language would give not only the benefit of learning to copy, but also the benefit of learning the character distributions typical of a given language.

To select words for the corpus word autoencoding task we use Wikipedia text dumps provided for the shared task. We filter out all words shorter than 4 characters. For each language we learn its alphabet from the letters that occur in training words of the original SIGMORPHON training sets and filter out all words that contain foreign characters. We use the remaining words to sample uniformly without repetition the required amount of autoencoding examples. The input and output formats are the same as for the previous approaches.

3.3 Data Mining for Inflected Pairs (DM)

Our next method, **DM**, mines the corpus data to create new training examples by (a) inferring new lemma-inflected form pairs and (b) predicting the tags of the inflected forms. We describe each step below.

Inferring Lemma-Word Form Pairs Although most work on unsupervised learning of morphology has focused on decomposing words into mor-

Word 1⇔Word 2	Sim.	Dif.
deceive⇔deception	*dece*	*ive ⇔ ption*
receive⇔reception	*rece*	*ive ⇔ ption*
perceive⇔perception	*perce*	*ive ⇔ ption*
conceive⇔conception	*conce*	*ive ⇔ ption*

Table 2: Pairs of related words, their similarities and the respective differences.

phemes, their constituent parts, e.g., (Kurimo et al., 2010; Hammarström and Borin, 2011), others have focused on finding morphologically related words and the orthographic patterns relating them (Schone and Jurafsky, 2000; Baroni et al., 2002; Neuvel and Fulop, 2002; Soricut and Och, 2015):

$$\text{walk} \Leftrightarrow \text{walking} \quad \varepsilon \Leftrightarrow \text{ing} \qquad (3)$$

We adopt the algorithm by Neuvel and Fulop (2002) to learn Word Formation Strategies (WFS)—frequently occurring orthographic patterns that relate whole words to other whole words. The input of this algorithm is a list of N words[4]. The algorithm works by comparing each of the N words to all other words. It first finds word *similarities* as the Longest Common Subsequence (LCS) between the two words. Then it finds word *differences* as the orthographic differences with respect to *similarities* (see Table 2 for examples). Finally, all word pairs with the same *differences* have their *similarities* and *differences* merged into one WFS. For example, words in Table 2 sanction the following WFS:

$$*\#\#\textbf{ceive} \Leftrightarrow *\#\#\textbf{ception} \qquad (4)$$

where * and # stand for the optional and mandatory character wild cards respectively. The interpretation of the WFS in Example 4 is: "a word that ends with *ceive* preceded by 2 to 3 characters predicts another word ending with *ception* preceded by the same 2 to 3 characters" (Neuvel and Fulop, 2002). Table 1 gives English WFS examples and sample word pairs that warranted their creation.

Tag Prediction To perform labeling we make use of two resources: (i) a word embedding based part of speech (POS) classifier; (ii) the WFS we learned previously.

---

[4] We choose N to be 40k and take the 40k most frequent words from each language's Wikipedia dump.

No	WFS	Examples
1	*********####d ⇔ *********####s	invited-invites, wired-wires, tried-tries
2	********####ed ⇔ ********####ing	trailed-trailing, folded-folding, melted-melting
3	********####e ⇔ *********####ing	violate-violating, liberate-liberating, raise-raising
4	**********####s ⇔ **********####al	comics comical, clinics-clinical, corrections-correctional

Table 1: Examples of word formation strategies and sample word pairs that warranted them.

Each of the original shared task training examples contains two word forms and a set of morphological tags including word POS information (see Example 1). We can use words with POS labels and word embeddings to train a POS classifier. Namely we train a support vector machine (SVM) (Cortes and Vapnik, 1995) to predict POS labels using word embeddings as features. We train word embeddings on the Wikipedia text dumps provided for the task. We use Fast-Text[5] by Bojanowski et al. (2016) to train 300 dimensional continuous bag of words embeddings (Mikolov et al., 2013) for all words occurring at least 5 times.

For each training example in the SIGMOR-PHON training data we examine each of the previously learned WFS. If the training example fits the WFS's orthographic constraints, we examine all word pairs that warranted the creation of this WFS. For a word pair to be labeled with the same morphological tags as the training example we require that both words are classified with the same part of speech as the original training example.

Input/Output Format To encode the additional training examples we use the same format as for the original ones (see §2) except we add a tag which signals that this example has been automatically extracted. We do this as a measure of caution to avoid ambiguities introduced by potentially erroneous training examples.

3.4 Using Multilingual Resources (MLT)

Recently, Kann et al. (2017) showed that training on a high-resource language can improve morphological inflection on a related low-resource language using an encoder-decoder system like the one here. This can be done using the same network as above, but training on inflection examples from multiple different languages—yet another form of multitask learning, since the model parameters are shared between languages. Following Kann et al. (2017), our multilingually trained system (**MLT**) uses the same input format as above, but with an additional tag prepended to each example indicating which language it is from.

Our setup is slightly different from that of Kann et al. (2017), since they had only 50 or 200 examples in each target language, and used only one or two other higher-resource languages for transfer. Here, we have similar amounts of data for each language (1000 examples in most cases), and use larger groups of related languages to train together (see §4).

4 Experiments

Datasets The official shared task data consists of sets for 52 different languages, of which 40 were released as development languages. We used these for our preliminary experiments to compare different systems and quantities of additional training data. The remaining 12 "surprise" languages were released shortly before the test phase of the shared task, and we report results for our best systems on these as well.[6] In the "medium" training data setting, which we focus on in this work, 1000 training instances are given for each language, except for Scottish Gaelic with only 681 instances. Additionally, development sets with 1000 instances are available for all languages except for Basque, Bengali, Haida, Welsh with 100 and Scottish Gaelic with 50.

MED Parameters In our experiments we use the same training method and hyper parameter settings as suggested by Kann and Schütze (2016). Namely, we use 100 hidden units for the encoder and decoder GRUs; 300 dimensions for encoder and decoder embeddings. For training we use stochastic gradient descent, Adadelta (Zeiler, 2012), with gradient clipping threshold of 1.0 and mini batch size of 20. When making predictions

---

[5]https://github.com/facebookresearch/fastText/

[6]A detailed list of languages can be found at https://sites.google.com/view/conll-sigmorphon2017/task, or see Figure 2.

we use beam-search decoding with a beam of size 12.

Baselines We compare our results with two baselines: the **SIGMORPHON** baseline[7] and **MED** baseline (see §2).

Additional Training Data We train the AE-CW, AE-RS and DM systems with increasing amounts of data: 1k, 2k, or 4k additional training examples. Four thousand training instances is the maximum number of mined training examples available for most languages. We train additional AE-CW and AE-RS systems with 8k and 16k additional training examples to see if any further performance gains are obtainable.

Multilingual Training We train together languages that belong to the same language family. This results in the following groupings: **Baltic** (Latvian, Lithuanian), **Celtic** (Scottish Gaelic, Welsh, Irish), **Germanic** (Danish, Dutch, English, Icelandic, Faroese, German, Swedish, Norwegian-Nynorsk, Norwegian-Bokmal), **Finnic** (Finnish, Estonian), **Iranian** (Persian, Sorani, Kurmanji), **Romance** (Catalan, French, Italian, Portuguese, Spanish, Romanian), **Semitic** (Arabic, Hebrew), **Slavic** (Bulgarian, Czech, Lower-Sorbian, Macedonian, Polish, Russian, Serbo-Croatian, Slovak, Slovene, Ukrainian).

We perform two different multilingual training experiments: First, we train **MLT** without any additional data. In this setting MED trained on individual languages gives a lower bound—MLT should work no worse than MED. We also train **MLT-AE-TD** in which the original training data is used to obtain up to twice as many autoencoding training examples for each language. In this setting the training file of Slavic languages, for example, contains 30K training examples (3K for each language). Here, AE-TD trained on individual languages gives a lower bound on the expected performance. In this setting we also train another stronger and fairer baseline (**AE-TD-RS-XK**), for which training files for individual languages contain exactly the same number of training examples as in the multilingual training case. For example, the training file for MLT-AE-TD when trained on the Baltic branch has 6k training examples—1k original and 2k AE-TD examples for each of

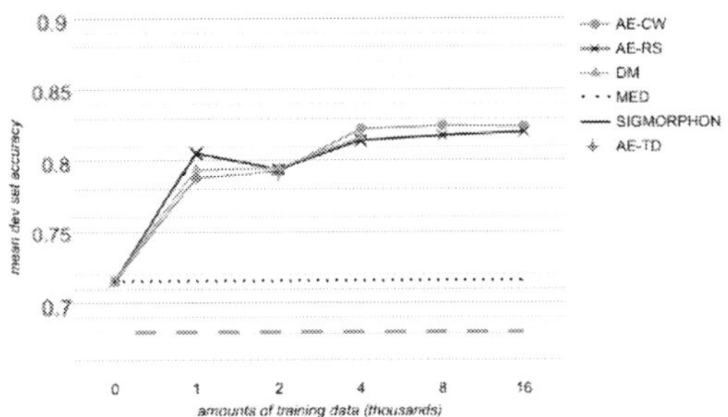

Figure 1: The average performance over the 40 development languages for each of the methods, as a function of the number of added examples.

System	Mean Accuracy
SIGMORPHON	65.67
MED	70.52
AE-TD	77.73
AE-CW-16K	**81.20**
AE-RS-16K	80.40

Table 4: The average performance over all languages except Haida and Khaling (see text).

the two Baltic languages (Latvian and Lithuanian). So, the Latvian training file for AE-TD-RS-3K also contains 6K training examples: 1K original and 2K training data autoencoding examples, plus an additional 3K random string autoencoding examples, which substitute for the absent Lithuanian training examples. The Lithuanian training file is constructed analogously.

5 Results and Discussion

5.1 Number of Added Examples

Figure 1 shows how the average performance over the 40 development languages varies with the number of added autoencoder examples, for AE-CW, AE-RS and DM methods. For all three methods, adding more data up to 4k examples helps a lot, after which performance rises more slowly and mostly levels off by about 16k extra examples. (These results contrast with the inflection results from the semi-supervised variational sequence autoencoder of Zhou and Neubig (2017), where even after 150k unlabeled examples, performance still appears to be increasing.) After controlling for the amount of additional data, we see only a small benefit from autoencoding corpus words (AE-CW) rather than random strings (AE-

---

[7]SIGMORPHON baseline: `https://github.com/sigmorphon/conll2017/tree/master/evaluation`

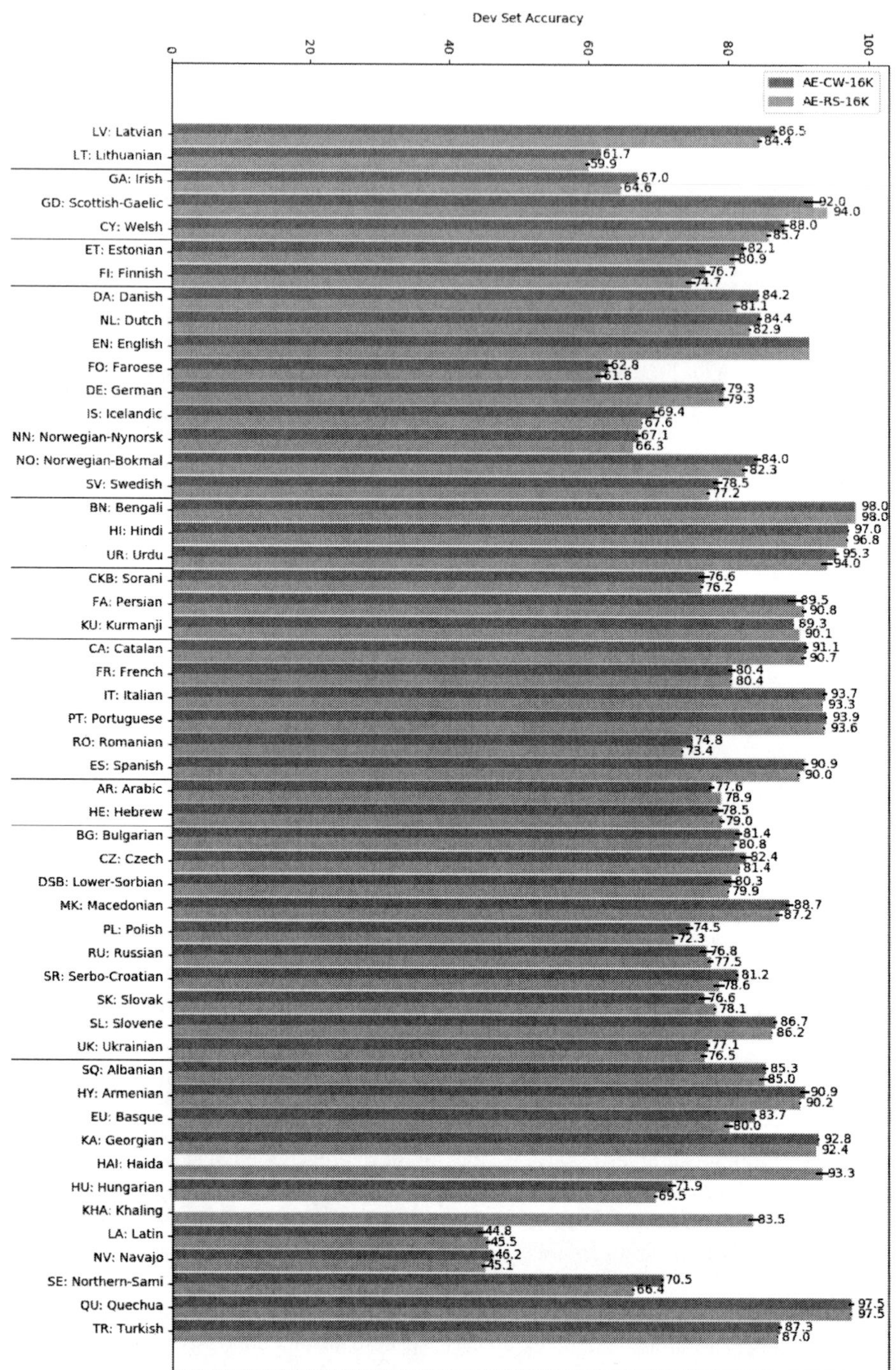

Figure 2: The accuracy of our best systems on all languages. We report the mean and standard error (shown as error bars) across three separate training runs for each language. Languages are grouped by their language families. From the top: Baltic, Celtic, Germanic, Finnic, Iranian, Romance, Semitic, Slavic and miscellaneous languages.

	MED	MLT	AE-TD	MLT-AE-TD	AE-TD-RS-XK
Baltic	63.25	**64.45**	69.15	70.80	**72.20**
Celtic	53.65	**56.09**	63.74	65.22	**68.17**
Germanic	66.53	**73.29**	73.83	75.87	**76.71**
Finnic	59.45	**68.65**	73.35	75.90	**76.77**
Iranian	75.83	**80.83**	81.53	83.60	**84.87**
Romance	80.72	**83.65**	84.90	86.10	**86.67**
Semitic	**71.60**	69.05	76.70	**77.30**	**77.30**
Slavic	63.78	**77.90**	75.65	**80.31**	79.47
Average	66.85	**71.74**	74.86	76.89	**77.77**

Table 3: Multilingual training. We report average development set accuracies, weighted by the number of examples in each development set. The letter X in AE-TD-RS-XK, stands for the number of random string autoencoding examples added (see §4 for more details).

RS).

Figure 1 suggests that on average, adding 1K, 2K or 4k mined training examples (DM curve) gives a similar performance gain to what adding the same amount of autoencoding examples would give (AE-CW and AE-RS).

To investigate the quality of the mined training examples we conduct an experiment where for each morphological tag in SIGMORPHON training data we pick an alternative lemma and target form among the mined examples with the same tag. We hypothesize that, if correct, mined examples should serve the same function as the original ones and the average performance should not change. On average this resulted in 500 swaps per language. The average MED performance on the modified training sets is about 10% lower than on the original training files.

This suggests, that—although noisy—the mined examples, when annotated with an additional "mining"-tag, work as model regularizers, thus benefiting MED's performance on the inflection task.

Obtaining autoencoding examples, however, is computationally simpler than mining additional training examples, hence given the similar effects the autoencoding approach seems preferable over the data mining.

5.2 Best Monolingual Systems

The average development set accuracy over 50 languages[8] of our best system AE-CW-16K is 81.2% (see Table 4) closely followed by AE-RS-16K with 80.4%. For comparison, this is about 15.5% and 10.6% absolute gain over the SIGMORPHON and MED baselines respectively. AE-TD on average performs only 3.5% worse than AE-CW-16K although using 87.5% fewer autoencoding examples and no external resources. Figure 2 shows the accuracy of our best systems on all languages. We report the average accuracy and standard error across three separate training runs for each language.

We conducted a paired-samples t-test to compare mean development set accuracies for 50 languages between AC-CW-16K and AC-RS-16K systems, using 3 runs each. The test suggested that there was a significant difference between accuracies of AC-CW-16K and AC-RS-16K ($T(49) = 4.04$, $p < 0.01$), although the difference is small relative to the gains over the baselines.

5.3 Multilingual Training

Table 3 shows results for multilingual training experiments. Due to the different development set sizes (see §4) we report **weighted average** development set accuracies. MLT without any additional data is better than the MED baseline for most related languages except Semitic languages, on average giving about 7% improvement over the MED baseline. MLT-AE-TD, the system in which the original training data is used to obtain autoencoding training examples on average outperforms the conservative AE-TD baseline by 2.5% absolute, but barely reaches the performance of AE-TD-RS-XK baseline. AE-TD-RS-XK baseline (for details see §4) gives performance for each individual language if all training examples of other languages in an MLT-AE-TD training file are replaced by random string autoencoding exam-

---

[8]Haida and Khaling do not have Wikipedia text dumps to train **AE-CW** and are thus excluded from all averages.

ples. Table 3 shows that on average MLT-AE-TD works no better than AE-TD-RS-XK. Currently, it is unclear whether the performance gains in MLT and MLT-AE-TD experiments are due to knowledge transfer from related languages as suggested by Kann et al. (2017), or because different languages serve as model regularizers with respect to each other. Performance on 6 out of 8 groups of related languages, however, suggests that random string autoencoding is not only simpler but also a better performing method than multilingual training.

5.4 Shared Task Submission: Test Results

We submitted two final systems to the medium-resource track of Subtask 1 (Inflection): **AE-RS-16K** for the restricted (main) track, and **AE-CW-16K** for the bonus track (where external monolingual corpora are permitted). The final systems are ensembles of 3 separate training runs, and the final answer is selected by majority voting (or chosen at random in case of a tie).

Although we did not tune any system to the high-resource track, we also submitted results there, using an analogous ensemble system with 16k autoencoder at random strings in addition to the 10k training examples. We did not submit to the low-resource track because the results from the AE-RS-16k method were below the baseline system on the development set.

In the high resource setting of the restricted track, our system achieved an average test set accuracy of 95.32%, which is an 17.51% absolute improvement over the Shared Task baseline, and the top performance of 18 submissions. In the medium resource setting AE-RS-16K gives 81.02%—an improvement of 16.32% absolute over the Shared Task baseline. This result, however, is 1.78% absolute lower than the best system's performance, so among 18 submissions AE-RS-16K takes the 6th place. In the medium resource setting of the bonus track among 2 submissions AE-CW-16K comes first with 82.37%. This is 1.35% better than our restricted track submission (AE-RS-16K), but still 0.43% worse than the top performing system in the restricted track.

6 Conclusion

We evaluated several ways to improve the morphological inflection performance of a state-of-the-art encoder-decoder model (MED) when relatively few labeled examples are available. In experiments on 52 languages, we showed that all methods considerably outperformed the MED baseline. Autoencoding corpus words (AE-CW) gave the largest improvement, but was only slightly better than autoencoding random strings (AE-RS). We found no benefit from cross-lingual knowledge transfer as compared to using an equivalent number of random string autoencoder examples.

Our results suggest that the main benefit of the various data augmentation methods is providing a strong bias towards learning the identity transformation and/or regularizing the model, with a slight additional benefit obtained by learning the typical character sequences in the language. These benefits can be achieved with very simple methods and few or no additional data resources.

References

Héctor Martínez Alonso and Barbara Plank. 2017. Multitask learning for semantic sequence prediction under varying data conditions. In *Proceedings of EACL*. Association for Computational Linguistics.

Dzmitry Bahdanau, Kyunghyun Cho, and Yoshua Bengio. 2015. Neural machine translation by jointly learning to align and translate. In *Proceedings of ICLR*.

Marco Baroni, Johannes Matiasek, and Harald Trost. 2002. Unsupervised discovery of morphologically related words based on orthographic and semantic similarity. In *Proceedings of the ACL-02 Workshop on Morphological and Phonological Learning*. Association for Computational Linguistics.

Piotr Bojanowski, Edouard Grave, Armand Joulin, and Tomas Mikolov. 2016. Enriching word vectors with subword information. *arXiv preprint arXiv:1607.04606* .

Marcel Bollmann, Joachim Bingel, and Anders Søgaard. 2017. Learning attention for historical text normalization by learning to pronounce. In *Proceedings of ACL*. Association for Computational Linguistics.

Corinna Cortes and Vladimir Vapnik. 1995. Support-vector networks. *Machine learning* 20(3):273–297.

Ryan Cotterell, Christo Kirov, John Sylak-Glassman, Géraldine Walther, Ekaterina Vylomova, Patrick Xia, Manaal Faruqui, Sandra Kübler, David Yarowsky, Jason Eisner, and Mans Hulden. 2017. The CoNLL-SIGMORPHON 2017 shared task: Universal morphological reinflection in 52 languages. In *Proceedings of the CoNLL-SIGMORPHON 2017 Shared Task: Universal Morphological Reinflection*. Association for Computational Linguistics.

Ryan Cotterell, Christo Kirov, John Sylak-Glassman, David Yarowsky, Jason Eisner, and Mans Hulden. 2016. The SIGMORPHON 2016 shared task–morphological reinflection. In *Proceedings of ACL*. Association for Computational Linguistics.

Andrew M Dai and Quoc V Le. 2015. Semi-supervised sequence learning. In *Advances in Neural Information Processing Systems*. pages 3079–3087.

Harald Hammarström and Lars Borin. 2011. Unsupervised learning of morphology. *Computational Linguistics* 37(2):309–350.

Herman Kamper, Micha Elsner, Aren Jansen, and Sharon Goldwater. 2015. Unsupervised neural network based feature extraction using weak top-down constraints. In *IEEE International Conference on Acoustics, Speech and Signal Processing (ICASSP)*. IEEE, pages 5818–5822.

Katharina Kann, Ryan Cotterell, and Hinrich Schütze. 2017. One-shot neural cross-lingual transfer for paradigm completion. In *Proceedings of ACL*. Association for Computational Linguistics.

Katharina Kann and Hinrich Schütze. 2016. MED: The LMU system for the SIGMORPHON 2016 shared task on morphological reinflection. In *Proceedings of ACL*. Association for Computational Linguistics.

Katharina Kann and Hinrich Schütze. 2017. Unlabeled data for morphological generation with character-based sequence-to-sequence models. *arXiv preprint arXiv:1705.06106* .

Mikko Kurimo, Sami Virpioja, Ville Turunen, and Krista Lagus. 2010. Morpho challenge competition 2005–2010: Evaluations and results. In *Proceedings of the 11th Meeting of the ACL Special Interest Group on Computational Morphology and Phonology*. Association for Computational Linguistics, SIGMORPHON '10, pages 87–95.

Minh-Thang Luong, Quoc V Le, Ilya Sutskever, Oriol Vinyals, and Lukasz Kaiser. 2016. Multi-task sequence to sequence learning. In *Proceedings of ICLR*.

Tomas Mikolov, Kai Chen, Greg Corrado, and Jeffrey Dean. 2013. Efficient estimation of word representations in vector space. *arXiv preprint arXiv:1301.3781* .

Sylvain Neuvel and Sean A Fulop. 2002. Unsupervised learning of morphology without morphemes. In *Proceedings of the ACL-02 workshop on Morphological and phonological learning-Volume 6*. Association for Computational Linguistics, pages 31–40.

Patrick Schone and Daniel Jurafsky. 2000. Knowledge-free induction of morphology using latent semantic analysis. In *Proceedings of the 2nd Workshop on Learning Language in Logic and the 4th Conference on Computational Natural Language Learning (CoNLL)*. Association for Computational Linguistics, pages 67–72.

Radu Soricut and Franz Josef Och. 2015. Unsupervised morphology induction using word embeddings. In *Proceedings of HLT-NAACL*. Association for Computational Linguistics, pages 1627–1637.

Matthew D Zeiler. 2012. Adadelta: an adaptive learning rate method. *arXiv preprint arXiv:1212.5701* .

Chunting Zhou and Graham Neubig. 2017. Multi-space variational encoder-decoders for semi-supervised labeled sequence transduction. *arxiv preprint arXiv:1704.01691* .

The LMU System for the CoNLL-SIGMORPHON 2017 Shared Task on Universal Morphological Reinflection

Katharina Kann and **Hinrich Schütze**

CIS

LMU Munich, Germany

kann@cis.lmu.de

Abstract

We present the LMU system for the CoNLL-SIGMORPHON 2017 shared task on universal morphological reinflection, which consists of several subtasks, all concerned with producing an inflected form of a paradigm in different settings. Our solution is based on a neural sequence-to-sequence model, extended by preprocessing and data augmentation methods. Additionally, we develop a new algorithm for selecting the most suitable source form in the case of multi-source input, outperforming the baseline by 5.7% on average over all languages and settings. Finally, we propose a fine-tuning approach for the multi-source setting, and combine this with the source form detection, increasing accuracy by a further 4.6% on average.

1 Introduction

Many of the world's languages have a rich morphology, i.e., make use of surface variations of lemmata in order to express certain properties, like the tense or mood of a verb. This makes a variety of natural language processing tasks more challenging, as it increases the number of words in a language drastically; a problem morphological analysis and generation help to mitigate. However, a big issue when developing methods for morphological processing is that for many morphologically rich languages, there are only few or no relevant training data available, making it impossible to train state-of-the-art machine learning models (e.g., (Faruqui et al., 2016; Kann and Schütze, 2016b; Aharoni et al., 2016; Zhou and Neubig, 2017)). This is the motivation for the CoNLL-SIGMORPHON-2017 shared task on uni-

versal morphological reinflection (Cotterell et al., 2017a), which animates the development of systems for as many as 52 different languages in 6 different low-resource settings for morphological reinflection: to generate an inflected form, given a target morphological tag and either the lemma (task 1) or a partial paradigm (task 2). An example is

$$(\text{use}, \text{V};3;\text{SG};\text{PRS}) \mapsto \text{uses}$$

In this paper, we describe the LMU system for the shared task. Since it depends on the language and the amount of resources available for training which method performs best, our approach consists of a modular system. For most medium- and high-resource, as well as some low-resource settings, we make use of the state-of-the-art encoder-decoder (Cho et al., 2014a; Sutskever et al., 2014; Bahdanau et al., 2015) network MED (Kann and Schütze, 2016b), while extending the training data in several ways. Whenever the given data are not sufficient, we make use of the baseline system, which can be trained on fewer instances.

While we submit solutions for every language and setting, our main focus is on task 2 of the shared task and the main contributions of this paper correspondingly address a multi-source input setting: (i) We develop CIS ("choice of important sources"), a novel algorithm for selecting the most appropriate source form for a target tag from a partially given paradigm, which is based on edit trees (Chrupała, 2008). (ii) We propose to cast the task of multi-source morphological reinflection as a domain adaptation problem. By fine-tuning on forms from a partial paradigm, we improve the performance of a neural sequence-to-sequence model for most shared task languages.

Our final methods, averaged over languages, outperform the official baseline by 7.0%, 18.5%, and 16.5% for task 1 and 8.7%, 10.1%, and

Proceedings of the CoNLL SIGMORPHON 2017 Shared Task: Universal Morphological Reinflection, pages 40–48,
Vancouver, Canada, August 3–4, 2017. ©2017 Association for Computational Linguistics

10.3% for task 2 for the low-, medium-, and high-resource settings, respectively.

Furthermore, our submitted sytem—a combination of our methods with the baseline system—surpasses the baseline's accuracy on test for both tasks as well as all languages and settings. Differences in performance are between 8.69% (task 1 low) and 17.94% (task 1 medium).

2 Morphological Reinflection

The paradigm of a lemma w_l is a set of tuples of inflected forms f_k and tags t_k describing the properties of the inflected word, which we formally denote as:

$$\pi(w_l) = \left\{ \left(f_k[w_l], t_k \right) \right\}_{t_k \in T(w_l)} \tag{1}$$

with $T(w_l)$ being the set of possible tags for w_l.

An example is the following paradigm of the Spanish lemma *soñar*:

$$\pi(\text{soñar}) = \left\{ \left(\textit{sueño}, \text{1SgPresInd} \right), \ldots, \left(\textit{soñaran}, \text{3PlPastSbj} \right) \right\}$$

The shared task has two subtasks: **task 1** consists of predicting a certain form $f_i[w_l]$, given the lemma w_l and the target tag t_i. For **task 2**, one or more source forms are given for each lemma (multi-source input). Thus, additional information about the way a lemma is inflected is known and can be leveraged.

3 Preprocessing Methods

We apply the following preprocessing methods.

String preprocessing. We determine for each language if it is predominantly prefixing or suffixing, using the same algorithm as the shared task baseline system (Cotterell et al., 2017a). For prefixing languages, we invert all words. An example for the prefixing language Navajo is:

$$\text{chidí} \rightarrow \text{ídihc}$$

New character handling. The source and target vocabularies for the languages are constructed using the respective training and development sets. Therefore, out-of-vocabulary symbols can appear in the test sets, resulting in symbols the model has no information about. In order to address this, we substitute such characters by a special NEW symbol and train the model on it by including it in the additional training samples we create, cf. §4.

In the output, NEW is substituted back by the new characters in the input in order of appearance. An example from the German development data is:

$$\text{Phloëm} \rightarrow \text{PhloNEWm}$$

Tag extension. Explicit information is usually handled better by machine learning methods than implicit information. Therefore, we search for optional subtag slots, in contrast to those that are always occupied by some value, e.g., an optional *negation* subtag, in contrast to the part-of-speech subtag which, for most languages, is always either *Verb*, *Noun* or *Adjective*, but never empty. For all optional subtags, we artificially introduce a negated form.

4 Training Data Augmentation Methods

Additional source-target form pairs. We collect all forms belonging to the same lemma. We then add additional samples by constructing source-target combinations for other sources than the lemma, using the members of each paradigm. For the two samples $lemma_i \rightarrow word_1$ and $lemma_i \rightarrow word_2$ we can introduce the new samples $word_1 \rightarrow word_2$ and $word_2 \rightarrow word_1$.[1]

Autoencoding samples. We further create samples for a sequence autoencoding task, i.e., we add mappings of words to themselves, with a special copy tag **A**. No morphological tags are given. This is a way to multi-task train on autoencoding the input string and reinflection, as we maximize the joint log-likelihood

$$\mathcal{L}(\boldsymbol{\theta}) = \sum_{(w_l, t_s, t_t) \in \mathcal{T}} \log p_{\boldsymbol{\theta}} \left(f_t(w_l) \mid e(f_s(w_l), t_t) \right)$$

$$\tag{2}$$

$$+ \sum_{w \in \mathcal{W}} \log p_{\boldsymbol{\theta}}(w \mid e(w))$$

for the training data $\mathcal{T}$, source and target tags t_s and t_t, a lemma w_l and an encoding function e depending on $\boldsymbol{\theta}$, as well as a set of strings $\mathcal{W}$. We apply two variants: autoencoding the lemmata and forms from the original training set, or using *random* strings for this. Random strings are produced in the following way. We first construct all possible bigrams $\mathcal{B}$ from the vocabulary of the language. We then combine those with a random sequence of characters r of a random length between

---

[1] The respective source and target tags are part of the input, but omitted here for clarity.

1 and 4 in the following way: $b_1 + b_2 + r + b_3 + b_4$ for $b_i \in \mathcal{B}$. Constructing random strings like this has the positive side-effect that we can add a NEW to the vocabulary.

Rule-based data generation. We imitate a rule-based system by, given a source form and a target form, defining the prefix (resp. suffix) of a word as the word minus the longest common suffix (resp. prefix). We then create an additional training example by generating a random string s and prepending (resp. appending) source and target prefixes (resp. suffixes) to s. For example, in German, we can find the following rule for the 2nd person singular form:

$$*en \rightarrow *st$$

From this we can create additional training instances like the following.

$$(\text{jfgdgfen, V;2;SG;PRS}) \mapsto \text{jfgdgfst}$$
$$(\text{Ahggen, V;2;SG;PRS}) \mapsto \text{Ahggst}$$

We apply this procedure to all pairs of a source and a target tag that appear less than t times in train for a certain threshold t.

5 System Architecture

We apply the encoder-decoder network MED (Kann and Schütze, 2016a), due to its success in last year's edition of the shared task (Cotterell et al., 2016). While we extend it by new training data augmentation methods and, for task 2, the additional algorithms described below, we do not make changes to the model's architecture. We will shortly describe MED and the shared task baseline system in this section.

5.1 MED

Encoder. The format of the input of the encoder is the same as in (Kann and Schütze, 2016a), but with a small modification to be able to handle unlabeled data: Given the set of morphological subtags M that each target tag is composed of (e.g., the tag *1SgPresInd* contains the subtags *1*, *Sg*, *Pres* and *Ind*), and the alphabet Σ of the language of application, our input is of the form $(\mathbf{A} \mid M^*) \Sigma^*$, i.e., it consists of *either* a sequence of subtags *or* the symbol $\mathbf{A}$ signaling that the input is not annotated and should be autoencoded, and (in both cases) the character sequence of the input word. All parts of the input are represented by embeddings.

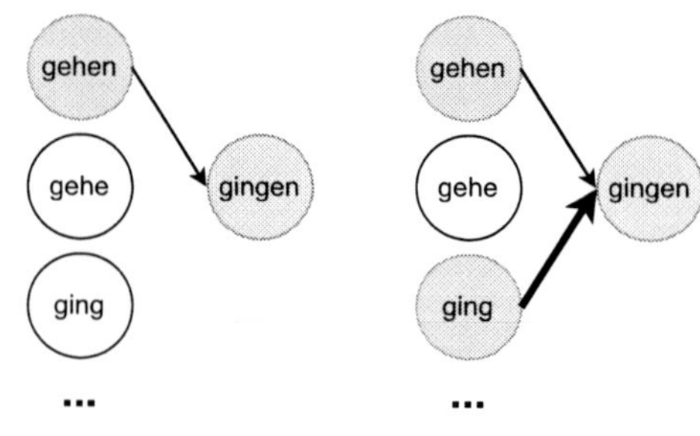

(a) The lemma is the only accepted source form.

(b) Additional source forms with a higher priority than the lemma have been determined.

Figure 1: Comparison of the traditional view (left) and the result of CIS (right). Possible source forms in green, the target form in blue. Thickness of the arrows represents priorities of source forms. Most forms of the paradigm have been omitted because of space limitations.

We encode the input $x = x_1, x_2, \ldots, x_{T_x}$ using a bidirectional gated recurrent neural network (GRU) (Cho et al., 2014b). We then concatenate the forward and backward hidden states to obtain the input h_i for the decoder.

Decoder. The decoder is a uni-directional attention-based GRU, defining a probability distribution over strings in Σ^*:

$$p(y \mid x) = \prod_{t=1}^{T_y} p(y_t \mid y_1, \ldots, y_{t-1}, s_t, c_t),$$

with s_t being the decoder hidden state for time t and c_t being a context vector, calculated using the encoder hidden states together with attention weights. A detailed description of the encoder-decoder model can be found in (Bahdanau et al., 2015).

5.2 Baseline System

The shared task baseline system (**BL**) is well-suited for low-resource settings. It first aligns each input and output string, and than extracts possible prefix or suffix substitution rules from the training data. At test time, it applies the most suitable one in the following way: Every input is searched for the longest contained prefix or suffix and the rule belonging to the affix and given target tag is applied to obtain the output. Whether prefixes or suffixes are used depends on the language and is determined using the training set.

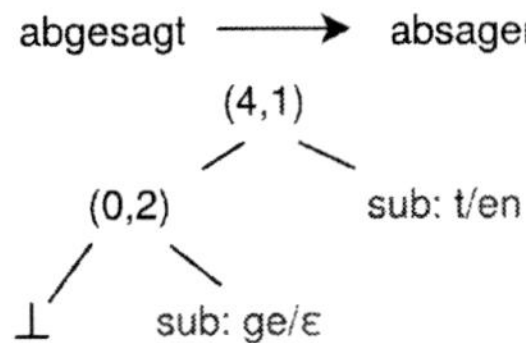

Figure 2: Edit tree for the transformation from *abgesagt* "canceled" to *absagen* "to cancel". Each node contains the length of the parts before and after the respective LCS, e.g., the leftmost node contains the length of the parts before and after the LCS of *abge* and *ab*. The prefix *sub* indicates that the node is a substitution operation.

6 Choice of Important Sources

As our **choice of important sources (CIS) algorithm** is based strongly on edit trees (Chrupała, 2008), we will introduce them first.

Edit trees. An edit tree $e(\sigma, \tau)$ is a way to specify a transformation between a source string σ and a target string τ (Chrupała, 2008). It is constructed by first determining the longest common substring (LCS) (Gusfield, 1997) of σ and τ and then modeling the prefix and suffix pairs of the LCS recursively. In the case of an empty LCS, $e(\sigma, \tau)$ corresponds to the substitution operation that replaces σ with τ. Figure 2 shows an example.

CIS. The entire task of paradigm completion is built upon the notion that the members of a paradigm are not independent. However, for many languages, some slots of a paradigm are more dependent on each other: For example, *gehen*, *gehe* and *ging* are all forms of the same German paradigm, but when aiming to produce the 3rd person plural past tense form *gingen*, the task is easier when starting from the (more similar) form *ging*. In fact, in many cases, the entire paradigm is *completely deterministic* when the right paradigm slots are known. A set of forms that determines all other inflected forms is called *principal parts*.

(Cotterell et al., 2017b) use this property of morphologically rich languages to induce topologies in order to jointly decode entire paradigms and to thus make use of all known forms. However, they suppose to be able to compute and use good estimates for the probabilities $p(f_i(w_l)|f_j(w_l))$ for source form $f_j(w_l)$ and target form $f_i(w_l)$, since they use at least 632 entire paradigms per part of speech and language for training. Using a minimum spanning tree, they approximate a solution to the maximum-a-posteriori

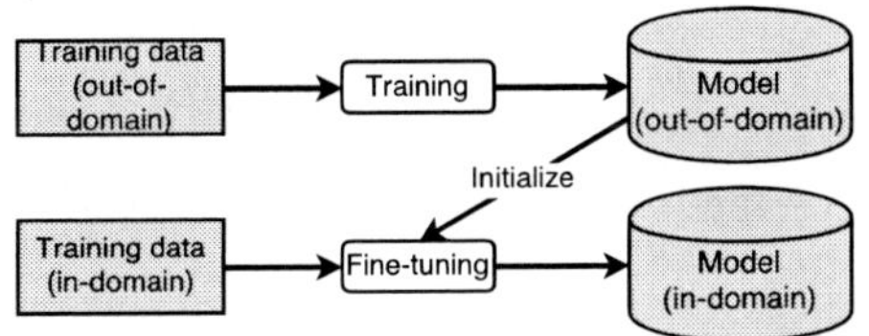

Figure 3: Overview of a fine-tuning setup. In our case, "in-domain" refers to the partial paradigm to be completed; "out-of-domain" refers to all other paradigms.

(MAP) inference problem.

In order to be able to apply our approach to low-resource settings, we focus instead on finding the *best source form* for each target form in a language, and CIS works as follows. We calculate edit trees for each pair $(f_j(w_l), f_i(w_l))$ for each lemma w_l in the training data. We then count the number of different edit trees for each pair of source and target tag (t_j, t_i) and build an *importance list* for each tag t_i, giving higher priorities to source tags with lower counts. The intuition behind this is that the fewer different edit trees appear in the training set, the more deterministic the paradigm slot i is, given a certain source slot j.

At test time, we find the form from the given slots of the paradigm which has the highest importance score, and use it to generate the target form. Note that, as the lemma is always given, there will never be a need to use a worse source form than the lemma.

7 Fine-Tuning for Multi-Source Input

For sequence-to-sequence models for neural machine translation, it has been shown that specialized models for a certain domain are able to obtain better performances than general ones (Luong and Manning, 2015). One way to perform such a *domain adaptation* is fine-tuning: a general model, which has been trained on out-of-domain data, is further trained on (newly) available in-domain data, cf. Figure 3. This brings the conditional probability $p(y_1, ..., y_m|x_1, ..., x_n)$ for an output sequence $(y_1, ..., y_m)$ given an input sequence $(x_1, ..., x_n)$ closer to the target distribution.

Here, we propose to improve multi-source morphological reinflection by treating each paradigm as a separate domain and performing "domain adaptation" everytime a new paradigm should be completed by the model.

In particular, we have one base model (for

$n \leq 1.5$	$1.5 < n < 10$	$10 \leq n$
danish	arabic	albanian
english	bengali	armenian
norwegian-bokmal	bulgarian	basque
norwegian-nynorsk	czech	catalan
	dutch	haida
	estonian	hindi
	faroese	italian
	finnish	khaling
	french	persian
	georgian	portuguese
	german	quechua
	hebrew	sorani
	hungarian	spanish
	icelandic	turkish
	irish	urdu
	kurmanji	welsh
	latin	
	latvian	
	lithuanian	
	lower-sorbian	
	macedonian	
	navajo	
	northern-sami	
	polish	
	romanian	
	russian	
	scottish-gaelic	
	serbo-croatian	
	slovak	
	slovene	
	swedish	
	ukrainian	

Table 1: Average amount n of sources given per paradigm, for the development set.

each setting and language), trained on all available training examples. The original training data corresponds to *out-of-domain data* in a domain adaptation setting. At test time, we construct for each partial paradigm $\mathcal{P}_{known}$ all possible training examples in the way described in the paragraphs about additional source-target form pairs and autoencoding in §4. Thus, for $|\mathcal{P}_{known}| = n$, we end up with (up to) $n * (n - 1) + N_a$ in-domain samples for fine-tuning where N_a is the number of autoencoding training samples. We then for each partial paradigm fine-tune the original base model on all examples constructed from $\mathcal{P}_{known}$, which match the *in-domain data* for domain adaptation. Thus, we end up with a different fine-tuned model for each partial paradigm in the test set.

Our method is expected to perform best in a setting in which many forms of each paradigm are given as input, e.g., when n is big. Table 1 indicates for which language we would therefore expect could performance.

8 Experiments

8.1 Systems

Task1. For task 1, we apply **MED***: MED in combination with all preprocessing methods mentioned in §3 and the following data augmentations. We create additional source-target form pairs where possible and create autoencoding samples, random ones as well as from the original data. Further, we create 5 additional rule-based samples for each existing sample of all source-target tag combinations that appear less than $t = 10$ times in the training set for a language.

We employ ensembles of 5 MED* models, which are trained for 90 (low and medium) or 45 (high) epochs. Ensembling is done by majority voting.

Task2. We again apply MED*. However, for task 2 we do not create rule-based samples.[2] Models for the low-resource, medium-resource and high-resource settings are trained for 45, 30 and 20 epochs, respectively. For task 2, we do not use ensembling.

At test time, we preprocess each newly incoming paradigm in the same way as the training data, except for the creation of random copy samples. We then *fine-tune* the base model for each new paradigm according to §7 for 25 additional epochs. Additionally, we choose the best source form for each required target tag and predict each inflected form for this input (**MED*+FT+CIS**).

The limited amount of data makes it impossible to obtain competitive performance using MED* for some languages and settings (especially for languages with only few given slots per paradigm), even after applying all data augmentation methods described above. Thus, we apply the baseline model for those cases, but combine it with CIS (cf. §6) to improve its performance (**BL+CIS**). We do not apply preprocessing or data augmentation methods for BL, as they would not influence its performance.

Shared task submission. The best approach depends on both the language and the setting. Thus, our final submission for each case is obtained by either BL, BL+CIS, the MED* ensemble, or MED*+FT+CIS, selected using the accuracy on the development set.

---

[2]Using rule-based examples for training leads to worse performance of the fine-tuned system, even though the base system turns out to be better. Thus, we do not use it.

	low			medium			high		
	BL	MED*	MED* (ENS)	BL	MED*	MED* (ENS)	BL	MED*	MED* (ENS)
albanian	**0.216**	0.102	0.129	0.661	0.849	**0.878**	0.781	0.966	**0.975**
arabic	0.215	0.237	**0.298**	0.400	0.804	**0.842**	0.477	0.930	**0.952**
armenian	0.378	0.444	**0.488**	0.766	0.897	**0.914**	0.891	0.972	**0.975**
bulgarian	0.331	0.437	**0.480**	0.750	0.814	**0.837**	0.900	0.969	**0.974**
catalan	0.552	0.560	**0.598**	0.832	0.903	**0.930**	0.942	0.981	**0.983**
czech	**0.408**	0.318	0.341	0.807	0.815	**0.856**	0.904	0.927	**0.937**
danish	0.598	0.636	**0.654**	0.781	0.830	**0.845**	0.891	0.934	**0.960**
dutch	**0.537**	0.500	0.521	0.717	0.828	**0.862**	0.868	0.968	**0.971**
english	0.762	0.831	**0.852**	0.902	0.928	**0.940**	0.950	0.964	**0.968**
faroese	0.307	0.347	**0.386**	0.587	0.595	**0.672**	0.747	0.817	**0.867**
finnish	**0.162**	0.120	0.147	0.425	0.682	**0.754**	0.785	0.939	**0.954**
french	0.630	0.579	**0.635**	0.761	0.789	**0.820**	0.836	0.889	**0.914**
georgian	0.712	0.802	**0.845**	0.900	0.925	**0.928**	0.940	0.991	**0.995**
german	0.537	0.541	**0.593**	0.715	0.772	**0.800**	0.812	0.894	**0.912**
hebrew	0.279	0.335	**0.366**	0.400	0.798	**0.831**	0.558	0.987	**0.991**
hindi	0.310	0.781	**0.782**	0.866	0.964	**0.974**	0.940	**1.000**	**1.000**
hungarian	0.172	0.300	**0.346**	0.417	0.708	**0.763**	0.711	0.856	**0.874**
icelandic	0.342	0.341	**0.364**	0.614	0.647	**0.689**	0.761	0.873	**0.913**
italian	0.449	0.392	**0.467**	0.738	0.920	**0.927**	0.799	**0.978**	0.974
latvian	**0.621**	0.483	0.536	0.851	0.834	**0.861**	0.910	0.965	**0.977**
lower-sorbian	0.343	0.451	**0.488**	0.705	0.788	**0.817**	0.860	0.966	**0.973**
macedonian	0.500	0.577	**0.664**	0.823	0.901	**0.913**	0.919	0.957	**0.964**
navajo	0.184	0.166	**0.198**	0.313	0.415	**0.460**	0.383	0.838	**0.897**
northern-sami	0.154	0.136	**0.174**	0.357	0.639	**0.711**	0.611	0.954	**0.968**
norwegian-nynorsk	0.508	0.489	**0.559**	0.633	0.671	**0.687**	0.783	0.883	**0.923**
persian	0.273	0.405	**0.457**	0.654	0.892	**0.913**	0.776	0.999	**1.000**
polish	0.419	0.366	**0.431**	0.752	0.751	**0.780**	0.894	0.909	**0.925**
portuguese	0.603	0.633	**0.684**	0.929	0.938	**0.944**	0.974	0.986	**0.993**
quechua	0.172	0.567	**0.615**	0.681	0.965	**0.977**	0.947	**1.000**	**1.000**
russian	**0.428**	0.319	0.366	0.750	0.763	**0.801**	0.820	0.909	**0.919**
scottish-gaelic	0.480	0.600	**0.620**	0.520	0.940	**0.960**	–	–	–
serbo-croatian	0.213	0.286	**0.324**	0.658	0.812	**0.844**	0.840	0.900	**0.920**
slovak	0.419	0.467	**0.495**	0.707	0.788	**0.795**	0.852	0.940	**0.960**
slovene	0.474	0.494	**0.522**	0.819	0.865	**0.883**	0.898	0.966	**0.981**
spanish	**0.586**	0.465	0.554	0.854	0.891	**0.910**	0.906	0.965	**0.974**
swedish	0.543	0.590	**0.607**	0.737	0.772	**0.796**	0.854	0.901	**0.914**
turkish	0.143	**0.280**	0.255	0.331	0.801	**0.852**	0.729	0.977	**0.982**
ukrainian	**0.729**	0.350	0.393	0.715	0.757	**0.775**	0.863	0.929	**0.934**
urdu	0.303	0.669	**0.687**	0.861	0.955	**0.962**	0.958	**0.996**	0.995
welsh	0.150	0.340	**0.460**	0.540	0.910	**0.920**	0.670	**0.990**	**0.990**
basque	0.000	0.140	**0.180**	0.020	0.860	**0.870**	0.060	**0.990**	**0.990**
bengali	0.440	0.610	**0.680**	0.750	**0.980**	**0.980**	0.840	**0.990**	**0.990**
estonian	0.226	0.242	**0.271**	0.624	0.796	**0.832**	0.762	0.985	**0.992**
haida	0.340	0.480	**0.570**	0.560	**0.920**	0.910	0.690	**0.970**	**0.970**
irish	**0.318**	0.188	0.222	0.447	0.626	**0.694**	0.543	0.891	**0.929**
khaling	0.039	0.157	**0.184**	0.184	0.879	**0.901**	0.538	0.995	**0.998**
kurmanji	**0.823**	0.818	0.620	0.884	0.904	**0.916**	0.922	0.934	**0.943**
latin	**0.160**	0.139	0.028	0.368	0.430	**0.489**	0.456	0.735	**0.795**
lithuanian	**0.235**	0.168	0.193	0.530	0.592	**0.618**	0.647	0.867	**0.906**
norwegian-bokmal	0.690	0.722	**0.743**	0.798	0.820	**0.838**	0.906	0.907	**0.925**
romanian	**0.441**	0.335	0.392	0.702	0.715	**0.764**	0.804	0.863	**0.893**
sorani	0.205	0.175	**0.232**	0.528	0.794	**0.823**	0.643	0.899	**0.910**
Average:	0.386	0.421	**0.456**	0.647	0.804	**0.832**	0.751	0.902	**0.916**

Table 2: Accuracies for task 1, for BL, MED* and MED* ensembles. Upper part: development languages; lower part: surprise languages.

8.2 MED Hyperparameters

We use the same hyperparameters for all MED models, i.e., all languages, tasks and amounts of resources. In particular, we keep them fixed to the following. Encoder and decoder RNNs each have 100 hidden units and the embeddings size is 300. For training we use ADADELTA (Zeiler, 2012) with minibatch size 20. Following Le et al. (2015), we initialize all weights in the encoder, decoder and the embeddings except for the GRU weights in the decoder to the identity matrix. Biases are initialized to zero. We use dropout with a coefficient of 0.5. As this is the model we use to produce test results for the shared task, we report

	Task 1	Task 2
Low	100	535
Medium	994	2285
High	9825	8578

Table 3: Average amount of training examples per task and resource quantity.

the best numbers obtained on the development set during training ("early stopping"). We compare the 1-best accuracy of all systems, i.e., the percentage of predictions that match the true answer exactly.

8.3 Data

The official shared task data consists of sets for 52 different languages, 2 tasks and 3 different settings with varying amount of resources.[3] An overview of the (averaged) amount of samples per task and setting is given in Table 3. Development and test sets are the same for all settings for each respective task and language. The gold labels for the test set are not published yet, so the experiments in this paper are performed on the development set.

8.4 Results

We compare our approaches to the official shared task baseline. Detailed results for task 1 and task 2 are shown in Table 2 and Table 4, respectively.

Task 1. Table 2 shows the results obtained by MED*, both for single models and ensembles. As can be seen, MED* already outperforms the baseline for the majority of languages in all settings; in average by 0.035, 0.157 and 0.151, respectively. MED*'s performance is worse for the low data quantity than for the others. This is an expected result, as neural networks are known to require a huge amount of training instances.

Ensembling increases the final accuracy for all settings, by an average of 0.035 (low), 0.028 (medium) and 0.014 (high).

Task 2. As can be seen in Table 4, combining BL and CIS outperforms BL on its own for many languages, especially in the low-resource setting. The highest improvements for the low-, medium- and high-resource setting are for Hungarian (0.362), Latin (0.440) and Latin (0.429), respectively. For some languages, e.g., Catalan, Danish or Urdu, choosing a good source form seems to not be important. For a few languages, results even get

---

[3]A list of all languages can be found in Tables 2 and 4.

worse. We will discuss some of those cases in §9. Overall, however, we obtain 0.087 (low), 0.066 (medium) and 0.019 (high) improvement on average over all languages, which clearly shows the usefulness of CIS.

MED* on its own does not achieve competitive performance for task 2. We attribute this to the limited number of different lemmata given for training, resulting in an overfitting model, learning, e.g., to produce certain character combinations for certain tags. However, MED*+FT+CIS outperforms both BL as well as BL+CIS for many languages in the medium- and high-resource settings and even in some low-resource scenarios. Comparing the obtained accuracies with Table 1, it gets obvious that languages with a higher amount of given source forms per paradigm achieve better results after fine-tuning, many times reaching a higher accuracy than BL, even in the low-resource setting. In contrast, fine-tuning works poorly for languages with ≤ 1.5 given source forms per paradigm. In total, using MED*+FT+CIS, we obtain an average improvement of 0.068 (low), 0.101 (medium) and 0.103 (high) over the baseline.

8.5 Official Shared Task Evaluation

Our submitted system obtained average accuracies of 0.4659 (low), 0.8264 (medium) and 0.947 (high) for task 1, and 0.6776 (low), 0.8202 (medium) and 0.8852 (high) for task 2, respectively. This corresponds to place 5 of 18, 3 of 19 and 7 of 15 for the high-, medium- and low-resource settings of task 1, respectively. Remarkably, the difference to the best system for the two higher settings is less than 0.01.

Among 3 submissions for task 2, our system comes first. It beats the baseline by 17.16 (low), 15.54 (medium) and 10.84 (high).

9 Remaining Challenges

Certain parts of our system do not perform as well for some languages as we would expect. In this section we will discuss those cases in more detail.

CIS. For some languages, e.g., Danish or English, CIS does not influence the performance. This might be due to those languages not having paradigm slots that are regularly closer to certain slots than others.

One other problem for the algorithm are training instances that consist of multiple separate words, e.g., the edit trees for "ride a bike" $\mapsto$

	low				medium				high			
	BL	BL+CIS	MED*	MED*+FT+CIS	BL	BL+CIS	MED*	MED*+FT+CIS	BL	BL+CIS	MED*	MED*+FT+CIS
albanian	0.160	0.249	0.000	**0.619**	**0.882**	0.280	0.016	0.865	0.942	0.434	0.240	**0.960**
arabic	0.380	0.428	0.011	**0.706**	0.553	0.704	0.059	**0.907**	0.566	0.733	0.533	**0.953**
armenian	0.722	0.855	0.001	**0.933**	0.785	0.962	0.210	**0.969**	0.856	0.806	0.517	**0.983**
bulgarian	0.553	**0.592**	0.006	0.571	0.640	0.646	0.200	**0.747**	0.819	0.810	0.677	**0.911**
catalan	**0.942**	0.938	0.000	0.877	0.958	**0.970**	0.266	0.962	0.965	0.976	0.759	**0.992**
czech	0.307	**0.346**	0.008	0.312	0.610	**0.635**	0.160	0.580	**0.841**	0.839	0.429	0.806
danish	**0.567**	**0.567**	0.284	0.287	**0.753**	**0.753**	0.541	0.410	**0.827**	**0.827**	0.673	0.680
dutch	0.588	**0.666**	0.057	0.608	0.796	**0.932**	0.509	0.796	0.845	0.965	0.812	**0.969**
english	**0.784**	**0.784**	0.544	0.576	0.832	0.832	**0.852**	0.784	0.900	0.900	0.900	**0.924**
faroese	0.513	**0.592**	0.000	0.171	0.559	**0.674**	0.234	0.578	0.651	0.738	0.430	**0.761**
finnish	0.517	**0.629**	0.017	0.581	0.720	0.743	0.143	**0.899**	0.709	0.772	0.470	**0.948**
french	0.864	0.876	0.000	**0.877**	0.893	0.936	0.379	**0.951**	0.982	0.959	0.824	**0.983**
georgian	0.793	**0.853**	0.000	0.834	0.900	**0.922**	0.532	0.909	0.933	0.954	0.793	**0.966**
german	0.610	**0.647**	0.123	0.625	0.662	0.748	0.255	**0.764**	0.705	0.813	0.619	**0.874**
hebrew	0.380	0.683	0.012	**0.786**	0.417	0.701	0.217	**0.895**	0.547	0.743	0.596	**0.950**
hindi	0.698	0.719	0.000	**0.970**	0.746	0.867	0.040	**0.970**	0.961	0.563	0.719	**1.000**
hungarian	0.255	0.617	0.000	**0.627**	0.453	0.823	0.238	**0.824**	0.585	0.877	0.503	**0.949**
icelandic	0.439	**0.546**	0.000	0.333	0.531	**0.683**	0.083	0.588	0.617	**0.753**	0.380	0.751
italian	0.769	**0.843**	0.000	0.809	0.839	0.901	0.075	**0.927**	0.901	0.896	0.503	**0.976**
latvian	0.790	**0.839**	0.001	0.565	0.852	**0.926**	0.330	0.825	0.877	**0.953**	0.705	0.951
lower-sorbian	0.362	**0.532**	0.003	0.509	0.670	**0.811**	0.302	0.769	0.866	**0.878**	0.650	0.867
macedonian	0.396	**0.562**	0.001	0.367	0.832	**0.858**	0.175	0.740	0.942	**0.964**	0.749	0.876
navajo	0.306	**0.404**	0.008	0.313	0.385	0.502	0.088	**0.517**	0.408	0.593	0.282	**0.650**
northern-sami	0.314	**0.485**	0.000	0.243	0.499	**0.841**	0.028	0.758	0.562	0.905	0.201	**0.912**
Norwegian-nynorsk	0.439	**0.445**	0.127	0.122	**0.604**	**0.604**	0.452	0.341	**0.610**	0.579	0.560	0.555
persian	0.822	0.159	0.000	**0.990**	0.911	0.185	0.203	**0.997**	0.889	0.190	0.854	**1.000**
polish	0.506	**0.596**	0.002	0.327	0.694	**0.787**	0.170	0.704	0.794	**0.831**	0.619	0.820
portuguese	0.951	**0.973**	0.001	0.934	0.969	**0.987**	0.243	0.969	0.975	**0.995**	0.741	0.991
quechua	0.973	**1.000**	0.000	0.972	0.973	0.973	0.234	**0.996**	0.972	**0.999**	0.796	**0.999**
russian	0.412	**0.503**	0.039	0.382	0.830	**0.843**	0.400	0.816	0.900	0.907	0.756	**0.915**
scottish-gaelic	0.449	**0.498**	0.004	0.441	0.441	**0.506**	0.087	0.490	–	–	–	–
serbo-croatian	0.285	0.291	0.001	**0.363**	0.570	0.601	0.095	**0.683**	0.863	0.850	0.166	**0.898**
slovak	0.647	**0.705**	0.006	0.447	0.720	**0.779**	0.295	0.659	0.777	**0.805**	0.530	0.789
slovene	0.616	**0.834**	0.000	0.583	0.767	**0.886**	0.352	0.834	0.798	**0.943**	0.636	0.933
spanish	0.787	0.882	0.000	**0.901**	0.911	0.895	0.192	**0.971**	0.954	0.908	0.717	**0.978**
swedish	0.421	**0.475**	0.049	0.208	0.635	**0.795**	0.282	0.643	0.723	**0.843**	0.583	0.789
turkish	0.124	0.624	0.000	**0.805**	0.613	0.876	0.303	**0.977**	0.825	0.921	0.697	**0.994**
ukrainian	0.523	**0.594**	0.007	0.411	**0.734**	0.709	0.285	0.655	**0.808**	0.760	0.452	0.773
urdu	0.670	0.670	0.010	**0.883**	0.680	0.680	0.027	**0.953**	**0.991**	0.488	0.221	0.982
welsh	0.601	0.349	0.000	**0.857**	0.693	0.864	0.127	**0.939**	0.752	0.903	0.258	**0.960**
basque	0.040	0.180	0.005	**0.890**	0.051	0.182	0.021	**0.891**	–	–	–	–
bengali	0.661	**0.928**	0.036	0.780	0.847	**0.963**	0.100	0.906	0.847	**0.965**	0.238	0.933
estonian	0.385	0.734	0.001	**0.806**	0.551	0.767	0.064	**0.953**	0.581	0.779	0.273	**0.951**
haida	0.554	0.810	0.000	**0.937**	0.802	0.849	0.002	**0.937**	–	–	–	–
irish	0.317	**0.439**	0.045	0.375	0.424	0.493	0.137	**0.592**	0.474	0.530	0.411	**0.692**
khaling	0.247	0.495	0.011	**0.973**	0.546	0.627	0.279	**0.992**	0.840	0.659	0.638	**0.996**
kurmanji	0.633	**0.648**	0.003	0.449	0.790	**0.798**	0.279	0.695	0.875	0.844	0.679	**0.878**
latin	0.336	**0.594**	0.000	0.157	0.449	**0.889**	0.112	0.691	0.493	**0.922**	0.301	0.820
lithuanian	0.536	**0.669**	0.006	0.487	0.615	**0.831**	0.059	0.744	0.662	**0.879**	0.302	0.876
norwegian-bokmal	0.417	**0.438**	0.396	0.306	**0.590**	**0.590**	0.576	0.340	**0.750**	**0.750**	0.715	0.667
romanian	0.151	**0.232**	0.008	0.062	0.630	**0.715**	0.077	0.561	0.773	**0.786**	0.284	0.744
soranı	0.534	0.532	0.000	**0.630**	0.661	0.561	0.065	**0.879**	0.646	0.599	0.488	**0.898**
Average:	0.520	**0.607**	0.035	0.588	0.682	0.748	0.220	**0.783**	0.783	0.802	0.549	**0.886**

Table 4: Accuracies for task 2. All systems are described in the text. Upper part: development languages; lower part: surprise languages.

"riding a bike" and "hike" $\mapsto$ "hiking" are not the same, even though they should be. Such cases potentially confuse the algorithm. A solution could be to detect training examples which consist of more than one token and split them up, in order to just consider the inflecting word.

Fine-tuning. For some settings and languages, e.g., Danish or Bokmål, the fine-tuned model obtains a lower accuracy than the base MED* model. While this might seem strange at first, when comparing to Table 1, it gets clear that this is mainly the case for languages where, besides the lemma, no forms of a paradigm are given. This results in the model being fine-tuned on autoencoding the lemma, and thus a strong bias to copy the input, which can hurt performance. A possible solution might be to apply a combination of fine-tuning and multi-domain training as proposed, e.g., by Chu et al. (2017) for neural machine translation. We leave respective experiments for future work.

10 Conclusion

We presented the LMU system for the CoNLL-SIGMORPHON 2017 shared task on universal morphological reinflection, which is based on an encoder-decoder network. We introduced two new methods for handling multi-source morphological reinflection: CIS, a source form selection algorithm based on edit trees and a fine-tuning approach similar in spirit to domain adaptation. On average over all participating languages, our approaches outperform the official shared task baseline for both tasks and all settings.

Acknowledgments

We would like to thank VolkswagenStiftung for supporting this research.

References

Roee Aharoni, Yoav Goldberg, and Yonatan Belinkov. 2016. Improving sequence to sequence learning for morphological inflection generation: The biumit systems for the sigmorphon 2016 shared task for morphological reinflection. In *SIGMORPHON*.

Dzmitry Bahdanau, Kyunghyun Cho, and Yoshua Bengio. 2015. Neural machine translation by jointly learning to align and translate. In *ICLR*.

Kyunghyun Cho, Bart Van Merriënboer, Dzmitry Bahdanau, and Yoshua Bengio. 2014a. On the properties of neural machine translation: Encoder-decoder approaches. *arXiv preprint 1409.1259* .

Kyunghyun Cho, Bart Van Merriënboer, Çalar Gülçehre, Dzmitry Bahdanau, Fethi Bougares, Holger Schwenk, and Yoshua Bengio. 2014b. Learning phrase representations using RNN encoder–decoder for statistical machine translation. In *EMNLP*.

Grzegorz Chrupała. 2008. *Towards a machine-learning architecture for lexical functional grammar parsing*. Ph.D. thesis, Dublin City University.

Chenhui Chu, Raj Dabre, and Sadao Kurohashi. 2017. An empirical comparison of simple domain adaptation methods for neural machine translation. *arXiv preprint 1701.03214* .

Ryan Cotterell, Christo Kirov, John Sylak-Glassman, Géraldine Walther, Ekaterina Vylomova, Patrick Xia, Manaal Faruqui, Sandra Kübler, David Yarowsky, Jason Eisner, and Mans Hulden. 2017a. The CoNLL-SIGMORPHON 2017 shared task: Universal morphological reinflection in 52 languages. In *CoNLL-SIGMORPHON*.

Ryan Cotterell, Christo Kirov, John Sylak-Glassman, David Yarowsky, Jason Eisner, and Mans Hulden. 2016. The SIGMORPHON 2016 shared task— morphological reinflection. In *SIGMORPHON*.

Ryan Cotterell, John Sylak-Glassman, and Christo Kirov. 2017b. Neural graphical models over strings for principal parts morphological paradigm completion. In *EACL*.

Manaal Faruqui, Yulia Tsvetkov, Graham Neubig, and Chris Dyer. 2016. Morphological inflection generation using character sequence to sequence learning. In *NAACL-HLT*.

Dan Gusfield. 1997. *Algorithms on strings, trees and sequences: computer science and computational biology*. Cambridge university press.

Katharina Kann and Hinrich Schütze. 2016a. MED: The LMU system for the SIGMORPHON 2016 shared task on morphological reinflection. In *SIGMORPHON*.

Katharina Kann and Hinrich Schütze. 2016b. Single-model encoder-decoder with explicit morphological representation for reinflection. In *ACL*.

Quoc V Le, Navdeep Jaitly, and Geoffrey E Hinton. 2015. A simple way to initialize recurrent networks of rectified linear units. *CoRR abs/1504.00941*.

Minh-Thang Luong and Christopher D Manning. 2015. Stanford neural machine translation systems for spoken language domains. In *IWSLT*.

Ilya Sutskever, Oriol Vinyals, and Quoc V Le. 2014. Sequence to sequence learning with neural networks. In *NIPS*.

Matthew D Zeiler. 2012. ADADELTA: An adaptive learning rate method. *CoRR abs/1212.5701*.

Chunting Zhou and Graham Neubig. 2017. Multi-space variational encoder-decoders for semi-supervised labeled sequence transduction. *arXiv preprint 1704.01691* .

Align and Copy: UZH at SIGMORPHON 2017 Shared Task for Morphological Reinflection

Peter Makarov[†*]   **Tatiana Ruzsics**[‡*]   **Simon Clematide**[†]

[†]Institute of Computational Linguistics, University of Zurich, Switzerland
[‡]CorpusLab, URPP Language and Space, University of Zurich, Switzerland

makarov@cl.uzh.ch   tatiana.ruzsics@uzh.ch   simon.clematide@cl.uzh.ch

Abstract

This paper presents the submissions by the University of Zurich to the SIGMORPHON 2017 shared task on morphological reinflection. The task is to predict the inflected form given a lemma and a set of morpho-syntactic features. We focus on neural network approaches that can tackle the task in a limited-resource setting. As the transduction of the lemma into the inflected form is dominated by copying over lemma characters, we propose two recurrent neural network architectures with hard monotonic attention that are strong at copying and, yet, substantially different in how they achieve this. The first approach is an encoder-decoder model with a copy mechanism. The second approach is a neural state-transition system over a set of explicit edit actions, including a designated COPY action. We experiment with character alignment and find that naive, greedy alignment consistently produces strong results for some languages. Our best system combination is the overall winner of the SIGMORPHON 2017 Shared Task 1 without external resources. At a setting with 100 training samples, both our approaches, as ensembles of models, outperform the next best competitor.

1 Introduction

This paper describes our approaches and results for Task 1 (without external resources) of the CoNLL-SIGMORPHON 2017 challenge on Universal Morphological Reinflection (Cotterell et al., 2017). This task consists in generating inflected

---

* These two authors contributed equally.

word forms for 52 languages given a lemma and a morphological feature specification (Sylak-Glassman et al., 2015) as input (Figure 1).

$$\begin{array}{c} \text{fliegen} \\ \{\text{VERB, PAST TENSE,} \\ \text{3RD PERSON, SINGULAR}\} \end{array} \quad \triangleright \quad \text{flog}$$

Figure 1: Morphological inflection generation task. A German language example.

There are three task setups: a low setting where training data are only 100 (!) samples, a medium setting with 1K training samples, and a high setting with 10K samples. We consider the problem of tackling morphological inflection generation at a low-resource setting with a neural network approach, which is hard for plain soft-attention encoder-decoder models (Kann and Schütze, 2016a,b). We present two systems that are based on the hard monotonic attention model of Aharoni and Goldberg (2017); Aharoni et al. (2016), which is strong on smaller-sized training datasets. We observe that to excel at a low-resource setting, a model needs to be good at copying lemma characters over to the inflected form— by far the most common operation of string transduction in the morphological inflection generation task.

In our first approach, we extend the hard monotonic attention model with a copy mechanism that produces a mixture distribution from the character generation and character copying distributions. This idea is reminiscent of the pointer-generator model of See et al. (2017) and the CopyNet model of Gu et al. (2016).

Our second approach is a neural state-transition system that explicitly learns the copy action and thus does away with character decoding altogether whenever a character needs to be copied over. This approach is inspired by shift-reduce parsing with

Proceedings of the CoNLL SIGMORPHON 2017 Shared Task: Universal Morphological Reinflection, pages 49–57,
Vancouver, Canada, August 3–4, 2017. ©2017 Association for Computational Linguistics

stack LSTMs (Dyer et al., 2015) and transition-based named entity recognition (Lample et al., 2016).

2 Preliminaries

In this section, we formally describe the problem of morphological inflection generation as a string transduction task. Next, we show how this task can be reformulated in terms of transduction actions. Finally, we discuss the string alignment strategies that we use to derive oracle actions.

2.1 Morphological inflection generation

Morphological inflection generation is an instance of the more general sequence transduction task, where the goal is to find a mapping of a variable-length sequence x to another variable-length sequence y. Specific to morphological inflection generation is that the input and output vocabularies—lemmas and inflected forms—are the same set of characters of one natural language, i.e. $\Sigma^x = \Sigma^y = \Sigma$. Formally, our task is to learn a mapping from an input sequence of characters $x_{1:n} \in \Sigma^*$ (the lemma) to an output sequence of characters $y_{1:m} \in \Sigma^*$ (the inflected form) given a set of morpho-syntactic features $f \subseteq \Phi$, where Φ is the alphabet of morpho-syntactic features for that language.

2.2 Task reformulation

To efficiently condition on parts of the input sequence, we use hard monotonic attention, which has been found highly suitable for this task (Aharoni and Goldberg, 2017; Aharoni et al., 2016). With *hard attention*, at each step, the prediction of an output element is based on attending to only one element from the input sequence as opposed to conditioning on the entire input sequence as in soft attention models.

Hard monotonic attention is motivated by the often monotonic alignment between the lemma characters and the characters of its inflected form: It suffices to only allow for the advancement of the attention pointer up in a sequential order over the elements of the input sequence. Thus, the sequence transduction process can be represented as a sequence of actions $a_{1:q} \in \Omega^*$ over an input string, where the set of actions Ω includes operations for writing characters and advancing the attention pointer. We can, therefore, reformulate the task of finding a mapping from an input sequence

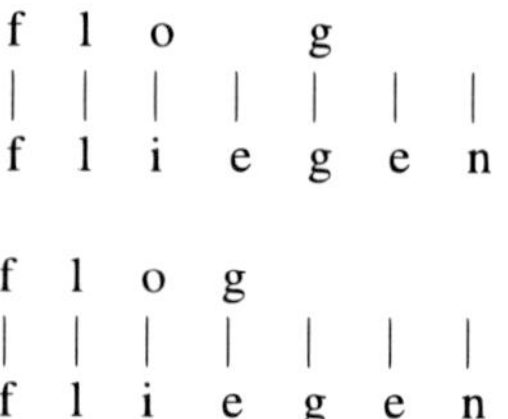

Figure 2: Examples of smart alignment (top) and naive alignment (bottom). In each example, inflected form is at the top, lemma at the bottom.

of lemma characters $x \in \Sigma^*$ to the output sequence of actions $\hat{a} \in \Omega^*$, given a set of morpho-syntactic features $f \subseteq \Phi$, such that:

$$\hat{a} = \arg\max_{a \in \Omega^*} P(a \mid x, f)$$

$$= \arg\max_{a \in \Omega^*} \prod_{t=1}^{|a|} P(a_t \mid a_{1:t-1}, x, f) \quad (1)$$

We use a recurrent neural network to estimate the probability distribution P in Equation 1 from training data. To derive the sequence of oracle actions from each training sample, we use two different character alignment strategies formally described below.

2.3 Character alignment strategies

We use two string alignment strategies that produce 0-to-1, 1-to-0, and 1-to-1 character alignments (Figure 2).

Smart alignment uses the Chinese Restaurant Process character alignment implementation distributed with the SIGMORPHON 2016 baseline system (Cotterell et al., 2016).[1] This is the aligner of Aharoni and Goldberg (2017).

Naive alignment aligns two sequences p and q, such that the length of p is greater or equal to the length of q, by producing 1-to-1 character alignments until it reaches the end of q, from which point it outputs 1-to-0 alignments (and 0-to-1 alignments once it reaches the end of p if $|q| > |p|$).

3 First approach: Hard attention model with copy mechanism (HACM)

Our first approach augments the hard monotonic attention model of Aharoni and Goldberg (2017)

---

[1] https://github.com/ryancotterell/
sigmorphon2016/tree/master/src/baseline

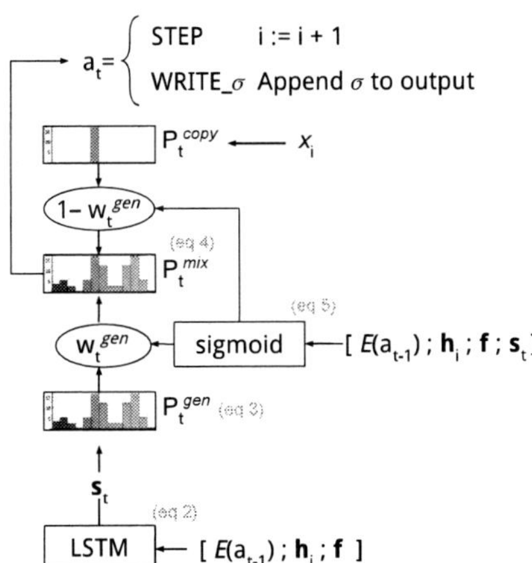

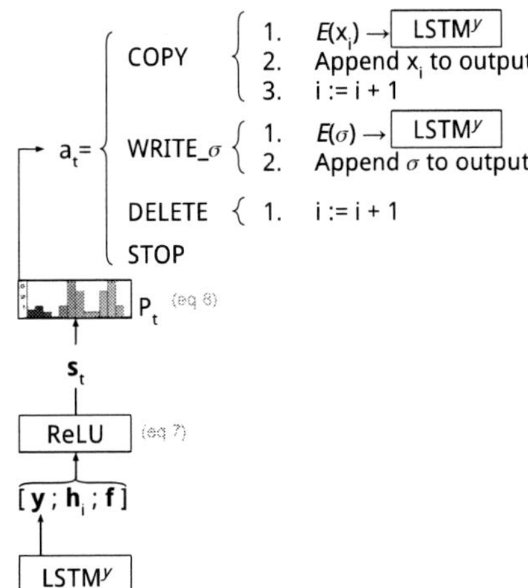

Figure 3: Overview of the architectures. Hard attention model with copy mechanism (HACM) on the left, hard attention model over edit actions (HAEM) on the right.

with a copy mechanism which adds a soft switch between generating an output symbol from a fixed vocabulary Σ^{train} and copying the currently attended input symbol x_i. In this section, we first review the architecture of the hard monotonic model and then present our copy mechanism.

3.1 Hard monotonic attention model

The hard monotonic attention model operates over two types of actions: WRITE_σ, $\sigma \in \Sigma$, for outputting the character σ and STEP which moves forward the attention pointer, i.e. $\Omega = \Sigma \cup \{\text{STEP}\}$. At each step, the model either generates an output symbol or starts to attend to the next encoded input character. The system learns to move the attention pointer by outputting a STEP action. To compute the sequences of oracle actions for each training pair of lemma and its inflected form, Aharoni and Goldberg (2017) apply a deterministic algorithm[2] to the output of the smart aligner.

Architecture The hard monotonic attention model uses a single-layer bidirectional LSTM encoder (Graves and Schmidhuber, 2005) to encode input lemma $x_{1:n}$ as a sequence of vectors $h_{1:n}, h_i \in \mathbb{R}^{2H}$, where H is the hidden dimension of the LSTM layer.

At all time steps t, the model maintains a state $s_t \in \mathbb{R}^H$ from which the most probable action a_t is predicted. The sequence of states is modeled

with a single-layer LSTM that receives, at time t, a concatenated input of:

1. the currently attended vector $h_i \in \mathbb{R}^{2H}$, where i is the attention pointer,

2. the concatenated vector of feature embeddings $f \in \mathbb{R}^{F \cdot |\Phi|}$, where F is the dimension of the feature embedding layer,

3. the embedding of the previous output action $E(a_{t-1}) \in \mathbb{R}^E$, where E is the dimension of the action embedding layer.

$$s_t = \text{LSTM}\big([E(a_{t-1}); h_i; f]\big) \qquad (2)$$

Let $\Sigma^{train} \subseteq \Sigma$ be the set of characters in training data. Then, the distribution P_t^{gen} for generating actions over the vocabulary $\Omega^{train} = \Sigma^{train} \cup \{\text{STEP}\}$ is modeled with the softmax function:

$$P_t^{gen} = \text{softmax}\big(\mathbf{W} \cdot s_t + \mathbf{b}\big) \qquad (3)$$

When the predicted action is STEP, the attention index gets incremented $i := i + 1$, and so at the next time step $t + 1$, the model attends to vector h_{i+1} of the bidirectionally encoded lemma sequence.

3.2 Copy mechanism

Our copying mechanism is based on using a mixture of a *generation* probability distribution from Equation 3 and a *copying* probability distribution.

---

[2] We refer the reader to Aharoni and Goldberg (2017) for the description of the algorithm.

1	2	3	4	5	6	7	8	9	10	11	12	13	14		t
⟨s⟩		f		l		o			g				⟨/s⟩		y
⟨s⟩	STEP	f	STEP	l	STEP	o	STEP	STEP	g	STEP	STEP	STEP	⟨/s⟩		a_t
⟨s⟩	⟨s⟩	f	f	l	l	i	i	e	g	g	e	n	⟨/s⟩		x_i
0	0	1	1	2	2	3	3	4	5	5	6	7	8		i

1	2	3	4	5	6	7	8	9		t
f	l			o	g					y
COPY	COPY	DELETE	DELETE	o	COPY	DELETE	DELETE	STOP		a_t
f	l	i	e	g	g	e	n	–		x_i
1	2	3	4	5	5	6	7	7		i

Table 1: Examples of generating German "flog" from "fliegen": HACM (left), HAEM (right). i is the attention pointer, x_i the currently attended lemma character, a the sequence of actions, y the output, t the index over actions.

At each time step t, the action $a \in \Omega^{train}$ is predicted from the following mixture distribution:

$$P_t(a) = w_t^{\text{gen}} P_t^{gen}(a) + (1 - w_t^{\text{gen}}) \mathbb{1}_{\{a=x_i\}}, \quad (4)$$

where x_i is the currently attended character of the lemma sequence x and $\mathbb{1}_{\{a=x_i\}} = P_t^{copy}(a)$ is a probability distribution for copying x_i.

The mix-in parameter of the generation distribution $w_t^{\text{gen}} \in \mathbb{R}$ is calculated from the concatenation of the state vector $\mathbf{s}_t$ and the input vector that produces this state. The resulting vector is fed through a linear layer to the logistic sigmoid function:

$$w_t^{\text{gen}} = \text{sigmoid}(\mathbf{v} \cdot [\mathbf{h}_i; \mathbf{f}; \mathbf{y}_{t-1}; \mathbf{s}_t] + c) \quad (5)$$

The mix-in parameter serves as a switch between a) generating a character from Σ^{train} according to the generation distribution P_t^{gen}, and b) copying the currently attended character $x_i \in \Sigma^{train}$.

At test time, we allow the copying of out-of-vocabulary (OOV) symbols by adding the following modification to the mixture distribution in Equation 4:

$$P_t(a) = \mathbb{1}_{\{a=x_i\}} \mathbb{1}_{\{x_i \in \Sigma \setminus \Sigma^{train}\}} + \left(w_t^{\text{gen}} P_t^{gen}(a) \right.$$
$$\left. + (1 - w_t^{\text{gen}}) \mathbb{1}_{\{a=x_i\}} \right) \mathbb{1}_{\{x_i \in \Sigma^{train}\}}$$
$$(6)$$

Therefore, if the currently attended symbol x_i is OOV, we copy it with probability one according to the distribution $\mathbb{1}_{\{a=x_i\}}$; otherwise, we use the mixture of generation P_t^{gen} and copy $\mathbb{1}_{\{a=x_i\}}$ distributions. Thus, the distribution P_t is built over an instance specific vocabulary $\Omega^{train} \cup \{x_i\}$. After copying the OOV symbol, we advance the attention pointer and use STEP as the previous predicted action.

The full architecture of the HACM system is shown schematically in Figure 3.

3.3 Learning

We train the system using cross-entropy loss, which, for a single input (x, y, f), equates to:

$$\mathcal{L}(\Theta; x, a, f) = - \sum_{t=1}^{|a|} \log P_t(a_t \mid a_{1:t-1}, x, f),$$
$$(7)$$

where x, y are lemma and inflected form character sequences, f the set of morpho-syntactic features, a the sequence of oracle actions derived from (x, y), Θ the model parameters and P_t is the probability distribution over actions from Equation 4.

4 Second approach: Hard attention model over edit actions (HAEM)

This neural state-transition system also uses hard monotonic attention but transduces the lemma into the inflected form by a sequence of explicit *edit* actions: COPY, DELETE, and WRITE_σ, $\sigma \in \Sigma$. The architectures of the two models are also different (Figure 3).

4.1 Semantics of edit actions

COPY If the system generates COPY, the lemma character at the attention index x_i is appended to the current output of the inflected form and the attention index is incremented $i := i + 1$. Therefore, unlike other neural morphological inflection generation systems, the copy character is not decoded from the neural network.

DELETE The system generates DELETE if it needs to increment the attention index.

WRITE_σ Whenever the system chooses to append a character $\sigma \in \Sigma$ to the current output of the inflected form, such that $\sigma \neq x_i$ where x_i is the lemma character at the attention index, it generates the corresponding WRITE_σ action.

Using this set of edit actions, the system can copy, delete, and substitute new characters. The substitution of a new character σ for a currently attended lemma character x_i, $\sigma \neq x_i$, is expressed as a sequence of one DELETE and one WRITE_σ action.

This action set directly compares to the $\Omega = \Sigma \cup \{\text{STEP}\}$ actions of the HACM model, which uses most basic actions to express edit operations. Crucially, in the HAEM system, character copying is a single action (which does not require character decoding) whereas it is typically a sequence of one WRITE_σ ($=\sigma$) and one STEP action in HACM.[3] Further, HAEM effectively deals with OOV characters through COPY and DELETE actions.

STOP Additionally, to signal the end of transduction, the system generates a STOP action.

4.2 Deriving oracle actions

We use the character alignment methods of Section 2.3 to deterministically compute sequences of oracle actions for each training example using Algorithm 1.

Algorithm 1: Derivation of oracle actions from alignment of lemma and form.

Input : A, list of 1-to-1, 0-to-1, and 1-to-0 alignments between lemma and form

Output: O, list of oracle actions

1 **foreach** $(t, s) \in A$ **do**
2   **if** $t = \epsilon$ **then**
3   O.append(WRITE_s)
4   **else if** $s = \epsilon$ **then**
5   O.append(DELETE)
6   **else if** $s = t$ **then**
7   O.append(COPY)
8   **else**
9   O.append(DELETE)
10   O.append(WRITE_s)
11   **end**
12 **end**

We then normalize all sub-sequences of only DELETE and WRITE_σ in such a way that all DELETEs come before all WRITE_σ actions. This simplifies unintuitive alignments produced by the smart aligner, especially at the low setting.

4.3 Architecture

Similarly to HACM, the input lemma is encoded as a sequence of vectors $\mathbf{h}_{1:n}, \mathbf{h}_i \in \mathbb{R}^{2H}$ with a single-layer bidirectional LSTM. Additionally, we use a single-layer LSTM to represent the predicted inflected form $y_{1:m}$, to which we refer as LSTM^y. In case the model outputs a character with WRITE_σ or COPY, LSTM^y gets updated with the embedding of this character.

At all time steps t, the system maintains a state $\mathbf{s}_t \in \mathbb{R}^H$ from which it predicts the most probable action a_t. The state sequence is derived differently. At time t, a concatenation of:

1. the currently attended vector $\mathbf{h}_i \in \mathbb{R}^{2H}$,

2. the set-of-features vector $\mathbf{f} \in \mathbb{R}^{|\Phi|}$,

3. the output of the latest state $\mathbf{y} \in \mathbb{R}^H$ of the inflected form representation LSTM^y,

passes through a rectifier linear unit (ReLU) layer (Glorot et al., 2011) to finally produce the state vector $\mathbf{s}_t$.

The probability distribution over valid actions[4] is then computed with softmax:

$$\mathbf{s}_t = \text{ReLU}\big(\mathbf{W} \cdot [\mathbf{y}; \mathbf{h}_i; \mathbf{f}] + \mathbf{b}\big) \tag{8}$$
$$P_t = \text{softmax}\big(\mathbf{V} \cdot \mathbf{s}_t + \mathbf{c}\big) \tag{9}$$

This describes the basic form of the HAEM system (Figure 3). In our experiments, we extend it to include two more representations: an LSTM that represents the action history, LSTM^a, and another LSTM that encodes a sequence of deleted lemma characters, LSTM^d. The deletion LSTM^d gets emptied once a WRITE_σ action is generated. In this way, we attempt to keep in memory a full representation of some sub-sequence of the lemma that needs to be replaced in the inflected form. In the extended system, the state $\mathbf{s}_t$ is thus derived from an input vector $[\mathbf{y}; \mathbf{h}_i; \mathbf{f}; \mathbf{a}; \mathbf{d}]$, where $\mathbf{a} \in \mathbb{R}^H$ is the output of the latest state of the action history LSTM^a and $\mathbf{d} \in \mathbb{R}^H$ the output of the latest state of the deletion LSTM^d.

The system is trained using the cross-entropy loss function as in Equation 7.

5 Experimental setup

We submit seven runs: a) two runs (1 and 2) for the HACM model; b) two runs (3 and 4) for the

---

[3] Except whenever the next alignment is 0-to-1 the HACM does not generate STEP. The HAEM system, however, increments the attention index on every COPY action.

[4] Some actions are not valid in certain states: The system cannot DELETE or COPY if the attention index is greater than the length of the lemma.

system	HACM		HAEM	
alignment	S	N	S	N
low	5		5	
medium	5		5	3
high	5		3	2

Table 2: Number of single models that we train for each language. N=Naive alignment, S=Smart alignment. E.g. for each language at the medium setting, there are 3 HAEM models trained on data aligned with naive alignment.

Run	Systems	Strategy
1	CM	MAX { $E(N_{CM})$, $E(S_{CM})$ }
2		ENSEMBLE_7 ($N_{CM} \cup S_{CM}$)
3	EM	MAX { $E(N_{EM})$, $E(S_{EM})$ }
4		ENSEMBLE_7 ($N_{EM} \cup S_{EM}$)
5	CM& EM	MAX { $E(N_{CM})$, $E(S_{CM})$, $E(N_{EM})$, $E(S_{EM})$ }
6		ENSEMBLE_4 ($N_{CM} \cup S_{CM} \cup N_{EM} \cup S_{EM}$)
7		MAX { Run 5, Run 6 }

Table 3: Aggregation strategies in submissions. CM=HACM, EM=HAEM, N_{CM}=the set of HACM models trained on naive-aligned data, S_{CM}=the set of HACM models trained on smart-aligned data, and similarly for HAEM.

HAEM model; and c) three runs (5, 6, and 7) that combine both systems. Detailed information on training regimes and the choice of hyperparameter values (e.g. layer dimensions, the application of dropout, etc.) for all the runs is provided in the Appendix. Crucially, for both systems and all settings and languages, we train models with both smart and naive alignments of Section 2.3. Table 2 shows the number of single models for each system, setting, and alignment.[5] We decode using greedy search.

We apply a simple post-processing filter that replaces any inflected form containing an endlessly repeating character with the lemma. This affects a small number of test samples—57 for HACM and 238 for HAEM across all languages and alignment regimes—and primarily at the low setting.

All runs aggregate the results of multiple single models, and we use a number of aggregation strategies. For system runs 1 through 4, these are:

Max strategy For each language l, we compute two ensembles over single models—one ensemble $E(S)$ over smart alignment models and one ensemble $E(N)$ over naive alignment models. We then pick the ensemble with the highest development set accuracy for l:

$$\hat{M} = \underset{M \in \{E(S), E(N)\}}{\arg\max} \ \mathrm{dev\,acc}(M) \qquad (10)$$

Ensemble_n strategy For each language l, we pick at most n models from all single models such that they have the best development set accuracies for l. We then compute one ensemble over them:

$$\hat{M} = E\left(\underset{M \in (S \cup N)}{\text{n-best}} \ \mathrm{dev\,acc}(M) \right) \qquad (11)$$

Runs 5, 6, and 7 are built with aggregation strategies that use as building blocks the MAX and ENSEMBLE_n strategies. Table 3 shows the strategies employed in each run.

At the high setting, Runs 5, 6, and 7 additionally feature a single run produced with Nematus (Sennrich et al., 2017), a soft-attention encoder-decoder system for machine translation. In all these runs, the Nematus run complements the HAEM models, which perform much worse at the high setting on average. We refer the reader to the Appendix for further information on data preprocessing, hyperparameter values, and training for the Nematus run.

6 Results and Discussion

Table 5 gives an overview on the average (macro) performance for each run on the official development and test sets at all settings. Accuracy measures the percentage of word forms that are inflected correctly (without a single character error). For the best system combination, we also report the average Levenshtein distance between the gold standard word form and the system prediction, which represents a softer criterion for correctness. Also, we include the performance of the shared task baseline system, which is a rule-based model that extracts prefix-changing and suffix-changing rules using alignments of each training sample with Levenshtein distance and associates the rules with the features of the sample.[6] All our official runs beat the baseline by a large margin on average in terms of accuracy and also in terms of Levenshtein distance. For all settings, we see an improvement by applying the more complex ensembling strategies (Table 3). It is the largest for low and the smallest for the high setting.

---

[5] Due to time restrictions, we could not produce the target of 5 HAEM models per setting and alignment.

[6] https://github.com/sigmorphon/
conll2017/tree/master/baseline

System	HACM		HAEM		HACM		HAEM		HACM & HAEM				BS	BS
Alignment/Run	N	S	N	S	1	2	3	4	5	6	7	7		
Metric	Acc	Acc	Acc	Acc	Acc	Acc	Acc	Acc	Acc	Acc	Acc	Lev	Acc	Lev
Development Set														
Low	43.8	41.3	45.8	44.3	46.5	47.6	48.9	49.5	49.2	51.1	**51.6**	1.3	*38.0*	2.1
Medium	75.8	81.4	70.7	80.0	81.9	82.6	80.5	81.1	82.2	83.4	**83.5**	0.3	*64.7*	0.9
High	93.3	94.6	*75.9*	89.6	95.0	95.3	89.8	90.1	95.2	95.3	**95.6**	0.1	*77.9*	0.5
Test Set														
Low					46.0	46.8	48.0	48.5	48.2	**50.6**	**50.6**	1.3	*37.9*	2.2
Medium					80.9	81.8	79.6	80.3	81.0	**82.8**	**82.8**	0.3	*64.7*	0.9
High					94.5	95.0	89.1	89.5	94.7	**95.1**	**95.1**	0.1	*77.8*	0.5

Table 4: Macro average results over all languages for all settings on the official development and test set. N=Naive alignment, S=Smart alignment, BS=Baseline system, Acc=Accuracy, Lev=Levenshtein.

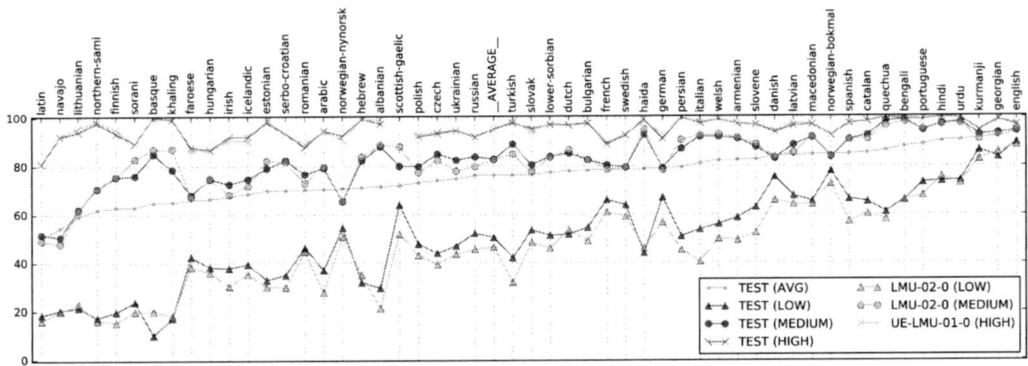

Figure 4: Test set accuracies of Run 7 (blue) and the next best system (yellow). The results are ordered by the averaged (low, medium, high) test set accuracies of Run 7.

At the low setting, HAEM outperforms HACM on average by 2-3 percentage points accuracy and is, therefore, especially suited for a low resource situation. At the medium setting, the performance of HACM is slightly better using smart alignments. The HAEM system does not seem to learn well with naive alignment for this amount of data. The poorer performance of HAEM whenever more training data are available is particularly obvious at the high-resource setting where the difference between HACM and HAEM is quite large.

At the low setting, both the HACM and HAEM ensembles (Run 2 and Run 4) outperform the next best competitor (LMU-02-0 with 46.59%) by 0.23 and 1.94 percentage points in average accuracy. The margin between Run 7 and the next best system is an impressive 4.02 percentage points.

At the medium setting, our best Run 7 also outperforms the next best competitor (LMU-02-0 with 82.64%) with a small margin of 0.16 per-centage points. At the high setting, our best Run 7 loses against UE-LMU-01-0 with a small margin of 0.20 percentage points.

The performance of our best system varies strongly across languages (Figure 4). This is not only due to typological differences, but probably also because some languages have only inflection patterns for a single part-of-speech category (e.g. verbs in English) and other languages include nouns and adjectives (sometimes with very imbalanced class distributions). Naive alignment generally works slightly better than smart alignment at the low setting (but sometimes fails detrimentally as in the case of Khaling, Navajo, or Sorani). For the medium and high settings, smart alignment strongly outperforms naive alignment for HAEM, and a bit less so for HACM. For a few languages such as Turkish, Haida or Norwegian-Nynorsk, naive alignment is consistently better than smart alignment.

As future work, we will experiment more with the HAEM model and try to improve its capabilities for high-resource settings. One obvious option would be to use more fine-grained actions, for instance, directly learn substitutions for certain characters. This system would probably also profit from more consistent alignments. Even with smart alignments, we observe linguistically inconsistent character alignments that might also prevent useful generalizations.

7 Related work

Some task-specific work has been published after the 2016 edition of the SIGMORPHON Reinflection Shared Task (Cotterell et al., 2016) that dealt with 10 languages, providing training material roughly at the size of the high setting of the 2017 task edition (a mean training data set size of 12,751 samples with a standard deviation of 3,303). The winning system of 2016 (Kann and Schütze, 2016a) showed that a standard sequence-to-sequence encoder-decoder architecture with soft attention (Bahdanau et al., 2014), familiar from neural machine translation, outperforms a number of other methods (as far as they were present in the task). Recently, Aharoni and Goldberg (2017) showed that hard monotonic attention works well when training data are scarce. Their approach exploits the almost monotonic alignment between the lemma and its inflected form. The HACM model extends this work with a copying mechanism similar to the pointer-generator model of See et al. (2017) and CopyNet of Gu et al. (2016). In HACM, the copying distribution, which is then mixed together with the generation distribution, is different: See et al. (2017) employ the soft-attention distribution whereas Gu et al. (2016) use a separately learned distribution. Our HACM model uses a simpler copying distribution that puts all the probability mass on the currently attended character. The logic of the HAEM model is similar to that of SIGMORPHON 2016's baseline which uses a linear classifier over hand-crafted features to predict edit actions. Grefenstette et al. (2015) extend an encoder-decoder model with neural data structures to better handle natural language transduction. Rastogi et al. (2016) present a neural finite-state approach to string transduction.

8 Conclusion

In this large-scale evaluation of morphological inflection generation, we show that a novel neural transition-based approach can deal well with an extreme low-resource setup. For a medium size training set of 1K items, HACM works slightly better. With abundant data (10K items), encoder/decoder architectures with soft attention are very strong, however, HACM achieves a comparable development set performance.

For optimal results, the ensembling of different system runs is important. We experiment with different ensembling strategies for eliminating bad candidates. At the low setting (100 samples), our best system combination achieves an average test set accuracy of 50.61% (an average Levenshtein distance (LD) of 1.29), at the medium setting (1K samples) 82.8% (LD 0.34), and at the high setting (10K samples) 95.12% (LD 0.11).

Acknowledgement

We would like to thank the SIGMORPHON organizers for the exciting shared task and Tanja Samardžić and two anonymous reviewers for their helpful comments. Peter Makarov has been supported by European Research Council Grant No. 338875.

References

Roee Aharoni and Yoav Goldberg. 2017. Morphological inflection generation with hard monotonic attention. In *ACL*.

Roee Aharoni, Yoav Goldberg, and Yonatan Belinkov. 2016. Improving sequence to sequence learning for morphological inflection generation: The BIU-MIT systems for the SIGMORPHON 2016 shared task for morphological reinflection. In *14th Annual SIGMORPHON Workshop on Computational Research in Phonetics, Phonology, and Morphology at ACL 2016*.

Dzmitry Bahdanau, Kyunghyun Cho, and Yoshua Bengio. 2014. Neural machine translation by jointly learning to align and translate. *CoRR* abs/1409.0473.

Ryan Cotterell, Christo Kirov, John Sylak-Glassman, Géraldine Walther, Ekaterina Vylomova, Patrick Xia, Manaal Faruqui, Sandra Kübler, David Yarowsky, Jason Eisner, and Mans Hulden. 2017. The CoNLL-SIGMORPHON 2017 shared task: Universal morphological reinflection in 52 languages. In *Proceedings of the CoNLL-SIGMORPHON 2017 Shared Task: Universal Morphological Reinflection*. ACL.

Ryan Cotterell, Christo Kirov, John Sylak-Glassman, David Yarowsky, Jason Eisner, and Mans Hulden. 2016. The SIGMORPHON 2016 Shared Task— Morphological Reinflection. In *Proceedings of the 14th SIGMORPHON Workshop on Computational Research in Phonetics, Phonology, and Morphology*. ACL.

Chris Dyer, Miguel Ballesteros, Wang Ling, Austin Matthews, and Noah A Smith. 2015. Transition-based dependency parsing with stack long short-term memory. In *ACL*.

Xavier Glorot, Antoine Bordes, and Yoshua Bengio. 2011. Deep sparse rectifier neural networks. In *Aistats*. volume 15.

Alex Graves and Jürgen Schmidhuber. 2005. Framewise phoneme classification with bidirectional LSTM and other neural network architectures. *Neural Networks* 18(5).

Edward Grefenstette, Karl Moritz Hermann, Mustafa Suleyman, and Phil Blunsom. 2015. Learning to transduce with unbounded memory. In *Advances in Neural Information Processing Systems*.

Jiatao Gu, Zhengdong Lu, Hang Li, and Victor O. K. Li. 2016. Incorporating copying mechanism in sequence-to-sequence learning. *CoRR* .

Katharina Kann and Hinrich Schütze. 2016a. MED: The LMU system for the SIGMORPHON 2016 shared task on morphological reinflection. In *14th Annual SIGMORPHON Workshop on Computational Research in Phonetics, Phonology, and Morphology at ACL 2016*.

Katharina Kann and Hinrich Schütze. 2016b. Single-model encoder-decoder with explicit morphological representation for reinflection. In *ACL*.

Guillaume Lample, Miguel Ballesteros, Sandeep Subramanian, Kazuya Kawakami, and Chris Dyer. 2016. Neural architectures for named entity recognition. In *NAACL*.

Pushpendre Rastogi, Ryan Cotterell, and Jason Eisner. 2016. Weighting finite-state transductions with neural context. In *NAACL-HLT*.

Abigail See, Peter J Liu, and Christopher D Manning. 2017. Get To The Point: Summarization with Pointer-Generator Networks. In *ACL*.

Rico Sennrich, Orhan Firat, Kyunghyun Cho, Alexandra Birch, Barry Haddow, Julian Hitschler, Marcin Junczys-Dowmunt, Samuel Läubli, Antonio Valerio Miceli Barone, Jozef Mokry, and Maria Nadejde. 2017. Nematus: a Toolkit for Neural Machine Translation. In *Proceedings of the Software Demonstrations of the 15th Conference of the European Chapter of the Association for Computational Linguistics*. ACL.

John Sylak-Glassman, Christo Kirov, David Yarowsky, and Roger Que. 2015. A language-independent feature schema for inflectional morphology. In *Proceedings of the 53rd Annual Meeting of the Association for Computational Linguistics and the 7th International Joint Conference on Natural Language Processing*. ACL.

Morphological Inflection Generation with Multi-space Variational Encoder-Decoders

Chunting Zhou and Graham Neubig
Language Technologies Institute
Carnegie Mellon University
`ctzhou,gneubig@cs.cmu.edu`

Abstract

This paper describes the CMU submission to shared task 1 of SIGMORPHON 2017. The system is based on the multi-space variational encoder-decoder (MSVED) method of Zhou and Neubig (2017), which employs both continuous and discrete latent variables for the variational encoder-decoder and is trained in a semi-supervised fashion. We discuss some language-specific errors and present result analysis.

1 Introduction

In morphologically rich languages, different affixes (i.e. prefixes, infixes, suffixes) can be combined with the lemma to reflect various syntactic and semantic features of a word. In many areas of natural language processing (NLP) it is important that systems are able to correctly analyze and generate different morphological forms, including previously unseen forms. The ability to accurately analyze and generate morphological forms is crucial to creating applications such as machine translation (Chahuneau et al., 2013) and information retrieval (Darwish and Oard, 2007). Accordingly, learning morphological reinflection patterns from labeled data is an important challenge.

The Universal Morphological Reinflection task at SIGMORPHON 2017 (Cotterell and Schütze, 2017) is an evaluation campaign aimed at systems that tackle the task of morphological inflection. It extends the SIGMORPHON 2016 Morphological Reinflection by conducting tasks in 52 languages instead of 10 Cotterell et al. (2016).

In our system submission, we utilize multi-space variational encoder-decoders (MSVEDs), which are a varitional encoder-decoder with both continuous and discrete latent variables (Zhou and Neubig, 2017). The continuous latent variable is expected to reflect the lemma form of a word and the discrete variables are used to induce the desired labels of the inflected word. The whole model is trained in a semi-supervised fashion. For the supervised part we are reducing the reconstruction error of generating the inflected word given the lemma and corresponding tags. For the unsupervised part, we introduce the discrete latent variables representing the morphological tags, and train an auto-encoder over unlabeled corpora. Thus, the training objective includes both the variational lower bound on the marginal log likelihood of the observed parallel training data and the monolingual data.

There are two tasks in SIGMORPHON 2017, which are morphology inflection (task 1) and paradigm completion (task 2) respectively. We participated in task 1, inflection generation, in which the goal is to output the inflected form of a lemma given a set of desired morphological tags.[1] Experimental results found that our model works relatively well on the shared task 1 without extensive tuning of hyper-parameters and language-specific features.

2 Methods

In this section we will detail the multi-space variational encoder-decoder model.

Notation: In morphological reinflection, the source sequence $\mathbf{x}^{(s)}$ consists of the characters in an inflected word (e.g., "`played`"), while the associated labels $\mathbf{y}^{(t)}$ describe some linguistic features (e.g., $y_{\text{pos}}^{(t)} = \text{Verb}$, $y_{\text{tense}}^{(t)} = \text{Past}$) that we

---

[1] We considered participation in task 2, but while the training data in the second task provides all inflection forms for each lemma, the number of different lemmas is rather smaller, which resulted in our model quickly overfitting to the training data when training the neural model. Therefore, we only took part in the first task this time.

58

Proceedings of the CoNLL SIGMORPHON 2017 Shared Task: Universal Morphological Reinflection, pages 58–65,
Vancouver, Canada, August 3–4, 2017. ©2017 Association for Computational Linguistics

hope to realize in the target. The target sequence $\mathbf{x}^{(t)}$ is therefore the characters of the re-inflected form of the source word (e.g., "`played`") that satisfy the linguistic features specified by $\mathbf{y}^{(t)}$. For this task, each discrete variable $y_k^{(t)}$ has a set of possible labels (e.g. `pos=V`, `pos=ADJ`, etc) and follows a multinomial distribution.

2.1 Preliminaries: Variational Autoencoder

The variational autoencoder (Kingma and Welling, 2014) is an efficient way to handle (continuous) latent variables in neural models. We describe it briefly here, and interested readers can refer to Doersch (2016) for details. The VAE learns a generative model of the probability $p(\mathbf{x})$ of observed data $\mathbf{x}$. The generative process consists of first generating a continuous latent variable $\mathbf{z}$ conditioned on the observed data $\mathbf{x}$, which is termed as the recognition model $q(\mathbf{z}|\mathbf{x})$ (encoder) and then use this latent variable to reconstruct the observation $\mathbf{x}$ known as the reconstruction (decoder) model $p(\mathbf{x}|\mathbf{z})$. VAE uses the variational inference to approximate the intractable posterior by learning a parametric posterior distribution for all observations.Th learning objective function is the variational lower bound on the marginal log likelihood of data:

$$\log p_\theta(\mathbf{x}) \geq \mathbb{E}_{\mathbf{z}\sim q_\phi(\mathbf{z}|\mathbf{x})}[\log p_\theta(\mathbf{x}|\mathbf{z})] - \\ \mathrm{KL}(q_\phi(\mathbf{z}|\mathbf{x})\|p(\mathbf{z})) \qquad (1)$$

To optimize the parameters with gradient descent, Kingma and Welling (2014) introduce a reparameterization trick that allows for training using simple backpropagation w.r.t. the Gaussian latent variables $\mathbf{z}$.

2.2 Multi-space Variational Encoder-Decoders

There are two cases to discuss when employing the variational encoder-decoder framework for labeled sequence transduction. First, when the labels of the inflected words are known as is the format of the training data in the shared task, we don't need to bother introduction the discrete latent variables for the inflected labels. We maximize the variational lower bound on the conditional log likelihood of observing $\mathbf{x}^{(t)}$ and $\mathbf{y}^{(t)}$ as follows:

$$\log p_\theta(\mathbf{x}^{(t)}, \mathbf{y}^{(t)}|\mathbf{x}^{(s)})$$
$$\geq \mathbb{E}_{\mathbf{z}\sim q_\phi(\mathbf{z}|\mathbf{x}^{(s)})} \log \frac{p_\theta(\mathbf{x}^{(t)}, \mathbf{y}^{(t)}, \mathbf{z}|\mathbf{x}^{(s)})}{q_\phi(\mathbf{z}|\mathbf{x}^{(s)})}$$
$$= \mathbb{E}_{\mathbf{z}\sim q_\phi(\mathbf{z}|\mathbf{x}^{(s)})}[\log p_\theta(\mathbf{x}^{(t)}|\mathbf{y}^{(t)}, \mathbf{z}) + \log p_\pi(\mathbf{y}^{(t)})] - $$
$$\mathrm{KL}(q_\phi(\mathbf{z}|\mathbf{x}^{(s)})\|p(\mathbf{z})) = \mathcal{L}_l(\mathbf{x}^{(t)}, \mathbf{y}^{(t)}|\mathbf{x}^{(s)}) \qquad (2)$$

which is a simple extension to the vanilla variational auto-enocders.

Second, in the case of unsupervised learning or when the labels of the inflected word is not observed, we only observe a word or a pair of words and we would like to maximize the log likelihood of the observed data by marginalizing over possible morphological labels, which is consisted to the supervised case above. In this scenario, we can introduce the discrete latent variables for the inflected labels which are used to infer the labels for the target word. Then when decoding the word, we condition both on the continuous and discrete latent variables. For the variational encoder-decoder (MSVED), the variational lower bound on the conditional log likelihood is affected by the recognition model, and thus is computed as:

$$\log p_\theta(\mathbf{x}^{(t)}|\mathbf{x}^{(s)})$$
$$\geq \mathbb{E}_{(\mathbf{y}^{(t)},\mathbf{z})\sim q_\phi(\mathbf{y}^{(t)},\mathbf{z}|\mathbf{x}^{(s)},\mathbf{x}^{(t)})} \log \frac{p_\theta(\mathbf{x}^{(t)}, \mathbf{y}^{(t)}, \mathbf{z}|\mathbf{x}^{(s)})}{q_\phi(\mathbf{y}^{(t)}, \mathbf{z}|\mathbf{x}^{(s)}, \mathbf{x}^{(t)})}$$
$$= \mathbb{E}_{\mathbf{y}^{(t)}\sim q_\phi(\mathbf{y}^{(t)}|\mathbf{x}^{(t)})}[\mathbb{E}_{\mathbf{z}\sim q_\phi(\mathbf{z}|\mathbf{x}^{(s)})}[\log p_\theta(\mathbf{x}^{(t)}|\mathbf{y}^{(t)}, \mathbf{z})]$$
$$- \mathrm{KL}(q_\phi(\mathbf{z}|\mathbf{x}^{(s)})\|p(\mathbf{z})) + \log p_\pi(\mathbf{y}^{(t)})$$
$$- \log q_\phi(\mathbf{y}^{(t)}|\mathbf{x}^{(t)})] = \mathcal{L}_u(\mathbf{x}^{(t)}|\mathbf{x}^{(s)}) \qquad (3)$$

While the unsupervised objective is trained by maximizing the following variational lower bound $\mathcal{U}(\mathbf{x})$ on the objective for unlabeled data:

$$\log p_\theta(\mathbf{x}) \geq \mathbb{E}_{(\mathbf{y},\mathbf{z})\sim q_\phi(\mathbf{y},\mathbf{z}|\mathbf{x})} \log \frac{p_\theta(\mathbf{x}, \mathbf{y}, \mathbf{z})}{q_\phi(\mathbf{y}, \mathbf{z}|\mathbf{x})}$$
$$= \mathbb{E}_{\mathbf{y}\sim q_\phi(\mathbf{y}|\mathbf{x})}[\mathbb{E}_{\mathbf{z}\sim q_\phi(\mathbf{z}|\mathbf{x})}[\log p_\theta(\mathbf{x}|\mathbf{z}, \mathbf{y})]$$
$$- \mathrm{KL}(q_\phi(\mathbf{z}|\mathbf{x})\|p(\mathbf{z})) + \log p_\pi(\mathbf{y})$$
$$- \log q_\phi(\mathbf{y}|\mathbf{x})] = \mathcal{U}(\mathbf{x}) \qquad (4)$$

Note that when labels are not observed, the inference model $q_\phi(\mathbf{y}|\mathbf{x})$ has the form of a discriminative classifier, thus we can use observed labels as the supervision signal to learn a better classifier. In this case we also minimize the following cross entropy as the classification loss:

$$\mathcal{D}(\mathbf{x}, \mathbf{y}) = \mathbb{E}_{(\mathbf{x},\mathbf{y})\sim p_l(\mathbf{x},\mathbf{y})}[-\log q_\phi(\mathbf{y}|\mathbf{x})] \qquad (5)$$

where $p_l(\mathbf{x}, \mathbf{y})$ is the distribution of labeled data.

To sum up, the semi-supervised model (**Semi-sup**) is trained to maximize the variational lower bounds and minimize the classification cross-entropy error of 5.

$$\mathcal{L}(\mathbf{x}^{(\mathbf{s})}, \mathbf{x}^{(\mathbf{t})}, \mathbf{y}^{(\mathbf{t})}, \mathbf{x}) = \alpha \cdot \mathcal{U}(\mathbf{x}) + \mathcal{L}_u(\mathbf{x}^{(s)}|\mathbf{x}^{(t)})$$
$$+ \mathcal{L}_l(\mathbf{x}^{(t)}, \mathbf{y}^{(t)}|\mathbf{x}^{(s)}) - \mathcal{D}(\mathbf{x}^{(t)}, \mathbf{y}^{(t)}) \quad (6)$$

The weight α controls the relative weight between the loss from unlabeled data and labeled data.

3 Learning MSVED

3.1 Learning Discrete Latent Variables

One challenge in training our model is that discrete random variables in a stochastic computation graph prevent the gradient from being back-propagated due to their non-differentiability, and marginalizing over all label combinations is also infeasible in our case.

To alleviate this problem, we use the recently proposed Gumbel-Softmax trick (Maddison et al., 2014; Gumbel and Lieblein, 1954) to create a differentiable estimator for categorical variables. In experiments, we start with a relatively large temperature and decrease it gradually.

3.2 Learning Continuous Latent Variables

We observe that with the vanilla implementation the KL cost quickly decreases to near zero, setting $q_\phi(\mathbf{z}|\mathbf{x})$ equal to standard normal distribution. In this case, the RNN decoder can easily degenerate into an RNN language model. Hence, the latent variables are ignored by the decoder and cannot encode any useful information. The latent variable $\mathbf{z}$ learns an undesirable distribution that coincides with the imposed prior distribution but has no contribution to the decoder. To force the decoder to use the latent variables, we take the following two approaches which are similar to Bowman et al. (2016).

KL-Divergence Annealing: We add a coefficient λ to the KL cost and gradually anneal it from zero to a predefined threshold $\lambda_{\mathbf{m}}$. At the early stage of training, we set λ to be zero and let the model first figure out how to project the representation of the source sequence to a roughly right point in the space and then regularize it with the KL cost. This technique can also be seen in (Kočiský et al., 2016; Miao and Blunsom, 2016).

Input Dropout in the Decoder: Besides annealing the KL cost, we also randomly drop out the

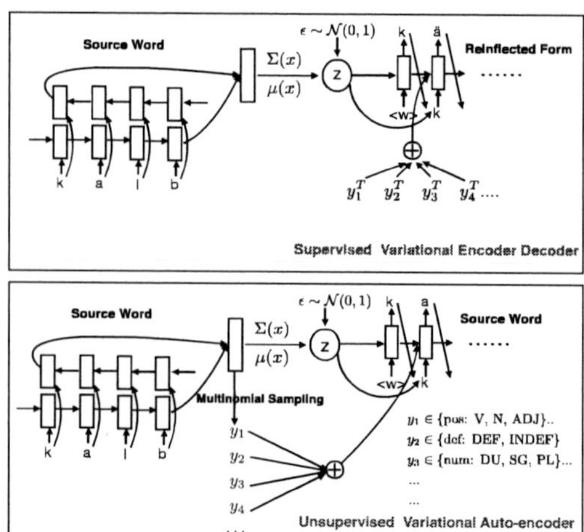

Figure 1: Model architecture for labeled and unlabeled data. For the encoder-decoder model, only one direction from the source to target is given. The classification model is not illustrated in the diagram.

input token with a probability of β at each time step of the decoder during learning. The previous ground-truth token embedding is replaced with a zero vector when dropped. In this way, the RNN decoder could not fully rely on the ground-truth previous token, which ensures that the decoder uses information encoded in the latent variables.

4 Architecture for Morphological Reinflection

The overall model architecture is shown in Fig. 1. Each character and each label is associated with a continuous vector. We employ Gated Recurrent Units (GRUs) for the encoder and decoder. We use only single directional GRUs as the encoder for the input word $\mathbf{x}^{(s)}$. $\mathbf{u}$ is the hidden representation of $\mathbf{x}^{(s)}$ which is the last hidden state of GRUs. and is used as the input for the inference model on $\mathbf{z}$. We represent $\mu(\mathbf{u})$ and $\sigma^2(\mathbf{u})$ as MLPs and sample $\mathbf{z}$ from $\mathcal{N}(\mu(\mathbf{u}), \mathrm{diag}(\sigma^2(\mathbf{u})))$, using $\mathbf{z} = \mu + \sigma \circ \epsilon$, where $\epsilon \sim \mathcal{N}(\mathbf{0}, \mathbf{I})$. Similarly, we can obtain the hidden representation of $\mathbf{x}^{(t)}$ and use this as input to the inference model on each label $\mathbf{y}_i^{(t)}$, which is also an MLP following a softmax layer to generate the categorical probabilities of target labels.

Other experimental setups: We apply temperature annealing in the Gumble-Softmax with the scheme $\max(0.5, \exp(-3e - 5 \cdot t))$ every 2000 updates where t is the update steps. We observe

Language	Dev	Test	Language	Dev	Test	Language	Dev	Test
Latin	66.2	66.2	Navajo	84.9	84.2	English	93.3	94.6
Icelandic	71.7	68.1	French	84.9	82.4	Lower-Sorbian	93.9	91.3
Irish	72.7	71.9	Armenian	85.3	82.3	Italian	94.2	92.6
Finnish	73.4	74.9	Latvian	85.6	87.5	Basque	95.0	97.0
Hungarian	74.5	73.6	Scottish-Gaelic	86.0	68.0	Estonian	95.1	93.7
Faroese	74.8	74.5	Bulgarian	86.3	86.7	Quechua	95.5	95.5
Russian	75.8	76.4	Macedonian	86.6	86.1	Khaling	96.2	94.8
Norwegian-Nynorsk	77.8	73.8	Northern-Sami	86.7	85.8	Hebrew	96.3	97.5
Polish	78.3	78.1	Slovene	87.3	87.8	Portuguese	96.4	96.4
German	79.3	78.7	Danish	88.1	85.4	Catalan	96.9	96.5
Swedish	80.2	80.6	Arabic	88.6	85.9	Urdu	98.4	97.9
Romanian	80.3	78.6	Sorani	89.6	87.8	Persian	98.6	98.7
Lithuanian	80.6	81.6	Slovak	89.6	87.9	Bengali	99.0	99.0
Serbo-Croatian	81.1	79.6	Turkish	90.4	90.3	Welsh	99.0	99.0
Norwegian-Bokmal	81.2	82	Dutch	91.2	88.9	Haida	99.0	97.0
Czech	83.1	81.9	Albanian	91.9	91.3	Hindi	99.9	99.6
Kurmanji	83.4	83.8	Georgian	92.5	92.3			
Ukrainian	84.5	84.0	Spanish	92.5	92.8	Average	87.18	86.21

Table 1: Results of the ensemble system on the development ang test sets of 52 languages.

Language	Src Word	Tgt Labels	Gold Tgt	Ours
Latin	trygon	Pos=N;Case=ABL;Num=PL	trȳgōnibus	trygōnibus
	largio	Mood=SBJV;Num=PL;Per=2;Tense=PST;Asp=PRF;Pos=V	largivissētis	largissētis
	compenso	Mood=SBJV;Num=SG;Per=3;Tense=PST;Asp=PFV;Pos=V	compensāverit	compenserit
Icelandic	háspil	Pos=N;Def=DEF;Case=GEN;Num=PL	háspilanna	hásplanna
	gallabuxur	Pos=N;Def=INDF;Case=GEN;Num=SG	gallabuxna	gallabölur
	lest	Pos=N;Def=DEF;Case=GEN;Num=SG L	lestarinnar	lestsins

Table 2: Examples of incorrect inflection generation words on the dev data.

Language	Settings	Dev Acc. (Single Model.)
Icelandic	vanilla Encoder-Decoder + attention, w/o data augmentation	81.0
	our model w/o data augmentation and Wiki	78.6
	our model (full)	71.7
Latin	vanilla Encoder-Decoder + attention, w/o data augmentation	74.6
	our model w/o data augmentation and Wiki	66.6
	our model (full)	66.2
Persian	vanilla Encoder-Decoder + attention, w/o data augmentation	99.6
	our model w/o data augmentation and Wiki	99.6
	our model (full)	98.6
Arabic	vanilla Encoder-Decoder + attention, w/o data augmentation	90.7
	our model w/o data augmentation and Wiki	91.3
	our model (full)	88.6

Table 3: Ablation experiments on the effects of data augmentation and WikiData.

that our model is not sensitive to the temperature in this task. All hyperparameters are tuned on the validation set, and include the following: For KL cost annealing, λ_m is set to be 0.2 for all language settings. For character drop-out at the decoder, we empirically set β to be 0.4 for all languages. We set the dimension of character embeddings to be 300, tag label embeddings to be 200, RNN hidden state to be 256, and latent variable $\mathbf{z}$ to be 150 or 100. We set α the weight for the unsupervised loss to be 0.8. We train the model with Adadelta (Zeiler, 2012) and use early-stop with a patience of 5. Our system is an ensemble of five models and the probability vector at each time step is obtained by averaging the output probabilities from each model

5 Experiments

5.1 Data pre-processing

Creating morphosyntactic tag maps: In our model, we treat the inference model on discrete labels in the form of discriminator, thus we need to know which label belongs to which morphosyntactic dimension. For example, *V* is a label of *Part-of-speech-tagging*. To obtain such mapping from a specific label to the morphosyntactic dimension, we leverage the Universal Morphological Feature Schema (Sylak-Glassman, 2016) and also add the missing schema from the training data to create the key-value pairs of morphosysntactic dimension and label. Then we reformat the labels provided in the data set into the key-value pairs to train a classifier for each morphosyntactic dimension.

Data Augmentation: We augment the data set in the similar way as Kann and Schütze (2016). By doing so, the training data is not limited to the form of lemma to inflected word but can also be any word pairs that share the same lemma. This helps our model generalize better and learn the latent continuous representations more effectively. The size of training data set after augmentation scales with a factor of 2 to 20 times compared with the original one.

Monolingual WikiData: We process the Wikipedia corpus provided by the shared task organizer as our unsupervised training data together with words in the training data. For each language, we first get the character vocabulary of the corresponding training data and only keep words in the Wiki corpus for which characters are all in the character set we obtained. All words that occur less than 20 times are eliminated. We also limit the number of words used during training to be the 50000 most frequent words.

5.2 Results and Analysis

The results on the dev and test data of the 52 languages are presented in 1. We obtain a generation accuracy above 80% over more than 25% languages and an average of 87.2% for both dev and test data. The generation accuracy is almost consistent on the dev and test data except that the test data accuracy of Scottish-Gaelic drops by near 21%. We find that only a medium volume of training data is provided for Scottish-Gaelic. This may be the reason why the model trained for Scottish-Gaelic can not generalize as well as other languages.

We do not tune the hyper-parameters for each language manually. However, we test on different dimensions for the continuous latent variables. The dimension size we have used included 100 and 150. And we observe significant improvement by using a larger dimension size of latent variables over a portion of languages including Faroese, Lithuanian, Navajo, Scottish-gaelic, Northern-sami, Slovene, Sorani, Slovak. However, we also observe that for some languages including Finnish, German, French, etc, the performance drops signficantly after increasing the size of continuous latent variable dimension. This indicates that for different languages, the continuous space required to encode the lemma and inflected information varies from language to language. We will further investigate this in the future work.

5.3 Effect of Data Augmentation and Using Wiki Data

While our performance was reasonable, it was not as good as that presented in our previous work (Zhou and Neubig, 2017), nor was it competitive with the highest-scoring models on the shared task. In order to examine the reason for this, we performed several ablations, the results of which are presented in Tab. 3

First, we first examined the effects of data augmentation and Wiki Data for semi-supervised learning on the performance of our model. By removing the augmented data from the training set, we observe a large gain in the generation accuracy. Besides, we find that Wiki Data for semi-supervised learning doesn't help much to increase the model's performance. The reasons for this will be examined further in the following section.

We additionally reimplemented a vanilla encoder-decoder model with attention that concatenates the input characters and target word tags together with a special token in the middle as the new input sequence to the encoder (Kann and Schütze, 2016). The results show that the vanilla encoder-decoder works better than our

Dimension	Label	Train Data	WikiData	Difference
Case	None	0.58	0.35	-0.22
	ACC	0.14	0.51	0.38
	NOM	0.14	0.12	-0.02
	GEN	0.14	0.01	-0.13
Possession	None	0.86	0.31	-0.55
	PSSD	0.14	0.69	0.55
Language-Specific-Features	None	0.90	0.42	-0.48
	LGSPEC1	0.10	0.58	0.48
Mood	None	0.68	0.10	-0.58
	IND	0.20	0.62	0.42
	IMP	0.02	0.03	0.01
	SBJV	0.10	0.25	0.15
Definiteness	None	0.57	0.60	0.03
	DEF	0.22	0.34	0.12
	NDEF	0.21	0.06	-0.15
Gender	None	0.53	0.52	-0.01
	FEM	0.23	0.27	0.04
	MASC	0.23	0.20	-0.03
Politeness	None	0.85	0.58	-0.28
	INFM	0.14	0.42	0.28
Number	None	0.01	0.16	0.15
	DU	0.22	0.34	0.12
	SG	0.47	0.31	-0.15
	PL	0.30	0.18	-0.11
Person	None	0.58	0.74	0.15
	1	0.06	0.02	-0.05
	3	0.18	0.17	-0.01
	2	0.17	0.08	-0.09
Tense	None	0.90	0.51	-0.40
	PST	0.10	0.49	0.40
Aspect	None	0.80	0.21	-0.59
	PRF	0.10	0.41	0.31
	IPFV	0.10	0.38	0.28
Part-of-Speech	None	0.00	0.03	0.03
	V+V.PTCP	0.01	0.29	0.28
	V+V.MSDR	0.00	0.15	0.14
	N	0.43	0.36	-0.07
	ADJ	0.14	0.14	-0.00
	V	0.42	0.03	-0.39
Voice	None	0.57	0.40	-0.18
	PASS	0.16	0.39	0.22
	ACT	0.27	0.22	-0.05

Table 4: The distribution of morphosyntactic tags for Arabic on Wikipedia and the shared task training data respectively. The linguistic tag classifier has an average accuracy of 93.36% on the Dev data.

model in some cases. We suspect that since task 1 is purely an inflection task and because semi-supervised learning did not provide a particularly large benefit, a simpler model that utilizes attention may be sufficient. This is in contrast to our previous findings, where semi-supervised learning was highly effective, and the proposed model out-performed the simpler attention-based baseline.

5.4 Analysis on the Distribution of Linguistic Tags of Wiki Data and Training Data

One potential reason for the lack of effectiveness of semi-supervised training is that the semi-supervised data that we used for training was not appropriate for the task at hand, or that we were not able to use it in the most effective way. In order to do so, we analyze the distribution of linguistic tags for words from the training data in the shared task and the Wiki Data provided by the organizer, with the hypothesis that if the distribution of tags for the Wiki Data is very different from the training and test data for the shared task, our predictions may be biased away from the testing distribution by incorporating the unsupervised Wiki data. To perform this examination, we use the tag classifier trained in our model to predict the labels for each word in the Wiki Data.

Dimension	Label	Train Data	WikiData	Difference
Mood	None	0.79	0.13	-0.66
	IMP	0.03	0.69	0.66
	SBJV	0.18	0.18	-0.00
Politeness	None	0.52	0.30	-0.22
	COL	0.48	0.70	0.22
Number	None	0.04	0.67	0.62
	SG	0.48	0.19	-0.30
	PL	0.47	0.15	-0.32
Person	None	0.04	0.28	0.24
	1	0.31	0.23	-0.08
	3	0.31	0.22	-0.09
	2	0.34	0.27	-0.07
Finiteness	None	0.98	0.33	-0.66
	NFIN	0.02	0.67	0.66
Tense	None	0.13	0.07	-0.07
	FUT	0.04	0.42	0.38
	PST	0.46	0.14	-0.32
	PRS	0.36	0.37	0.01
Aspect	None	0.39	0.37	-0.01
	PROG	0.18	0.07	-0.11
	PRF	0.17	0.03	-0.14
	IPFV	0.18	0.09	-0.08
	PFV	0.09	0.44	0.35
Part-of-Speech	None	0.00	0.44	0.44
	V+V.PTCP	0.03	0.18	0.15
	V	0.97	0.38	-0.59

Table 5: The distribution of morphosyntactic tags for Persian on Wikipedia and the shared task training data respectively. The linguistic tag classifier has an average accuracy of 95.26% on the Dev data.

The percentages of each label within each morphosyntactic dimension for Arabic and Persian are listed in Tab. 4 and Tab. 5. We found that the distribution of the linguistic tags for the Wiki Data and the training data in the shared task are not always consistent. For example, in Arabic, the distributions of predicted tags with respect to case, possession, part-of-speech, and several other classes differ significantly from the original training data. Such difference suggests that either the words in the unlabeled Wiki Data have very different characteristics than our training set, or our tag classifier is not functioning properly to identify the tags. Either case would be detrimental to semi-supervised learning. The problem is even more stark for Persian: in Persian the only labeled words in the training data are verbs, so all non-verb words in the Wiki Data will receive an incorrect analysis, which is obviously not conducive to learning anything useful. As a recommendation for the future, when performing semi-supervised learning for morphology where the labeled data only represents a subset of the phenomena in the language, it is likely necessary to first identify which of the available unlabeled data is appropriate for semi-supervised learning before applying such methods.

5.5 Case Study on Inflected Words

In Tab. 1, we notice that the performance on Latin is relatively poor compared with other languages. Latin is a highly inflected languages with three distinct genders, seven noun cases, four verb conjugations, four verb principal parts, six tenses, three persons, three moods, two voices, two aspects and two numbers. In addition to this, we found that the data set size after augmentation was only enlarged 2 times. We examine some errors made by our system on two worst performed languages Latin and Icelandic in Tab. 2. As shown in the table, we found that the inflections of Latin and Icelandic have more suffix variations from the lemma. We guess our model still lacks the ability to capture more complicated inflections for such languages. We might consider adding the dependencies between different inflections for multiple target labels in our future work.

6 Conclusion and Future Work

In this work, we further examine the method proposed in (Zhou and Neubig, 2017) for the shared task of SIGMORPHON 2017 on 52 languages and demonstrate the effectiveness of this approach. We will further improve our model's sophistication by investigating strategies for choosing appropriate semi-supervised data, and examining the model's performance on languages with a high inflection level.

Acknowledgments

This work has been supported in part by an Amazon Academic Research Award. We thank Matthew Honnibal for pointing out that the data distribution of Wikipedia corpus might be biased.

References

Samuel R Bowman, Luke Vilnis, Oriol Vinyals, Andrew M Dai, Rafal Jozefowicz, and Samy Bengio. 2016. Generating sentences from a continuous space. *Proceedings of CoNLL* .

Victor Chahuneau, Eva Schlinger, Noah A Smith, and Chris Dyer. 2013. Translating into morphologically rich languages with synthetic phrases. Association for Computational Linguistics.

Ryan Cotterell, Christo Kirov, John Sylak-Glassman, David Yarowsky, Jason Eisner, and Mans Hulden. 2016. The sigmorphon 2016 shared task—morphological reinflection. In *Proceedings of the 2016 Meeting of SIGMORPHON*. Association for Computational Linguistics, Berlin, Germany.

Ryan Cotterell and Hinrich Schütze. 2017. Joint semantic synthesis and morphological analysis of the derived word. *arXiv preprint arXiv:1701.00946* .

Kareem Darwish and Douglas W Oard. 2007. Adapting morphology for arabic information retrieval. In *Arabic Computational Morphology*, Springer, pages 245–262.

Carl Doersch. 2016. Tutorial on variational autoencoders. *arXiv preprint arXiv:1606.05908* .

Emil Julius Gumbel and Julius Lieblein. 1954. Statistical theory of extreme values and some practical applications: a series of lectures. *US Government Printing Office Washington* .

Katharina Kann and Hinrich Schütze. 2016. Med: The lmu system for the sigmorphon 2016 shared task on morphological reinflection. In *In Proceedings of the 14th SIGMORPHON Workshop on Computational Research in Phonetics, Phonology, and Morphology*. Berlin, Germany.

D.P. Kingma and M. Welling. 2014. Auto-encoding variational bayes. In *The International Conference on Learning Representations*.

Tomáš Kočiský, Gábor Melis, Edward Grefenstette, Chris Dyer, Wang Ling, Phil Blunsom, and Karl Moritz Hermann. 2016. Semantic parsing with semi-supervised sequential autoencoders. *the 2016 Conference on Empirical Methods in Natural Language Processing (EMNLP)* .

Chris J Maddison, Daniel Tarlow, and Tom Minka. 2014. A* sampling. In *Advances in Neural Information Processing Systems*. pages 3086–3094.

Yishu Miao and Phil Blunsom. 2016. Language as a latent variable: Discrete generative models for sentence compression. *the 2016 Conference on Empirical Methods in Natural Language Processing (EMNLP)* .

John Sylak-Glassman. 2016. The composition and use of the universal morphological feature schema (unimorph schema) .

Matthew D Zeiler. 2012. Adadelta: an adaptive learning rate method. *arXiv preprint arXiv:1212.5701* .

Chunting Zhou and Graham Neubig. 2017. Multi-space variational encoder-decoders for semi-supervised labeled sequence transduction. In *The 55th Annual Meeting of the Association for Computational Linguistics (ACL)*. Vancouver, Canada. https://arxiv.org/abs/1704.01691.

ISI at the SIGMORPHON 2017 Shared Task on Morphological Reinflection

Abhisek Chakrabarty and **Utpal Garain**
Computer Vision and Pattern Recognition Unit
Indian Statistical Institute
203 B.T. Road, Kolkata-700108, India
abhisek0842@gmail.com, utpal@isical.ac.in

Abstract

We present a system for morphological reinflection based on the LSTM model. Given an input word and morphosyntactic descriptions, the problem is to classify the proper edit tree that, applied on the input word, produces the target form. The proposed method does not require human defined features and it is language independent also. Currently, we evaluate our system only for task 1 without using any external data. From the test set results, it is found that the proposed model beats the baseline on 15 out of the 52 languages in high resource scenario. But its performance is poor when the training set size is medium or low.

1 Introduction

The morphological reinflection task is to generate the variant of a source word, given the morphosyntactic descriptions of the target word. This year's shared task (Cotterell et al., 2017) is divided into two sub-tasks. Task 1 demands to inflect the isolated word forms based on labelled training data. For example, given the source form 'communicate' and the features 'V;3;SG;PRS', one has to predict the target form 'communicates'. Whereas, in task 2, partially filled incomplete paradigms are provided. The goal is to complete them using a restricted number of full paradigms. For each of the tasks, 3 separate training files are given per language, which differ in size (low/medium/high), in order to analyze systems' generalization ability in low and high resource situations. The competition is spread over 52 languages. For each language, a finite set of morphological tags are provided, from which the target inflections are taken. Evaluation is done separately under each of the three different training sets. To make the shared task competition fair, use of external resources are forbidden for the main competition track. However, for those systems which make use of external monolingual corpora, a list of approved external corpora selected from the Wikipedia text dumps are provided.

So far, there have been several efforts on reinflection employing statistical learning based methods (Dreyer and Eisner, 2011; Durrett and DeNero, 2013; Ahlberg et al., 2015; King, 2016) and string transduction (Nicolai et al., 2015). These methods entail feature definition which is hard to generalize for all of the world's languages.

In this article, we introduce a long short-term memory (LSTM) network architecture to handle the morphological reinflection task. The proposed method is language independent and does not require features to be defined manually. Our model is related to the encoder-decoder based approaches such as (Aharoni et al., 2016; Faruqui et al., 2016; Kann and Schütze, 2016a,b), but the main difference is that the proposed network is not designed to generate sequence of characters as output. Rather, we formulate the problem as to classify the transformation process required to convert a source form to its target form (Chakrabarty et al., 2017). Our goal is to model such a system which receives an input word and the morphological tags and returns the proper transformation that induces the target word. The source-target transformation is accomplished using edit tree (Chrupala et al., 2008; Müller et al., 2015). Initially all edit trees are extracted from the labelled pairs in the training data and then the distinct candidates from them are marked as the class labels. We feed the character sequence of the input word through the LSTM network to encode it and finally, the encoded representation is jointly trained with the input tags to classify the correct edit tree.

Currently, we assess our system only for task 1

Proceedings of the CoNLL SIGMORPHON 2017 Shared Task: Universal Morphological Reinflection, pages 66–70,
Vancouver, Canada, August 3–4, 2017. ©2017 Association for Computational Linguistics

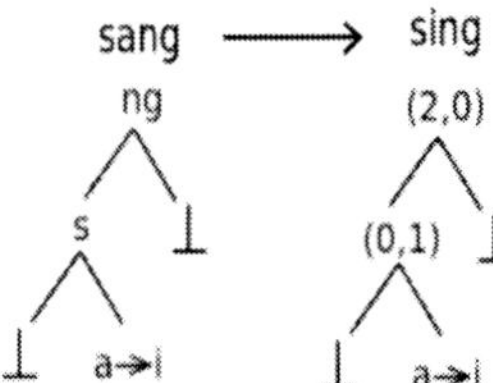

Figure 1: Edit tree for the source-target pair 'sang-sing'.

on all 52 languages, though it can be used for task 2 also. No external data such as the Wikipedia dumps provided by the SIGMORPHON committee has been exploited in the present work. The results obtained from the test sets indicate that the proposed method is resource intensive. When the training size is high, it achieves over the baseline system on 15 out of the 52 languages. But on medium and low amount training data, the performance is poor beating the baseline on 5 and 4 languages only.

2 Methodology

Edit Trees: An edit tree encodes a transformation which maps a source string to a target string. Given a source-target pair, the process of finding the corresponding edit tree is as follows. At first, the longest common substring (LCS) between them is found and then the prefix and suffix pairs of the LCS are recursively modelled in the same manner. The edit tree does not encode the LCS itself. Instead, it contains the length of the prefix and suffix in the source string for generalization. When no LCS is found between the source and the target strings, they are kept as a substitution node.

Figure 1 shows an example of edit trees between the source-target pair 'sang-sing'. The LCS between them is 'ng'. In the source string, the prefix length of the LCS is 2 (for 'sa') and the suffix length is 0. So, the root of the edit tree keeps the information $(2, 0)$. The left subtree of the root represents the edit tree between the prefix pair of the LCS in the source and the target string i.e. for 'sa-si' and following the same way, the right subtree remains empty.

Note that, to generalize the transformation pattern, the LCS is not stored in the edit tree. Con-

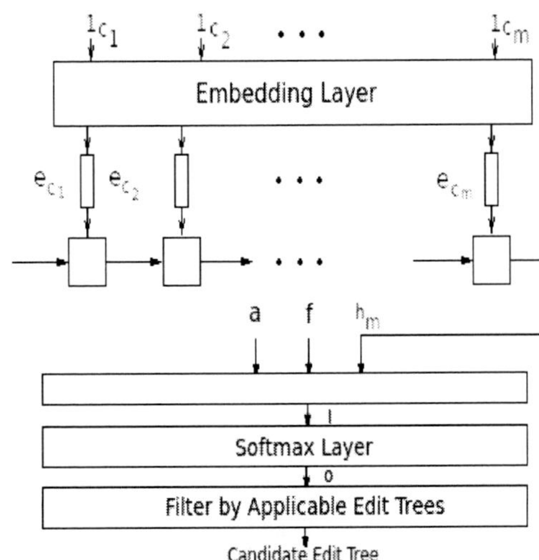

Figure 2: The model architecture.

sider the two source-target pairs 'gives-give' and 'takes-take' where the transformation rule is same i.e. to omit the ending 's' character. The root of the corresponding edit tree contains $(0, 1)$. If the LCS were stored in the root, then the tree could not be generalized for all the pairs like 'comes-come', 'sleeps-sleep' etc. where the same rule works.

2.1 The System Description

The architecture of our system is presented in Figure 2. At first, we use the LSTM network to make a syntactic embedding of the source word, that captures the morphological regularities. A character alphabet of the concerned language is defined as C. Let the input word w consists of the character sequence $c_1, \ldots, c_m$ where the word length is m and each character c_i is represented as a one hot encoded vector $\mathbf{1}_{c_i}$. The particular dimension of $\mathbf{1}_{c_i}$ referring to the index of c_i in the alphabet C, is set to one and the other dimensions are made zero. $\mathbf{1}_{c_1}, \ldots, \mathbf{1}_{c_m}$ are passed to an embedding layer $\mathbf{E}_c \in \mathbb{R}^{d_c \times |C|}$, which projects them to d_c dimensional vectors $\mathbf{e}_{c_1}, \ldots, \mathbf{e}_{c_m}$, by doing the operation $\mathbf{e}_{c_i} = \mathbf{E}_c \cdot \mathbf{1}_{c_i}$ where '·' denotes matrix multiplication.

When the sequence of vectors $\mathbf{e}_{c_1}, \ldots, \mathbf{e}_{c_m}$ is given to the LSTM network, it computes the state sequence $\mathbf{h}_1, \ldots, \mathbf{h}_m$ using the following equations:

$$\mathbf{f}_t = \sigma(\mathbf{W}_f \mathbf{e}_{c_t} + \mathbf{U}_f \mathbf{h}_{t-1} + \mathbf{V}_f \mathbf{c}_{t-1} + \mathbf{b}_f)$$
$$\mathbf{i}_t = \sigma(\mathbf{W}_i \mathbf{e}_{c_t} + \mathbf{U}_i \mathbf{h}_{t-1} + \mathbf{V}_i \mathbf{c}_{t-1} + \mathbf{b}_i)$$
$$\mathbf{c}_t = \mathbf{f}_t \odot \mathbf{c}_{t-1}$$
$$+ \mathbf{i}_t \odot tanh(\mathbf{W}_c \mathbf{e}_{c_t} + \mathbf{U}_c \mathbf{h}_{t-1} + \mathbf{b}_c)$$
$$\mathbf{o}_t = \sigma(\mathbf{W}_o \mathbf{e}_{c_t} + \mathbf{U}_o \mathbf{h}_{t-1} + \mathbf{V}_o \mathbf{c}_t + \mathbf{b}_o)$$
$$\mathbf{h}_t = \mathbf{o}_t \odot tanh(\mathbf{c}_t),$$

σ denotes the sigmoid function and $\odot$ stands for the element-wise (Hadamard) product. LSTM utilizes an extra memory $\mathbf{c}_t$ that is controlled by three gates - input ($\mathbf{i}_t$), forget ($\mathbf{f}_t$) and output ($\mathbf{o}_t$). $\mathbf{W}$, $\mathbf{U}$, $\mathbf{V}$ (weights), $\mathbf{b}$ (bias) are the parameters. Eventually, we take the final state $\mathbf{h}_m$ as the encoded representation of w.

In addition to the source word, we have morphosyntactic features in hand to predict the target form. From the training data, all distinct features are sorted out to make a feature dictionary F. For a training sample, the given features are mapped to $|F|$ dimensional feature vector $\mathbf{f} = (f_1, \ldots, f_{|F|})$ where $f_i = 1$ if the ith feature in the dictionary is present in the input features, otherwise f_i is set to 0. Thus, $\mathbf{f}$ becomes a numeric representation of the input features for the present training sample.

Another important point is that, for any arbitrary input word, all unique edit trees in the training data are not applicable due to incompatible substitutions. For example, the edit tree for the source-target pair 'sang-sing' (shown in Figure 1) cannot be applied on the word 'sleep'. In spite of all unique edit trees are set as the class labels, few of them are applicable for an input word to the model. To sort out this issue, we put the information over which classes the model should distribute the output probability mass while training.

Let $T = \{t_1, \ldots, t_k\}$ be the distinct edit trees set extracted from the training data. For the input word w, its applicable edit trees vector is defined as $\mathbf{a} = (a_1, \ldots, a_k)$ where $\forall j \in \{1, \ldots, k\}$, $a_j = 1$ if t_j is applicable for w, otherwise 0. Hence, $\mathbf{a}$ holds the applicable edit tree information for w. Finally, we combine the LSTM output $\mathbf{h}_m$, feature vector $\mathbf{f}$ and applicable tree vector $\mathbf{a}$ together for the edit tree classification task as following,

$$\mathbf{l} = softplus(\mathbf{L}^h \mathbf{h}_m + \mathbf{L}^f \mathbf{f} + \mathbf{L}^a \mathbf{a} + \mathbf{b}),$$

where 'softplus' is the activation function $f(x) = ln(1 + e^x)$ and $\mathbf{L}^h, \mathbf{L}^f, \mathbf{L}^a$ and $\mathbf{b}$ are the network parameters. Next, $\mathbf{l}$ is passed through the softmax layer to get the output labels for w.

To pick the maximum probable edit tree for an input word, we exploit the prior information about applicable classes. Let $\mathbf{o} = (o_1, \ldots, o_k)$ be the output of the softmax layer. The particular edit tree $t_j \in T$ is considered as the right candidate, where

$$j = \mathrm{argmax}_{j' \in \{1,\ldots,k\} \,\wedge\, a_{j'}=1}\, o_{j'}$$

In this way, we choose the maximum probable class over the applicable classes only.

Language- Training Set Size	Our Model's Acc. (%)	Baseline Acc. (%)
albanian-high	79.1	78.9
arabic-high	60.2	50.7
armenian-high	89.5	87.2
dutch-high	90.2	87.0
georgian-high	94.4	93.8
hebrew-high	71.1	54.0
hindi-high	99.1	93.5
hungarian-high	77.5	68.5
icelandic-high	78.2	76.3
irish-high	60.6	53.0
italian-high	91.1	76.9
khaling-high	56.0	53.7
russian-high	86.1	85.7
turkish-high	73.5	72.6
urdu-high	98.2	96.5
english-medium	91.1	90.9
french-medium	73.9	72.5
hebrew-medium	46.6	37.5
italian-medium	75.7	71.6
scottish-gaelic-medium	62.0	48.0
albanian-low	21.6	21.1
danish-low	61.9	58.4
khaling-low	6.1	3.1
serbo-croatian-low	24.2	18.4

Table 1: Our model's performance on the test datasets for those languages where it beats the baseline system.

3 Experimentation

Parameters of the Model: For all 52 languages, we limit each word length to maximum 25 characters. Null characters are padded to the smaller words at the end and for words having more than 25 characters, extra characters are omitted. We represent each character as 25 length sequence of one hot encoded character vectors that are passed to the embedding layer. The output dimension of the embedding layer is set as the length of the one hot encoded character vectors i.e. $|C|$, size of the character alphabet of the concerned language.

Hyper parameters of the model are given as follows. The number of neurons in the hidden layer

Language- Training Set Size	Our Model's Acc. (%)	Baseline Acc. (%)
albanian-high	79.4	78.1
arabic-high	60	47.7
armenian-high	89.2	89.1
dutch-high	88	86.8
georgian-high	94.6	94
hebrew-high	72.3	55.8
hindi-high	99.1	94
hungarian-high	75.8	71.1
icelandic-high	80.6	76.1
irish-high	62.4	54.3
italian-high	91.6	79.9
khaling-high	56.2	53.8
russian-high	85.6	82
turkish-high	74.4	72.9
urdu-high	97.4	95.8
georgian-medium	90.4	90
hebrew-medium	47.3	40
italian-medium	78.2	73.8
scottish-gaelic-medium	68	52
danish-low	60.2	59.8
khaling-low	5	3.9
serbo-croatian-low	26.7	21.3
welsh-low	17	15

Table 2: Our model's performance on the development datasets for those languages where it beats the baseline system.

of LSTM is set to 64 for all languages. We apply online learning in our model. Number of epochs and the dropout rate are set to 150 and 0.2 respectively. We use 'Adagrad' (Duchi et al., 2011) optimization algorithm for training. Categorical cross-entropy function is used to measure the loss in our model.

3.1 Results

As stated in section 1, our method overperforms the baseline system on 15 out of the 52 languages in high resource configuration for the test sets. Whereas, in medium and low resource situations separately, it beats the baseline on 5 and 4 languages respectively. We provide these results in Table 1. The results show that the proposed method is resource intensive.

We also provide our model's performance on the development datasets in Table 2. The results are quite similar to the results given in Table 1. When the training size is high, the proposed model beats the baseline on 15 languages. For medium and low resource scenario, it achieves over the baseline on 4 languages only.

References

Roee Aharoni, Yoav Goldberg, and Yonatan Belinkov. 2016. Improving sequence to sequence learning for morphological inflection generation: The biu-mit systems for the sigmorphon 2016 shared task for morphological reinflection. In *Proceedings of the 14th SIGMORPHON Workshop on Computational Research in Phonetics, Phonology, and Morphology*. Association for Computational Linguistics, Berlin, Germany, pages 41–48. http://anthology.aclweb.org/W16-2007.

Malin Ahlberg, Markus Forsberg, and Mans Hulden. 2015. Paradigm classification in supervised learning of morphology. In *Proceedings of the 2015 Conference of the North American Chapter of the Association for Computational Linguistics: Human Language Technologies*. Association for Computational Linguistics, Denver, Colorado, pages 1024–1029. http://www.aclweb.org/anthology/N15-1107.

Abhisek Chakrabarty, Onkar Arun Pandit, and Utpal Garain. 2017. Context sensitive lemmatization using two successive bidirectional gated recurrent networks. In *Proceedings of the 55th Annual Meeting of the Association for Computational Linguistics*. Association for Computational Linguistics, Vancouver, Canada.

Grzegorz Chrupala, Georgiana Dinu, and Josef van Genabith. 2008. Learning morphology with morfette. In *Proceedings of the Sixth International Conference on Language Resources and Evaluation (LREC'08)*. European Language Resources Association (ELRA), Marrakech, Morocco. http://www.lrec-conf.org/proceedings/lrec2008/pdf/594$_{paper.pdf}$.

Ryan Cotterell, Christo Kirov, John Sylak-Glassman, Géraldine Walther, Ekaterina Vylomova, Patrick Xia, Manaal Faruqui, Sandra Kübler, David Yarowsky, Jason Eisner, and Mans Hulden. 2017. The CoNLL-SIGMORPHON 2017 shared task: Universal morphological reinflection in 52 languages. In *Proceedings of the CoNLL-SIGMORPHON 2017 Shared Task: Universal Morphological Reinflection*. Association for Computational Linguistics, Vancouver, Canada.

Markus Dreyer and Jason Eisner. 2011. Discovering morphological paradigms from plain text using a dirichlet process mixture model. In *Proceedings of the 2011 Conference on Empirical Methods in Natural Language Processing*. Association for Computational Linguistics, Edinburgh, Scotland, UK., pages 616–627. http://www.aclweb.org/anthology/D11-1057.

John Duchi, Elad Hazan, and Yoram Singer. 2011. Adaptive subgradient methods for online learning and stochastic optimization. *Journal of Machine Learning Research* 12(Jul):2121–2159. http://www.jmlr.org/papers/v12/duchi11a.html.

Greg Durrett and John DeNero. 2013. Supervised learning of complete morphological paradigms. In *Proceedings of the 2013 Conference of the North American Chapter of the Association for Computational Linguistics: Human Language Technologies*. Association for Computational Linguistics, Atlanta, Georgia, pages 1185–1195. http://www.aclweb.org/anthology/N13-1138.

Manaal Faruqui, Yulia Tsvetkov, Graham Neubig, and Chris Dyer. 2016. Morphological inflection generation using character sequence to sequence learning. In *Proceedings of the 2016 Conference of the North American Chapter of the Association for Computational Linguistics: Human Language Technologies*. Association for Computational Linguistics, San Diego, California, pages 634–643. http://www.aclweb.org/anthology/N16-1077.

Katharina Kann and Hinrich Schütze. 2016a. Med: The lmu system for the sigmorphon 2016 shared task on morphological reinflection. In *Proceedings of the 14th SIGMORPHON Workshop on Computational Research in Phonetics, Phonology, and Morphology*. Association for Computational Linguistics, Berlin, Germany, pages 62–70. http://anthology.aclweb.org/W16-2010.

Katharina Kann and Hinrich Schütze. 2016b. Single-model encoder-decoder with explicit morphological representation for reinflection. In *Proceedings of the 54th Annual Meeting of the Association for Computational Linguistics (Volume 2: Short Papers)*. Association for Computational Linguistics, Berlin, Germany, pages 555–560. http://anthology.aclweb.org/P16-2090.

David King. 2016. Evaluating sequence alignment for learning inflectional morphology. In *Proceedings of the 14th SIGMORPHON Workshop on Computational Research in Phonetics, Phonology, and Morphology*. Association for Computational Linguistics, Berlin, Germany, pages 49–53. http://anthology.aclweb.org/W16-2008.

Thomas Müller, Ryan Cotterell, Alexander Fraser, and Hinrich Schütze. 2015. Joint lemmatization and morphological tagging with lemming. In *Proceedings of the 2015 Conference on Empirical Methods in Natural Language Processing*. Association for Computational Linguistics, Lisbon, Portugal, pages 2268–2274. http://aclweb.org/anthology/D15-1272.

Garrett Nicolai, Colin Cherry, and Grzegorz Kondrak. 2015. Inflection generation as discriminative string transduction. In *Proceedings of the 2015 Conference of the North American Chapter of the Association for Computational Linguistics: Human Language Technologies*. Association for Computational Linguistics, Denver, Colorado, pages 922–931. http://www.aclweb.org/anthology/N15-1093.

Experiments on Morphological Reinflection: CoNLL-2017 Shared Task

Akhilesh Sudhakar
BITS, Pilani, India
akhileshs.s4@gmail.com

Anil Kumar Singh
IIT (BHU), Varanasi, India
nlprnd@gmail.com

Abstract

We present two systems for the task of morphological inflection, i.e., finding a target morphological form, given a lemma and a set of target tags. Both are trained on datasets of three sizes: low, medium and high. The first uses a simple Long Short-Term Memory (LSTM) for low-sized dataset, while it uses an LSTM-based encoder-decoder based model for the medium and high sized datasets. The second uses a simple Gated Recurrent Unit (GRU) for low-sized data, while it uses a combination of simple LSTMs, simple GRUs, stacked GRUs and encoder-decoder models, depending on the language, for medium-sized data. Though the systems are not very complex, they give accuracies above baseline accuracies on high-sized datasets, around baseline accuracies for medium-sized datasets but mostly accuracies lower than baseline for low-sized datasets.

1 Introduction

The CoNLL-SIGMOPRHON 2017 shared task Cotterell et al. (2017) consists of two subtasks out of which we participate only in the first subtask, which involves generating a target inflected form from a given lemma with its part-of-speech. For instance, the word *writing* is the present continuous inflected form of the lemma *write*. The models were trained on three differently-sized datasets. The low-sized datasets had around 100 training samples, the medium-sized datasets had around 1000 training samples and the high-sized datasets had around 10000 samples for most languages. Datasets were provided for a total of 52 languages.

2 Background

Prior to neural network based approaches to morphological reinflection, most systems used a 3-step approach to solve the problem: 1) String alignment between the lemma and the target (morphologically transformed form), 2) Rule extraction from spans of the aligned strings and 3) Rule application to previously unseen lemmas to transform them. Durrett and DeNero (2013) and Ahlberg et al. (2014; 2015) used the above approaches, with each of them using different string alignment algorithms and different models to extract rules from these alignment tables. However, in these kinds of systems, the types of rules to be generated must be specified, which should also be engineered to take into account language-specific transformational behaviour.

Faruqui et al. (2016) proposed a neural network based system which abstracts away the above steps by modeling the problem as one of generating a character sequence, character-by-character. Akin to machine translation systems, this system uses an encoder-decoder LSTM model as proposed by Hochreiter and Schmidhuber (1997). The encoder is a bidirectional LSTM, while the decoder LSTM feeds into a softmax layer for every character position in the target string. A beam search is used to create many output sequences and the best one is chosen based on predicted scores from the softmax layer. This model takes into account the fact that the target and the root word are similar, except for the parts that have been changed due to inflection, by feeding the root word directly to the decoder as well. A separate neural net is trained for every language.

3 System Description

We have modeled our system based on the system proposed by Faruqui et al. (2016), as described

Proceedings of the CoNLL SIGMORPHON 2017 Shared Task: Universal Morphological Reinflection, pages 71–78,
Vancouver, Canada, August 3–4, 2017. ©2017 Association for Computational Linguistics

in the previous section. However we have made some modifications to the above system, to account for the three different sizes of datasets and to account for the behaviour of morphological transformations of independent languages. We submitted two submissions for the shared task, each of which we describe in the following sections.

In all the models, some structural and hyperparametrical features remain the same. The characters in the root word are represented using character indices, while the morphological features of the target word are represented using binary vectors. Each character of the root word is then embedded as a character embedding of dimension 64, to form the root word embedding. If an encoder is used, it is bidirectional and the the input word embeddings feed into it. The output of the encoder (if any), concatenated with the root word embedding, feeds into the decoder. All recurrent units have hidden layer dimensions of 256, meaning that they transform the input to a vector of dimension 256. Over the decoder layer is a softmax layer that is used to predict the character that must occur at each character position of the target word. In order to maintain a constant word length, we use paddings of '0' characters. All models use categorical cross-entropy as the loss function and the Adam optimizer as reported by Kingma and Ba (2014) for optimization.

3.1 First Submission

3.1.1 Low-sized Dataset

For training the model on the low-sized dataset, we did not use any encoder and we used a simple LSTM with a single layer as the recurrent unit (Figure 1).

3.1.2 Medium-sized Dataset

For training the model on the medium-sized dataset, we used a bidirectional LSTM as the encoder and a simple LSTM with a single layer as the decoder (Figure 2).

3.1.3 High-sized Dataset

For training the model on the high-sized dataset, we used a bidirectional LSTM as the encoder and a simple LSTM with a single layer as the decoder (Figure 2).

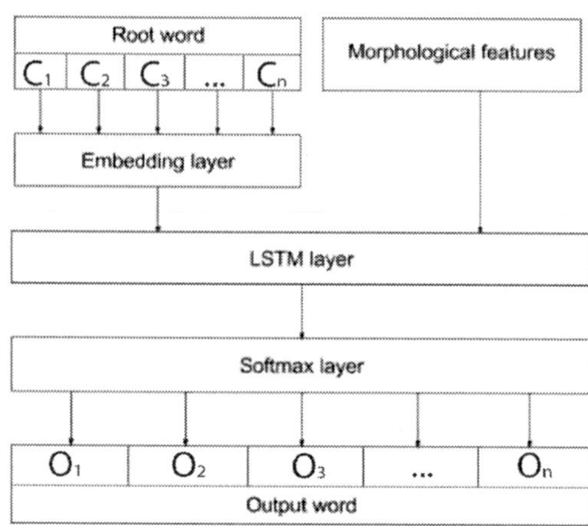

Figure 1: $C_1, .., C_n$ represent characters of the root word while $O_1, .., O_n$ represent characters of the output word

3.2 Second Submission

3.2.1 Low-sized Dataset

For training the model on the low-sized dataset, we did not use any encoder and we used a simple GRU, as reported by Cho et al. (2014), with a single layer as the recurrent unit (Figure 3).

3.2.2 Medium-sized Dataset

For medium-sized dataset, we used different model configurations for different languages. Four different kinds of configurations were used:

1) Bidirectional LSTM as the encoder and a simple LSTM with a single layer as the decoder (Figure 2) 2) Bidirectional GRU as the encoder and a simple GRU with a single layer as the decoder (Figure 4) 3) No encoder and a simple GRU with a single layer as the recurrent unit (Figure 3) 4) Bidirectional GRU as the encoder and a deep GRU (two GRUs stacked one above the other) as the decoder (Figure 5)

The specific configuration used for each language has been listed in Table 1. The configuration numbers indicated in the table are according to those mentioned above.

3.2.3 High-sized Dataset

For high-sized data, we were unable to complete experiments for the second submission due to lack of time. However, we have been able to perform

Configuration	Language List
1	Arabic, Basque, Bengali, Catalan, Georgian, Latin, Quechua, Urdu
2	Kurmanji
3	Bulgarian, Czech, Estonian, Faroese, German, Icelandic, Irish, Latvian, Lithuanian, Norwegian-Bokmal, Persian, Polish, Swedish
4	Albanian, Armenian, Danish, Dutch, English, Finnish, French, Haida, Hebrew, Hindi, Hungarian, Italian, Khaling, Lower-Sorbian, Macedonian, Navajo, Northern-Sami, Norwegian-Nynorsk, Portuguese, Romanian, Russian, Scottish-Gaelic, Serbo-Croatian, Slovak, Slovene, Sorani, Spanish, Turkish, Ukrainian, Welsh

Table 1: Configurations for different languages for medium-sized data for submission-2.

Language	B	S-1(T)	S-2(T)
Norwegian-Bokmal	69.0	52.6	62.7
Danish	59.8	46.1	49.8
Urdu	30.3	31.2	43.7
Hindi	31.0	33.4	40.8
Swedish	54.3	40.6	39.4

Table 2: Accuracies for top-5 languages for low data.

Language	BL	S-1	S-2
Quechua	68.1	93.0	93.0
Bengali	75.0	91.0	91.0
Portuguese	92.9	86.0	89.6
Urdu	86.1	88.0	88.0
Georgian	90.0	87.7	87.7

Table 3: Accuracies for top-5 languages for medium data.

Language	BL	S-1
Basque	6.0	100.0
Welsh	67.0	99.4
Hindi	94.0	99.3
Persian	77.6	98.9
Portuguese	97.4	98.5

Table 4: Accuracies for top-5 languages for high data.

Language	BL	S-1	S-2
Norwegian-Bokmal	0.489	0.71	0.55
Danish	0.669	0.95	0.87
Swedish	0.884	1.08	1.09
Norwegian-Nynorsk	0.928	1.41	1.23
Dutch	0.69	1.42	1.24

Table 5: Levenshtein distances for top-5 languages for low data.

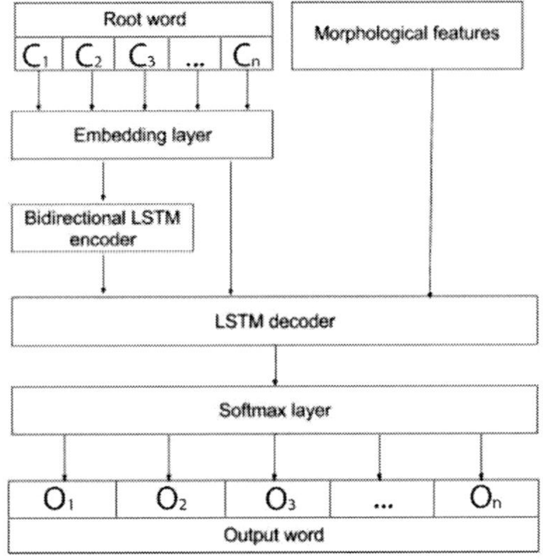

Figure 2: $C_1, .., C_n$ represent characters of the root word while $O_1, .., O_n$ represent characters of the output word

some ablation studies on high-size datasets, which have been discussed in the analysis section.

4 Evaluation

4.1 Results on Test Set

The evaluation results were obtained using the evaluation script and the test set provided by the shared task organizers. Baseline accuracies were also obtained from the baseline model provided. The best five baseline accuracies, accuracies for the first submission and accuracies for the second submission can be found in Table 2, Table 3 and Table 4 for each of the three dataset sizes: low, medium and high respectively. Similar results for Levenshtein distances can be found in Table 5, Table 6 and Table 7. In these tables, BL stands for Baseline, S-1 stands for Submission-1 and S-2 stands for Submission-2.

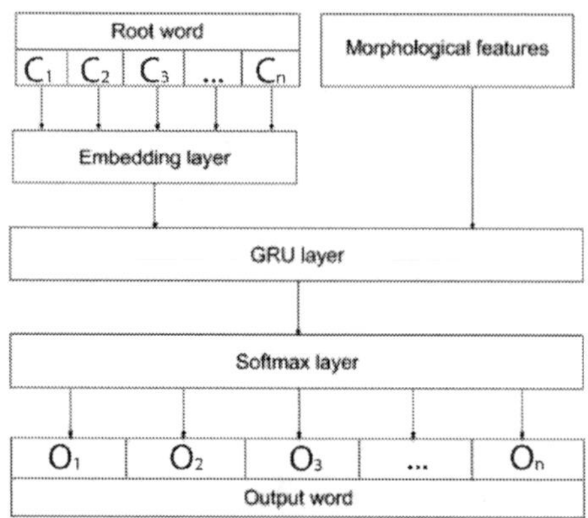

Figure 3: $C_1, .., C_n$ represent characters of the root word while $O_1, .., O_n$ represent characters of the output word

Language	BL	S-1	S-2
Portuguese	0.103	0.21	0.16
Bengali	0.44	0.19	0.19
Quechua	1.706	0.28	0.28
Welsh	1.02	0.4	0.29
Georgian	0.225	0.32	0.32

Table 6: Levenshtein distances for top-5 languages for medium data.

The complete set of accuracies and Levenshtein distances for all languages have been included in Appendix-1 (tables 8 to 10), sorted by accuracies. The main observation from these tables is that languages belonging to the same language family tend to get similar similar results by our system, which is intuitively valid (although there are many exceptions). For example, Romance and Slavic languages tend to occur together in these tables.

However, it is not evident from these tables that morphologically more complex languages should be harder to learn, which seems to be counter-

Language	BL	S-1
Basque	3.32	0.0
Serbo-Croatian	0.36	0.0
Welsh	0.45	0.01
Hindi	0.075	0.02
Persian	0.567	0.02

Table 7: Levenshtein distances for top-5 languages for high data.

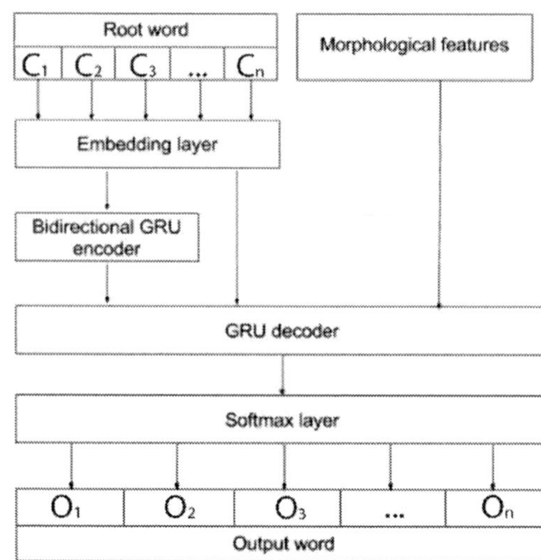

Figure 4: $C_1, .., C_n$ represent characters of the root word while $O_1, .., O_n$ represent characters of the output word

intuitive. For example, Turkish is above French. This may be because of hyperparameters or configurations selected for different languages (which were different, in an attempt to maximize accuracy on the development data).

Figures 6 to 10 show the correlation between accuracy and Levenshtein distance for all three sizes of datasets for submission-1 and for low and medium sizes of datasets for submission-2.

4.2 Ablation Studies

While we were unable to run an exhaustive hyperparameter search due to lack of time, we performed some experiments, where the choice of hyperparameters was guided by intuitions developed from analysis of the dataset and results obtained on smaller subsets of the data. We have presented some key observations from our analysis in the ensuing sub-sections.

4.2.1 Early Stop Patience

We observed that for low-sized datasets, both the models (LSTM as well as GRU based) required that at least 10 epochs be run before early stop, every time no progress is detected on the validation set. Setting this patience to less than 5, resulted in near 0 accuracies for most languages and printing of nonsensical target words. For medium-sized datasets, this patience value can be set to around

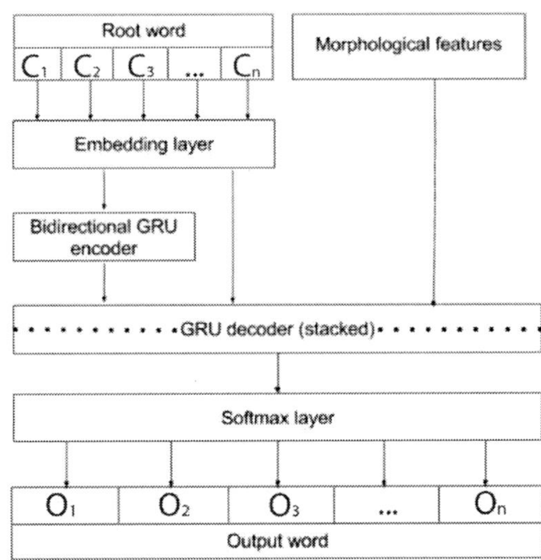

Figure 5: $C_1, .., C_n$ represent characters of the root word while $O_1, .., O_n$ represent characters of the output word

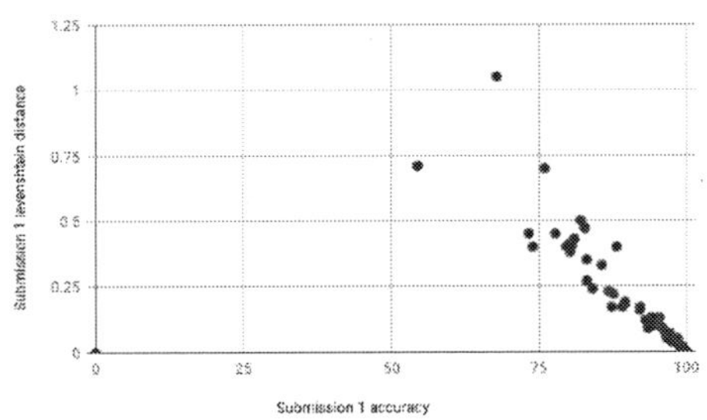

Figure 6: Accuracy vs. Levenshtein Distance for high data (submission-1)

6-8 while for high-sized datasets, it can be set to around 3-4. However, in order to ensure best results, we set our patience value to 10 across all models, training sizes and languages in the final system.

4.2.2 External Feature Categories

In last year's version of the shared task, the morphological features in the dataset were annotated along with the category of each feature. For instance, a sample training feature set from last year is: 'pos=N,def=DEF,case=NOM/ACC/GEN,num=SG'. This year, however, the category of each feature was not provided, i.e., the same example above would appear in this year's format as:

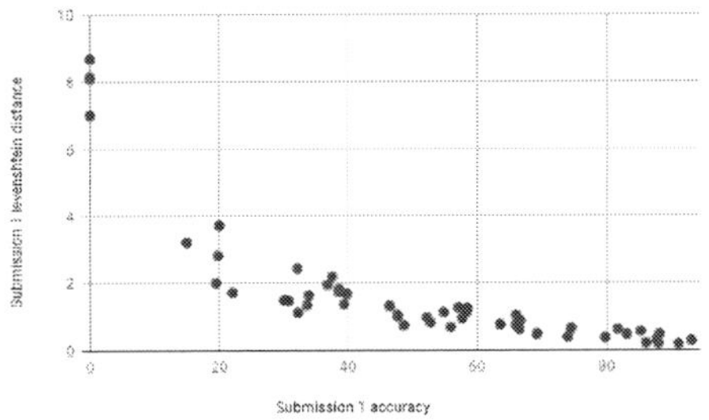

Figure 7: Accuracy vs. Levenshtein Distance for medium data (submission-1)

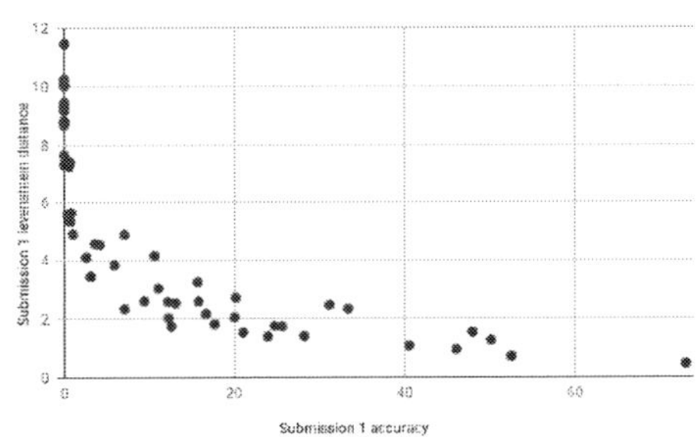

Figure 8: Accuracy vs. Levenshtein Distance for low data (submission-1)

'N,DEF,NOM/ACC/GEN,SG'. Our studies show that while it is conceptually true that the presence of feature categories means exploring a shorter search space, the absence of them does not make a difference to the accuracies obtained for high and medium sized datasets. In the case of low-sized datasets, marginally better accuracies (around 0.5-1%) were obtained when the categories were incorporated into the dataset (this was done manually). However, this might also be the effect of random initialization of parameters.

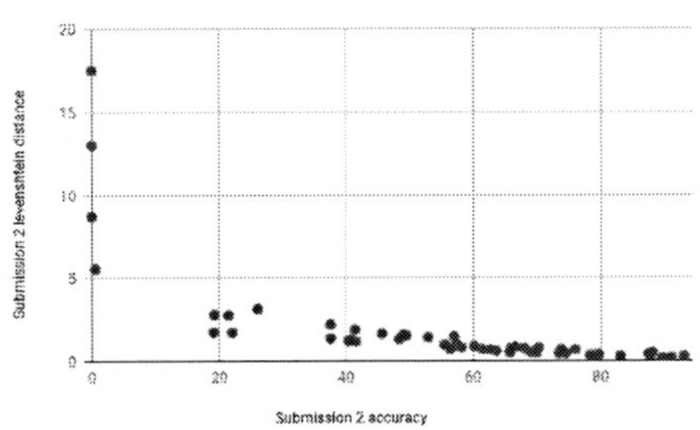

Figure 9: Accuracy vs. Levenshtein Distance for medium data (submission-2)

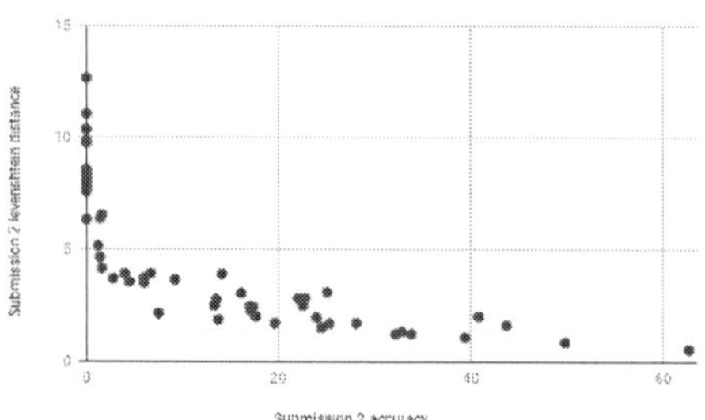

Figure 10: Accuracy vs. Levenshtein Distance for low data (submission-2)

4.2.3 Choice of Recurrent Unit

Simple Recurrent Neural Networks (RNNs) performed the poorest on all sizes of datasets. For low-sized datasets, in almost all cases, using a GRU gave better results than using an LSTM. On an average, the accuracy increased by 2.33% when shifting from LSTM to GRU as the choice of recurrent unit.

In the case of medium-sized datasets, 8 out of 52 languages performed better with an LSTM than a GRU, while the rest showed better performance with a GRU.

4.2.4 Convolutional Layers

We also ran experiments using convolutional layers, in which the root word was convolved and the convolution was concatenated along with the root word and passed to the encoder layer (if any). The rest of the network structure remained the same. For low-sized and medium-sized datasets, adding convolutional layers resulted in the accuracy dropping to near 0. For high-sized datasets, we were unable to finish running the experiments on all languages due to lack of time. However for the few languages on which we performed convolutional ablation studies, it did seem to improve accuracy by around 1.5% on an average.

4.2.5 Stacking Recurrent Units

Deeper models (more than one layer of LSTM/GRU) resulted in drastic accuracy drops for low-sized datasets. For medium-sized datasets, 30 out of 52 languages showed an accuracy improvement upon stacking two GRU layers, while the accuracy drop in the rest 22 was not drastic but appreciable.

5 Conclusions

There are two main conclusions. One is that different configurations of deep neural networks work well for different languages. The second is that deep learning may not be the right approach for low-sized data.

Results for low-size were poor for almost all languages. It is to be noted that we used purely deep learning. If deep learning is augmented with other transduction, rule-based or knowledge-based methods, the results for low-size could perhaps be improved.

For high-sized data, for one language (Basque), we even got an accuracy of 100%. For medium, the highest was 93% and for low, the highest was 69%.

References

Malin Ahlberg, Markus Forsberg, and Mans Hulden. 2014. Semi-supervised learning of morphological paradigms and lexicons. In *Proc. of the 14th Conference of the European Chapter of the Association for Computational Linguistics:Language Technology (Computational Linguistics)*. Gothenburg, Sweden, pages 569–578.

Malin Ahlberg, Markus Forsberg, and Mans Hulden. 2015. Paradigm classification in supervised learning of morphology. In *Proc. of the 2015 Conference of the North American Chapter of the Association for Computational Linguistics: Human Language Technologies*. Denver, Colorado, pages 1024–1029.

Kyunghyun Cho, Bart van Merrienboer, Caglar Gulcehre, Fethi Bougares, Holger Schwenk, and Yoshua Bengio. 2014. Learning phrase representations using rnn encoder-decoder for statistical machine translation. In *Proc. of EMNLP 2014*.

Ryan Cotterell, Christo Kirov, John Walther Géraldine Sylak-Glassman, Ekaterina Vylomova, Patrick Xia, Manaal Faruqui, Sandra Kübler, David Yarowsky, Jason Eisner, and Mans Hulden. 2017. The conll-sigmorphon 2016 shared task: Universal morphological reinflection in 52 languages. In *Proc. of the CoNLL-SIGMORPHON 2017 Shared Task: Universal Morphological Reinflection*. Vancouver, Canada.

Greg Durrett and John DeNero. 2013. Supervised learning of complete morphological paradigms. In *Proc. of the 2013 Conference of the North American Chapter of the Association for Computational Linguistics: Human Language Technologies*. Atlanta, Georgia, pages 1185–1195.

Manaal Faruqui, Yulia Tsvetkov, Graham Neubig, and Chris Dyer. 2016. Morphological inflection generation using character sequence to sequence learning. In *Proc. of NAACL*.

Sepp Hochreiter and Jürgen Schmidhuber. 1997. Long short-term memory. *Neural Comput.* 9(8):1735–1780.

Diederik P. Kingma and Jimmy Ba. 2014. Adam: A method for stochastic optimization. *CoRR* abs/1412.6980.

Acknowledgement

We would like to thank Shaili Jain, Aanchal Chaurasia and Himanshu Karu for their help in our experiments in this shared task.

Appendix-1

In Tables 8 to 10 (on this page and the next), BA stands for baseline accuracy, BLD for baseline Levenshtein Distance, S1A for submission-1 accuracy, S1LD for submission-1 Levenshtein Distance, S2A for submission-2 accuracy and S2LD for submission-2 Levenshtein Distance. All three tables are sorted by submission-1 accuracy, since we have results for all dataset sizes for this submission.

Language	BA	BLD	S1A	S1D
Basque	6	3.32	100	0
Welsh	67	0.45	99.4	0.01
Hindi	94	0.075	99.3	0.02
Persian	77.6	0.567	98.9	0.02
Portuguese	97.4	0.034	98.5	0.03
Quechua	94.7	0.106	98.5	0.05
Bengali	84	0.28	98	0.05
Georgian	94	0.111	97.5	0.04
Khaling	53.8	0.816	97.4	0.04
Catalan	94.2	0.145	97.2	0.07
Hebrew	55.8	0.551	96.7	0.05
Ukrainian	86.3	0.289	96.4	0.07
Haida	69	0.61	96	0.09
Albanian	78.1	0.606	95.4	0.13
Italian	79.9	0.624	95.3	0.1
Estonian	76.2	0.447	94.8	0.11
Macedonian	91.9	0.152	94.6	0.12
Bulgarian	90	0.16	94.3	0.1
English	95	0.09	94.3	0.1
Sorani	64.3	0.696	94.3	0.11
Armenian	89.1	0.215	94	0.12
Swedish	85.4	0.255	94	0.13
Northern-Sami	61.1	0.813	93.6	0.12
Kurmanji	92.2	0.088	93.5	0.09
Lower-Sorbian	86	0.27	93.1	0.12
Dutch	86.8	0.201	92.1	0.16
Latvian	91	0.253	92.1	0.17
Czech	90.4	0.196	89.6	0.19
Slovene	89.8	0.183	89.5	0.18
Danish	89.1	0.184	89.2	0.17
Arabic	47.7	1.481	88.2	0.4
Urdu	95.8	0.065	87.6	0.22
Spanish	90.6	0.206	87.3	0.17
Turkish	72.9	0.772	86.7	0.23
Navajo	38.3	2.105	85.6	0.33
Norwegian-Bokmal	90.6	0.154	84.1	0.24
German	81.2	0.643	83.1	0.35
Lithuanian	64.7	0.466	83.1	0.27
Russian	82	0.61	82.8	0.47
Polish	89.4	0.232	82	0.5
Slovak	85.2	0.248	81	0.43
Finnish	78.5	0.361	80.5	0.4
French	83.6	0.299	80.3	0.38
Hungarian	71.1	0.622	80.2	0.41
Icelandic	76.1	0.466	79.7	0.4
Faroese	74.7	0.553	77.8	0.45
Romanian	80.4	0.647	76	0.7
Norwegian-Nynorsk	78.3	0.383	73.3	0.45
Irish	54.3	1.064	67.9	1.05
Latin	45.6	0.86	54.5	0.71

Table 8: Results for all languages for high data, sorted by submission-1 accuracy

Language	BA	BLD	S1A	S1D	S2A	S2D
Quechua	68.1	1.706	93	0.28	93	0.28
Bengali	75	0.44	91	0.19	91	0.19
Urdu	86.1	0.287	88	0.47	88	0.47
English	90.2	0.159	87.9	0.2	0	8.74
Georgian	90	0.225	87.7	0.32	87.7	0.32
Portuguese	92.9	0.103	86	0.21	89.6	0.16
Hindi	86.6	0.186	85.2	0.56	87.4	0.42
Haida	56	1.24	83	0.47	0	17.48
Kurmanji	88.4	0.234	81.6	0.62	19.2	1.72
Catalan	83.2	0.337	79.7	0.38	79.7	0.38
Turkish	33.1	2.854	74.5	0.65	0	12.97
Welsh	54	1.02	74	0.4	83	0.29
Macedonian	82.3	0.323	69.3	0.5	79.1	0.32
Danish	78.1	0.336	69.2	0.47	0.5	5.53
Spanish	85.4	0.322	66.7	0.89	73.9	0.68
Dutch	71.7	0.403	66.5	0.62	74.6	0.44
Basque	2	5.11	66	0.75	66	0.75
Scottish-Gaelic	52	0.76	66	1.04	76	0.68
French	76.1	0.45	63.6	0.77	69.7	0.61
Italian	73.8	0.743	58.5	1.26	70.3	0.8
Armenian	76.6	0.442	58.4	1.14	68.1	0.78
Latvian	85.1	0.278	57.7	0.95	60.2	0.88
Persian	65.4	1.068	57.1	1.27	57	1.46
Hebrew	40	0.933	55.9	0.69	65.8	0.51
Bulgarian	75	0.445	54.8	1.13	55.5	0.98
Slovak	70.7	0.533	52.8	0.82	63.7	0.6
Khaling	18.4	1.909	52.2	0.97	58.2	0.81
Norwegian-Bokmal	79.8	0.311	48.7	0.74	78.3	0.33
Hungarian	41.7	1.559	47.7	1.05	62.8	0.68
Swedish	73.7	0.452	47.7	1	70	0.49
Sorani	52.8	1.053	46.5	1.31	57.5	0.95
Estonian	62.4	0.779	39.9	1.68	45.7	1.63
Russian	75	0.737	39.4	1.37	66.6	0.83
Serbo-Croatian	65.8	0.884	38.7	1.83	49.5	1.52
Czech	80.7	0.434	38.6	1.74	52.9	1.41
Arabic	40	1.787	37.6	2.2	37.6	2.2
Romanian	70.2	0.848	36.9	1.95	49	1.57
Northern-Sami	35.7	1.445	34	1.64	40.8	1.26
Lithuanian	53	0.714	33.7	1.34	37.6	1.34
Slovene	81.9	0.33	32.3	1.13	73.5	0.45
Albanian	66.1	1.175	32.2	2.44	41.5	1.88
Ukrainian	71.5	0.538	30.8	1.47	61.5	0.7
German	71.5	0.798	30.1	1.49	57.3	0.93
Latin	36.8	1.103	22.1	1.72	22.1	1.72
Irish	44.7	1.457	20.1	3.71	26.1	3.11
Navajo	31.3	2.495	19.9	2.82	19.3	2.78
Polish	75.2	0.533	19.6	2.01	48.4	1.33
Finnish	42.5	1.353	15	3.21	21.5	2.75
Faroese	58.7	0.891	0	8.13	40.4	1.2
Icelandic	61.4	0.763	0	8.09	41.6	1.16
Lower-Sorbian	70.5	0.587	0	7.01	69	0.52
Norwegian-Nynorsk	63.3	0.634	0	8.68	56.4	0.71

Table 9: Results for all languages for medium data, sorted by submission-1 accuracy

Language	BA	BLD	S1A	S1D	S2A	S2D
English	76.2	0.415	73	0.46	0	8.14
Norwegian-Bokmal	69	0.489	52.6	0.71	62.7	0.55
Kurmanji	82.3	0.459	50.2	1.27	0	7.77
Scottish-Gaelic	48	0.68	48	1.54	0	8.32
Danish	59.8	0.669	46.1	0.95	49.8	0.87
Swedish	54.3	0.884	40.6	1.08	39.4	1.09
Hindi	31	3.798	33.4	2.34	40.8	2.02
Urdu	30.3	4.201	31.2	2.48	43.7	1.63
Dutch	53.7	0.69	28.2	1.42	33.8	1.24
German	53.7	1.111	25.6	1.75	0	8.59
Catalan	55.2	1.091	24.7	1.76	25.2	1.71
Norwegian-Nynorsk	50.8	0.928	23.9	1.41	32.1	1.23
Slovene	47.4	0.862	21	1.54	0	7.6
Spanish	58.6	1.229	20.1	2.72	22.5	2.51
Bengali	44	1.49	20	2.05	28	1.72
Lower-Sorbian	34.3	1.264	17.6	1.82	19.6	1.72
Latvian	62.1	0.806	16.6	2.18	17.6	2.02
Russian	42.8	1.311	15.7	2.61	17.3	2.46
Czech	40.8	1.869	15.6	3.27	16.1	3.05
Icelandic	34.2	1.541	13	2.53	13.3	2.5
Slovak	41.9	1.029	12.5	1.75	0	6.32
Ukrainian	40.7	1.001	12.2	2.04	13.7	1.87
Polish	41.9	1.551	12.1	2.59	17.1	2.29
Bulgarian	33.1	1.572	11	3.05	13.5	2.78
Persian	27.3	3.357	10.5	4.17	14.1	3.9
Faroese	30.7	1.585	9.3	2.62	4.5	3.56
Haida	34	6.03	7	4.89	25	3.1
Hebrew	27.9	1.312	7	2.36	7.5	2.15
Romanian	44.1	1.551	5.8	3.85	1.6	4.15
Serbo-Croatian	21.3	2.735	4.1	4.55	9.2	3.66
Estonian	22.6	2.93	3.5	4.58	6.7	3.93
Lithuanian	23.5	1.916	3	3.46	0	8.44
Northern-Sami	15.4	2.359	2.5	4.12	4	3.92
Basque	0	6.46	1	4.91	6	3.73
Arabic	21.5	3.049	0.8	5.66	0	9.76
Quechua	17.2	6.691	0.7	5.34	22.7	2.84
Finnish	16.2	4.217	0.7	7.41	1.6	6.53
Irish	31.8	2.698	0.6	7.26	0	9.89
Navajo	18.4	3.432	0.4	5.61	1.2	5.16
Portuguese	60.3	0.956	0	9.31	32.8	1.35
Macedonian	50	1.006	0	8.68	24.4	1.52
French	63	0.781	0	8.8	23.9	1.96
Armenian	37.8	2.218	0	9.17	22	2.82
Welsh	15	1.6	0	8.77	17	2.47
Latin	16	2.838	0	9.44	6	3.49
Khaling	3.9	4.298	0	7.32	2.8	3.71
Albanian	21.6	4.439	0	10.23	1.4	6.36
Sorani	20.5	3.363	0	7.64	1.4	4.64
Georgian	71.2	0.585	0	8.82	0	7.96
Hungarian	17.2	2.049	0	10.07	0	11.04
Italian	44.9	1.998	0	10.02	0	10.38
Turkish	14.3	4.319	0	11.45	0	12.65

Table 10: Results for all languages for low data, sorted by submission-1 accuracy

If you can't beat them, join them:
the University of Alberta system description

Garrett Nicolai, Bradley Hauer, Mohammad Motallebi, Saeed Najafi, Grzegorz Kondrak

Department of Computing Science
University of Alberta, Edmonton, Canada
`{nicolai,bmhauer,motalleb,snajafi,gkondrak}@ualberta.ca`

Abstract

We describe our approach and experiments in the context of the CoNLL-SIGMORPHON 2017 Shared Task on Universal Morphological Reinflection. We combine a discriminative transduction system with neural models. The results on five languages show that our approach works well in the low-resource setting. We also investigate adaptations designed to handle small training sets.

1 Introduction

In this paper, we describe our system as participants in the CoNLL-SIGMORPHON 2017 Shared Task on Universal Morphological Reinflection (Cotterell et al., 2017). Our focus is on the sub-task of inflection generation under the low-resource scenario, in which the training data is limited to 100 labeled examples, with and without monolingual corpora. Our principal approach follows Nicolai et al. (2015), performing discriminative string transduction with a modified version of the DIRECTL+ program (Jiampojamarn et al., 2008). Taking into account the results of the SIG-MORPHON 2016 Shared Task on Morphological Reinflection (Cotterell et al., 2016), we investigate ways to combine the strengths of DIRECTL+ with those of neural models. In addition, we experiment with various adaptations designed to handle small training sets, such as splitting and reordering morphological tags, and synthetic training data.

We derive inflection models for five languages: English, German, Persian, Polish, and Spanish. These languages display varying degrees of inflectional complexity, but are mostly suffixing, fusional languages. We combine three systems for each language: a discriminative transduction system, an ensemble of neural encoder-decoder models, and the affix-matching baseline provided by the task organizers. We test two methods of system combination: linear combination and an SVM reranker. The results demonstrate that our transduction approach is strongly competitive in the low-resource setting. Further gains can be obtained via tag reordering heuristics and system combination.

2 Methods

We follow Nicolai et al. (2015, 2016) in approaching inflection generation as discriminative string transduction. After aligning source lemmas to target word forms, conversion operations are extracted and applied to transform a lemma-tag sequence into an inflected form. In this section, we describe several novel adaptations to the low-resource setting, as well as the system combination methods.

2.1 String transduction

We perform string transduction with a modified version of DIRECTL+, a tool originally designed for grapheme-to-phoneme conversion.[1] DIRECTL+ is a feature-rich, discriminative character string transducer that searches for a model-optimal sequence of character transformation rules for its input. The core of the engine is a dynamic programming algorithm capable of transducing many consecutive characters in a single operation. Using a structured version of the MIRA algorithm (McDonald et al., 2005), training attempts to assign weights to each feature so that its linear model separates the gold-standard derivation from all others in its search space.

From aligned source-target pairs, our version of DIRECTL+ extracts statistically-supported feature templates: source context, target n-gram, and joint

---

[1] https://github.com/GarrettNicolai/DTL

Proceedings of the CoNLL SIGMORPHON 2017 Shared Task: Universal Morphological Reinflection, pages 79–84,
Vancouver, Canada, August 3–4, 2017. ©2017 Association for Computational Linguistics

n-gram features. Context features conjoin the rule with indicators for all source character n-grams within a fixed window of where the rule is being applied. Target n-grams provide indicators on target character sequences, describing the shape of the target as it is being produced, and may also be conjoined with our source context features. Joint n-grams build indicators on rule sequences, combining source and target context, and memorizing frequently-used rule patterns. We also add an abstract copy feature that corresponds to preserving the source characters unchanged.

We perform source-target pair alignment with a modified version of the M2M aligner (Jiampojamarn et al., 2007). The program applies the Expectation-Maximization algorithm with the objective to maximize the conditional likelihood of its aligned source and target pairs. In order to encourage alignments between identical characters, we modify the aligner to generalize all identity transformations into a single match operation, which corresponds to the transduction copy feature.

2.2 Tag splitting

Training instances in the inflection generation task consist of a lemma and a tag sequence which specifies the inflection slot. Tag sequences consist of smaller units, which we refer to as *subtags*, that determine specific aspects of the inflection. For example, the tag sequence "V;PTCP;PST;FEM;SG" indicates that the target form is a verbal (V) feminine (FEM) singular (SG) past (PST) participle (PTCP).

In the small training data scenario, it is not practical to treat tag sequences as atomic units, as we did in Nicolai et al. (2016), because many tag sequences may be represented by only a single training instance, or not at all. We follow Kann and Schütze (2016) in separating each tag sequence into its component subtags, in order to share information across inflection slots. Our system treats each subtag as an indivisible atomic symbol. An example is shown in Figure 1.

From the linguistic point of view, tag splitting may seem counter-intuitive, as composite inflectional affixes in fusional languages can rarely be separated into individual morphemes. However, on the character level, many affixes share letter substrings across inflection slots. For example, the Spanish word *lavemos* could be analyzed as

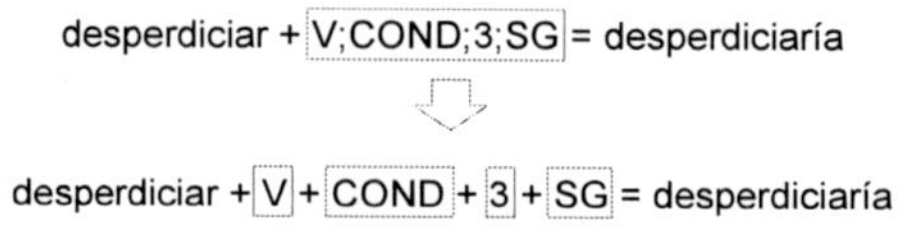

desperdiciar + V;COND;3;SG = desperdiciaría

desperdiciar + V + COND + 3 + SG = desperdiciaría

Figure 1: Splitting a tag into subtags to mitigate data sparsity.

`lav+e+mos`, where the three substrings correspond to the stem, the subjunctive marker, and the first-person ending, respectively. In the single-tag setting, a model must learn the subjunctive inflection for each person; in the split-tag setting, the model can learn the subjunctive modification separately from the personal suffixes.

After splitting the tags, we perform an additional operation of prepending the part-of-speech symbol to each subtag, in order to distinguish between identically named subtags that correspond to different parts of speech (e.g., V:SG vs. N:SG).

2.3 Subtag reordering

Because our alignment and transduction systems are monotonic, tag splitting introduces the issue of subtag ordering. The provided data files are not always consistent in terms of the relative order in which subtags appear in sequence. We enforce the consistency by establishing a global ordering of all subtags in a given language. Our objective is to make as few changes as possible with respect to the original tag sequences. We achieve this by adapting the set ordering algorithm of Hauer and Kondrak (2016), which uses a beam search to minimize the number of subtag swaps within the tag sequences. We then reorder all tag sequences that are inconsistent with the resulting ordering. Our development experiments suggest that the consistent ordering never leads to a decrease in accuracy with respect to the original ordering.

We also investigate ways of optimizing the subtag order. For example, it would make sense for the gender subtag to precede the number subtag in Spanish past participles (e.g., *cortadas*). Since the number of possible orderings is exponential, testing a separate transduction model for each of them is infeasible. Instead, we consider the five orderings with the highest M2M-aligner alignment score on the training set, and select the one that results in the highest accuracy on the development set.

2.4 Particle handling

Some languages, including Spanish, German, and Polish, contain particles that complicate the inflection process. For example, some Spanish verbs contain the reflexive particle *se* (e.g. *levantarse*), which may be detached, inflected, and moved to the front (e.g. *me levanto*). In order to simplify our inflection model, we treat these particles as atomic characters. In this approach, *se* is a single-symbol affix of the lemma which is substituted by *me* and transposed in the output sequence. These particles were identified via language-specific rules, and processed prior to training.

2.5 RNNs and synthetic training data

Recurrent encoder-decoder neural networks (RNNs) can generate a target sequence given an input sequence. Sutskever et al. (2014) introduce this sequence-to-sequence architecture for machine translation. Kann and Schütze (2016) adapt RNNs to perform morphological reinflection by training the models on the character level.

RNNs are sensitive to the amount of training data. In our preliminary experiments, RNNs performed poorly in the low-resource setting. In order to increase the accuracy of the RNNs, we supplement the training data with morphological analyses generated by a DIRECTL+ model trained on the 100 training forms, and applied to randomly-chosen words from an unlabeled corpus using the method of Nicolai and Kondrak (2017). Many of these analyses are incorrect, but overall they provide information to the neural model that enforces inflectional patterns observed in the original training data. This process is shown schematically in Figure 2.

Because RNNs train with a stochastic learning algorithm, they are very dependent upon their initialization method (Goodfellow et al., 2016). In order to improve the stability of the RNNs, we ensemble five distinct models, each initialized with a different random seed. We produce an n-best list from each network, and combine them with equal weighting. This ensembling process is a common technique intended to stabilize neural networks, and lessen the impact of local optima. Our development experiments confirmed that ensembling can reduce the error rate over individual networks by more than 20%, while reducing the variance by half.

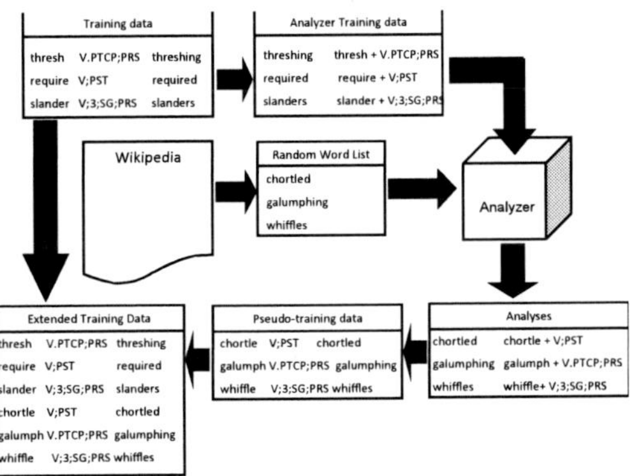

Figure 2: Generation of synthetic training data for RNNs.

2.6 Language models

Transduction models trained on small amounts of data often produce output forms that violate the phonotactic constraints of a language. Character-level language models offer the possibility of reducing the number of implausible outputs. For each language, we produce a list of word types from the first million lines of the provided Wikipedia corpus, and create a 4-gram character language model using the CMU language modeling toolkit.[2] This language model, however, is very noisy, because the corpus contains many hyperlinks and filenames.

We attempt to improve the quality of the language models using the following two methods. The first method is to disregard the corpus, and instead produce a small language model derived exclusively from the target forms in the training data. The second method, which we refer to as affix-matching, is to use only those word types in the corpus that match the affixes seen in training. We identify the affixes by extracting any character sequence in the training set that is aligned to a subtag by M2M-aligner.

2.7 System combination

In an attempt to leverage their unique strengths, we combine DIRECTL+ with a neural network ensemble. Both approaches produce ranked n-best lists. In addition, we include the provided baseline system, which produces a single output form for each input instance. A diagram of our two system combination methods is shown in Figure 3.

---

[2] http://www.speech.cs.cmu.edu/SLM/toolkit.html

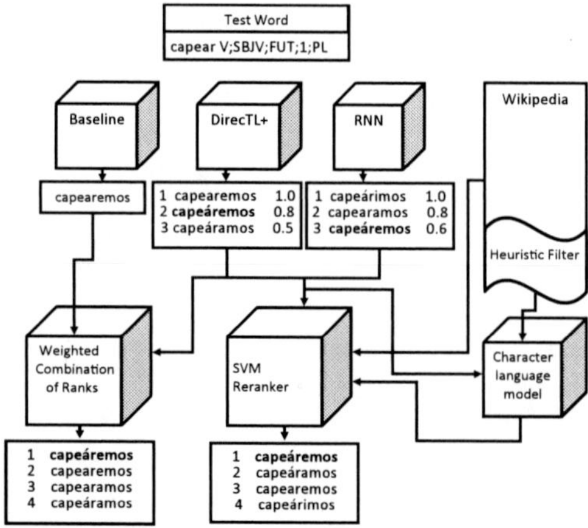

Figure 3: Two methods of system combination. Correct outputs are shown in bold.

The first method is a simple linear combination, which selects the prediction with the highest weighted average of the three ranks. Combining ranks, rather than numerical scores, circumvents issues with scaling, and allows the integration of the baseline, which produces no score.

The second combination method is the reranking of the n-best list produced by DIRECTL+ using other system outputs as features. By framing the reranking of an n-best list as a classification task (Joachims, 2002), we can also leverage other sources of information, such as the language model described in Section 2.6. Our SVM reranker includes four features: (1) the normalized score produced by DIRECTL+, (2) the normalized score produced by the RNN ensemble, (3) a binary indicator of the presence of a prediction in a corpus, and (4) the normalized probability assigned to the prediction by a character language model. The general objective is to promote high-scoring predictions shared by multiple systems that occur in the corpus or look like real words.

3 Experiments

We conduct experiments on five languages: English (EN), German (DE), Persian (FA), Polish (PL), and Spanish (ES). The training data in the low-resource setting of the inflection generation task is limited to 100 instances. The DIRECTL+ models are trained on the subtag sequences made consistent with the method described in Section 2.3. For two languages, we identified best subtag orderings that are different from the initial

orderings; the Spanish ordering was found with the alignment-based method. while the Persian ordering was hand-crafted by a native speaker using linguistic analysis.

Our other systems take advantage of the first one million lines of the Wikipedia dumps from 2017/03/01 provided by the task organizers. Our RNN models are trained on the original training set augmented with 16,000 synthetic instances generated by the DIRECTL+ morphological analyzers, as described in Section 2.5. For the language models that inform our SVM reranker, we use the entire Persian corpus, training data only for English and Polish, and the affix-match method for German and Spanish (Section 2.6). The reranker is trained using 2-fold cross-validation on the training data.

3.1 Development results

Our development results are summarized in Table 1. We see that our DIRECTL+ models (DTL) substantially outperform the official baseline (BL). even without subtag reordering. The only exception is Persian, in which the best ordering strategy (BO) makes a dramatic difference. Further, modest gains are obtained via linear combination (LC) and reranking (RR) of the best individual systems.

	BL	RNN	DTL	BO	LC	RR
EN	76.2	76.3	88.0		88.0	88.0
DE	53.7	43.3	66.6		68.6	68.8
FA	27.3	8.1	23.9	40.8	41.4	40.7
PL	41.9	36.0	48.2		49.3	49.0
ES	58.6	38.9	65.8	68.3	68.3	68.4

Table 1: Results on the development sets.

The most striking outcome is the disappointing performance of the RNN ensembles, which in most cases is well below the baseline, even with the addition of the synthetic data.[3] In this context, it is not surprising that system combination only minimally improves over DIRECTL+ by itself.

Based on the development results, we decided to submit 3 versions for each of the 5 languages (DTL, LC, and RR) plus two runs that correspond to the best subtag ordering (BO) for Spanish and Persian.

---

[3]Without synthetic data, our RNN ensembles completely fail on this task in the low-resource setting.

3.2 Test results

Our results on the test set are shown in Table 2. The numerical tags of the submitted runs are shown in the top row. In the cases of incorrect files being mistakenly submitted, we provide the actual results, which may differ from the official ones. With the exception of Persian, our results are among the best in the low-resource setting.

			01	02	03	04
	BL	RNN	DTL	BO	LC	RR
EN	80.6	78.4	90.6		90.6	90.3
DE	55.3	57.1	66.0		66.8	66.2
FA	24.5	8.1	*19.5*	*38.3*	*39.0*	*37.7*
PL	42.3	28.2	45.2		45.3	45.9
ES	57.1	37.9	64.6	*68.2*	*68.0*	*67.3*

Table 2: Results on the test sets. Runs corrected after the submission deadline are in italics.

The system combination results largely confirm the development experiments. Notably, the simple linear combination, which has no access to language models, performs slightly better on average than the SVM reranker, and seems to be more stable as well. One possible explanation is the necessary subdivision of an already small training set in order to train the reranker, which further reduces the amount of the training data. The linear combination requires no training, but its weights are tuned on a relatively large development set.

3.3 Error analysis

English is characterized by a relatively simple inflectional morphology, with only 5 verbal inflection slots. Most words are regular, and pose no problem even to an inflection model trained on only 100 instances. The errors tend to reflect irregular verbs, as well as orthographic rules, such as the consonant doubling in *splitting*. The current RNN-based systems are unlikely to achieve significantly better results in the low-resource setting.

A number of German errors can be attributed to implicit information that can only be learned by observing multiple forms. For example, the genitive singular suffix differs depending on the gender of the noun. Certain suffixes, such as -in, often indicate the gender of a noun to be feminine. However, the only genitive feminine singular in the training data does not end in -in, and thus, our system fails to correctly predict the genitive singular of *Köchin*.

Persian results seem to be affected by subtag orderings to a greater degree than other languages. The verbal morphology demonstrates some agglutinative properties, where individual subtags may match their own affix. One of the authors handcrafted a subtag ordering, which turned out to be much more effective than the orderings derived by our algorithmic methods. The other sources of difficulty that set Persian apart are the differences between formal and colloquial inflectional forms, which are both represented in the training data, as well as the preponderance of multi-word inflection forms (86% of the test instances), which complicates the task of the language model.

Many Polish outputs are non-words, which we expected to be filtered out by the language model. In many cases, the reranker has no chance to succeed, as none of the models includes the correct form in its top-n list. In other cases, the signal from the language model is not strong enough to overrule the top DIRECTL+ prediction.

An interesting type of error in Spanish are forms that involve orthographically illegal bigrams like ze. DIRECTL+ has a set of bigram features on the target side, but their weights are established on the training set, which is too small to learn such constraints. In the future, we would like to investigate ways to integrate the unlabeled corpus information directly into the DIRECTL+ generation process.

The languages that we consider in this paper are mostly fusional. Another avenue for future work is adapting our approach to other types of languages.

4 Conclusion

Kann and Schütze (2016) show that the neural network models achieve high accuracy on the morphological reinflection task, given a sufficiently large training set. However, the effectiveness of neural models in the low-resource setting is yet to be demonstrated. In this paper, we have described an attempt to combine our string transduction tool with a reimplementation of the neural approach, which turned out to be largely unsuccessful due to the weakness of the latter. Nevertheless, we are satisfied with several novel ideas that we have developed for the shared task, and with the entire learning experience for the members of our team. The overall results confirm the competitiveness of our string transduction approach in the low-resource setting.

Acknowledgments

This research was supported by the Natural Sciences and Engineering Research Council of Canada, Alberta Innovates – Technology Futures, and Alberta Advanced Education.

References

Ryan Cotterell, Christo Kirov, John Sylak-Glassman, Géraldine Walther, Ekaterina Vylomova, Patrick Xia, Manaal Faruqui, Sandra Kübler, David Yarowsky, Jason Eisner, and Mans Hulden. 2017. The CoNLL-SIGMORPHON 2017 shared task: Universal morphological reinflection in 52 languages. In *Proceedings of the CoNLL-SIGMORPHON 2017 Shared Task: Universal Morphological Reinflection*. Association for Computational Linguistics, Vancouver, Canada.

Ryan Cotterell, Christo Kirov, John Sylak-Glassman, David Yarowsky, Jason Eisner, and Mans Hulden. 2016. The SIGMORPHON 2016 shared task—morphological reinflection. In *Proceedings of the 14th SIGMORPHON Workshop on Computational Research in Phonetics, Phonology, and Morphology*. pages 10–22. http://www.aclweb.org/anthology/W16-2002.

Ian Goodfellow, Yoshua Bengio, and Aaron Courville. 2016. *Deep Learning*. MIT Press. http://www.deeplearningbook.org.

Bradley Hauer and Grzegorz Kondrak. 2016. Decoding anagrammed texts written in an unknown language and script. *Transactions of the Association of Computational Linguistics* 4:75–86. http://aclweb.org/anthology/Q16-1006.

Sittichai Jiampojamarn, Colin Cherry, and Grzegorz Kondrak. 2008. Joint processing and discriminative training for letter-to-phoneme conversion. In *ACL*. pages 905–913. http://www.aclweb.org/anthology/P/P08/P08-1103.

Sittichai Jiampojamarn, Grzegorz Kondrak, and Tarek Sherif. 2007. Applying many-to-many alignments and hidden markov models to letter-to-phoneme conversion. In *NAACL-HLT*. pages 372–379. http://www.aclweb.org/anthology/N/N07/N07-1047.

Thorsten Joachims. 2002. Optimizing search engines using clickthrough data. In *Proceedings of the Eighth ACM SIGKDD International Conference on Knowledge Discovery and Data Mining*. ACM, New York, NY, USA, KDD '02, pages 133–142. https://doi.org/10.1145/775047.775067.

Katharina Kann and Hinrich Schütze. 2016. MED: The LMU system for the SIGMORPHON 2016 shared task on morphological reinflection. In *Proceedings of the 14th SIGMORPHON Workshop on Computational Research in Phonetics, Phonology, and Morphology*. pages 62–70. http://www.aclweb.org/anthology/W16-2010.

Ryan McDonald, Koby Crammer, and Fernando Pereira. 2005. Online large-margin training of dependency parsers. In *Proceedings of the 43rd Annual Meeting of the Association for Computational Linguistics (ACL'05)*. Association for Computational Linguistics, pages 91–98. http://aclweb.org/anthology/P05-1012.

Garrett Nicolai, Colin Cherry, and Grzegorz Kondrak. 2015. Inflection generation as discriminative string transduction. In *Proceedings of the 2015 Conference of the North American Chapter of the Association for Computational Linguistics: Human Language Technologies*. Association for Computational Linguistics, pages 922–931. http://aclweb.org/anthology/N15-1093.

Garrett Nicolai, Bradley Hauer, Adam St Arnaud, and Grzegorz Kondrak. 2016. Morphological reinflection via discriminative string transduction. In *Proceedings of the 14th SIGMORPHON Workshop on Computational Research in Phonetics, Phonology, and Morphology*. pages 31–35. http://www.aclweb.org/anthology/W16-2005.

Garrett Nicolai and Grzegorz Kondrak. 2017. Morphological analysis without expert annotation. In *Proceedings of the 15th Conference of the European Chapter of the Association for Computational Linguistics: Volume 2, Short Papers*. Association for Computational Linguistics, Valencia, Spain, pages 211–216. http://www.aclweb.org/anthology/E17-2034.

Ilya Sutskever, Oriol Vinyals, and Quoc V Le. 2014. Sequence to sequence learning with neural networks. In Z. Ghahramani, M. Welling, C. Cortes, N. D. Lawrence, and K. Q. Weinberger, editors, *Advances in Neural Information Processing Systems 27*, Curran Associates, Inc., pages 3104–3112. http://papers.nips.cc/paper/5346-sequence-to-sequence-learning-with-neural-networks.pdf.

Character Sequence-to-Sequence Model with Global Attention for Universal Morphological Reinflection

Qile Zhu, Yanjun Li, Xiaolin Li
Large-scale Intelligent Systems Laboratory
NSF Center for Big Learning
University of Florida
`{valder, yanjun.li}@ufl.edu, andyli@ece.ufl.edu`

Abstract

This paper presents a neural network based approach for the CoNLL-SIGMORPHON-2017 Shared Task 1 on morphological reinflection. We propose an encoder-decoder architecture to model this morphological reinflection problem. For an input word, every character is encoded through a Bi-directional Gated Recurrent Unit (GRU) network. Another GRU network is deployed as a decoder to generate the inflection. We participate in Task 1, which includes 52 languages without using external resources. In each language, three training sets are provided (high, medium, and low respectively represent the amount of training data; Scottish Gaelic only has medium and low), totally 155 training sets. Due to time constraints, we only search for optimized parameters of our model based on the Albanian dataset. The source code of our model is available at https://github.com/valdersoul/conll2017.

1 Introduction

A linguistic paradigm is the complete set of related word forms associated with a given lexeme. Within the paradigm, inflected word forms of lexemes are defined by the requirements of syntactic rules. A word's form reflects syntactic and semantic features that are expressed by the word, such as the conjugations of verbs, and the declensions of nouns (Cotterell et al., 2017). For example, every English count noun has both singular and plural forms, known as the inflected forms of the noun. Different languages have various degrees of inflection. Some can be highly inflected, such as Latin, Greek, Spanish, Biblical Hebrew, and Sanskrit, and some can be weakly inflected, such as English. An example is shown in table 1.

	inflection	tags
release	release	V;NFIN
release	releases	V;3;SG;PRS
release	releasing	V;V.PTCP;PRS
release	released	V;PST
release	released	V;V.PTCP;PST

Table 1: An example of an inflection table from word "release".

The issue of analyzing and generating different morphological forms has received considerable critical attention. Errors in the understanding of morphological forms can seriously harm performance in the machine translation and question answering systems. On the other hand, applying inflection generation as a post-processing step has been shown to be beneficial to reducing the data sparsity when translating morphologically-rich languages (Minkov et al., 2007).

For the CoNLL-SIGMORPHON-2017 Shared Task 1 (Cotterell et al., 2017) on morphological reinflection, given a lemma (the dictionary form of a word) and target morphosyntactic descriptions, a target inflected form is required to be generated across 52 different languages. In each of these languages, there are three training sets (high, medium, and low) representing different amount of training data (Scottish Gaelic only has medium and low).

2 Related Work

Inflection generation can be modeled as string transduction and consists of three major components: (1) Aligning characters forms; (2) Extracting string transformation rules; (3) Applying rules to new root forms (Faruqui et al., 2016).

Recently, end-to-end deep learning approaches achieve state-of-the-art performance across many different datasets. LMU system ranked first in SIGMORPHON shared task (Kann and Schütze,

Proceedings of the CoNLL SIGMORPHON 2017 Shared Task: Universal Morphological Reinflection, pages 85–89,
Vancouver, Canada, August 3–4, 2017. ©2017 Association for Computational Linguistics

2016). It used an encoder-decoder structure with attention mechanism to do translation from root word to its inflection. At the same time, convolutional neural networks have been leveraged to extract features from root words (Ostling, 2016). Faruqui et al. (2016) added language model interpolation into the encoder-decoder structure and trained the neural network in both supervised and semi-supervised settings, and achieved state-of-the-art performance in Spanish verb and Finnish noun and adjective datasets.

Our system leverages a sequence-to-sequence model similar to Faruqui et al. (2016). For each language and training set, we train a separate model using a character-level bidirectional GRU encoder and a single layer GRU decoder with a global attention model (Luong et al., 2015).

3   Model

Our system for this Shared Task 1 is based on an encoder-decoder model proposed by Bahdanau et al. (2014) for neural machine translation. The RNN unit we use in our system is GRU (Cho et al., 2014). Fig. 1 shows our overall architecture.

The GRU reads an input sequence and encodes each input as a fixed length vector h_i, which is computed by

$$z_t = \sigma_g(W_z x_t + U_z h_{t-1} + b_z) \tag{1}$$

$$r_t = \sigma_g(W_r x_t + U_r h_{t-1} + b_r) \tag{2}$$

$$\hat{h}_t = tanh(r_t \circ U h_{t-1} + W_h x_t) \tag{3}$$

$$h_t = (1 - z_t) \circ \hat{h}_t + z_t \circ h_{t-1} \tag{4}$$

To obtain global information of each input, we use a bidirectional GRU and concatenate each hidden state as one vector, $h_i = [\overrightarrow{h}_i; \overleftarrow{h}_i]$ to be the output of encoder's hidden state. For the decoder, we use a single layer GRU. Our model has two input streams, one is the characters and the other is the morphological tags. We only encode the input characters, and make the morphological tags as another input feature to contribute to the outputs. We pad the morphological tagging sequences to the length of the longest tags in the training sets, and feed them into a fully connected network to produce the feature.

In neural machine translation, the input and output sequences are semantically equivalent. However, morphological inflection of a word has different semantics (Faruqui et al., 2016). So we make the encoded input sequence as a part of the input of

decoder together with the morphological tags (including part-of-speech; POS). To get the hidden state of decoder at time step t, we use the previous hidden state h_{t-1}, the decoder input y_{t-1}, the encoder state of the root word e, and the representation of morphological tagging sequence of target form p to compute:

$$h_t = g(h_{t-1}, \{y_{t-1}, e, p\}) \tag{5}$$

where g is the GRU decoder function.

Another difference from machine translation is that our input and output sequence characters may be very similar except the inflections. Take the words *release*, *releasing*, and *released* from English as an example, these three words only differ in the ending characters. To make full use of this similarity, we also add the corresponding input character as a part of the decoder's input, so h_t is computed as

$$h_t = g(h_{t-1}, \{y_{t-1}, x_t, e, p\}) \tag{6}$$

To solve the variable length of input and output sequences, we add paddings as x_t indicating null input.

In the decoding phase, we use a global attention model based on the hidden state of decoder and all the hidden states from the encoder (Luong et al., 2015) to calculate the context vector c_t at time step t as:

$$c_t = \sum_{j=1}^{T_x} \alpha_{tj} h_j \tag{7}$$

where α_{tj} is the attention weights, h_j is the output of each hidden state from the encoder. The weights are computed as

$$score_{tj} = tanh((W_a h_t + b_a)^T \cdot h_j) \tag{8}$$

$$\alpha_{tj} = \frac{exp(score_{tj})}{\sum_i exp(score_{ti})} \tag{9}$$

This context vector can be treated as a fixed representation of what has been read from the source for this time step. We concatenate it with the decoder state h_t and feed it through another fully connected network to produce the output distribution (Fig. 2):

$$P_y = softmax(W[c_t; h_t] + b) \tag{10}$$

The loss for time step t is the negative log likelihood of the target w_t:

$$loss_t = -log(P(w_t)) \tag{11}$$

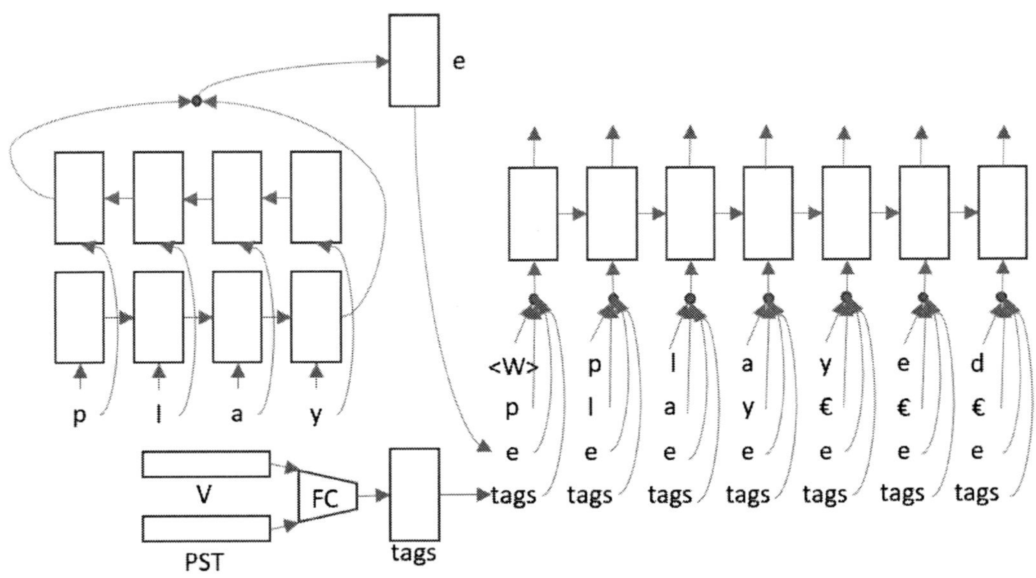

Figure 1: The overall architecture of our approach (without the global attention model and ϵ is the padding character).

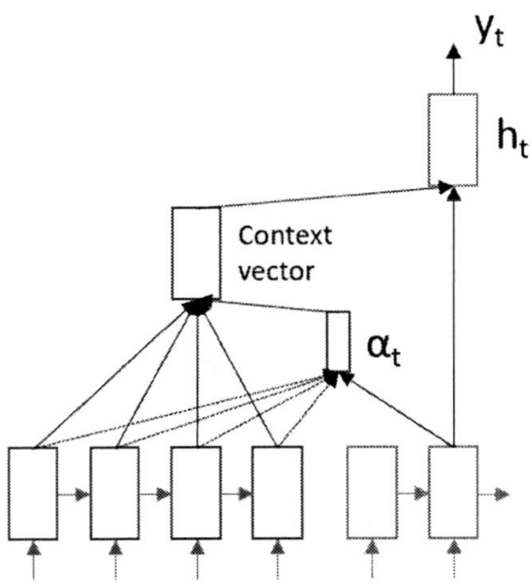

Figure 2: The attention model.

and the overall loss for the whole sequence is computed by:

$$loss = \frac{1}{T} \sum_{t=0}^{T} loss_t \qquad (12)$$

When decoding, we use beam search of size 4 to generate possible output character sequences and rank them by the average probability of characters.

4 Experimental Evaluation

4.1 Data Format

The data provided by Task 1 is the root word and its target morphological tags. We add some special symbols to the character set for every language: "UNK" represents the unknown character, "PAD" is the padding character, "START" denotes the starting of a sequence and "END" represents the ending of a sequence. We only add "START" and "END" to the output sequences. Because the input is fixed, and it is not necessary to make the encoder aware of when the sequence will finish. Although the starting character is not considered in the loss, the ending character is taken into account.

4.2 Training Setting

Due to time limits, we only use the Albanian dataset to do parameter searching. As shown in table 2, we leverage three different groups of parameters based on the variety of the training sets (high/medium/low) for Task 1. We use the same embedding size for characters and morphological tags. The length of morphological tags of a training sample differs from each other, so we pad them to the longest one in each training corpus. We also use a dropout layer after the embedding layer to prevent overfitting.

	Embedding Size	Hidden Size
High	100	200
Medium	100	50
Low	50	20

Table 2: The embedding size and hidden size for three different settings.

	Dropout Rate
High	[0.55, 0.6, 0.65, 0.7, 0.75, 0.8, 0.85]
Medium	[0.4, 0.45, 0.5, 0.55, 0.6, 0.65, 0.7]
Low	[0.3, 0.35, 0.4, 0.45, 0.5, 0.55, 0.6]

Table 3: The dropout rates used for three different settings.

For training, we use Adam algorithm (Kingma and Ba, 2014) and set different minibatch sizes according to various training settings (high/medium/low). Compared to high setting, there are much less training samples in the medium and low. Thus it will take more time to converge if we set the minibatch size too large. We also use early stopping (Caruana et al., 2000) based on the performance of development sets.

4.3 Ensemble

We use different dropout rates to train multiple models in the same training set. Table 3 shows our dropout rates for different models. To select the best result, we use the voting strategy from different models and pick up the answer that appears most likely.

4.4 Results

All the results in this section are evaluated in accuracy for different languages, computed over the official test data. Tables 4, 5, and 6 show the results of our model in different settings.

High			
Top 10		Bottom 10	
Urdu	99.4	French	79.1
Hindi	99.1	Hungarian	78.7
Welsh	98	Serbo Croatian	78.6
Quechua	97.1	Icelandic	78
Haida	97	Romanian	77.3
Khaling	96.6	Faroese	77
Persian	96.3	Finnish	74.4
Basque	96	Irish	73.1
Bengali	96	Navajo	68.5
Estonian	94.8	Latin	54.7

Table 4: Top 10 and bottom 10 performance in the high setting of Task 1.

Medium			
Top 10		Bottom 10	
Bengali	93	Icelandic	57.9
Urdu	90.8	Romanian	57.5
Quechua	90.7	Arabic	55.8
English	88.3	Faroese	52
Hindi	86.8	Northern Sami	50.4
Kurmanji	86.3	Lithuanian	49.2
Portuguese	84.3	Finnish	37.3
Turkish	83.2	Irish	35.4
Haida	81	Latin	30.9
Catalan	80.6	Navajo	28.9

Table 5: Top 10 and bottom 10 performance in the medium setting of Task 1.

Low			
Top 10		Bottom 10	
English	74.7	Finnish	7.6
Norwegian Bokmal	73.6	Latin	7.4
Kurmanji	71.1	Haida	7
Danish	59.7	Northern Sami	4.9
Wwedish	51.7	Albanian	4.5
Urdu	46.9	Khaling	3.2
French	46.2	Arabic	1.5
Norwegian Nynorsk	45.8	Basque	1
Portuguese	44.5	Navajo	0.3
Scottish Gaelic	44	Sorani	0.1

Table 6: Top 10 and bottom 10 performance in the low setting of Task 1.

In each training setting (high/medium/low), we use the same parameters for all languages, instead of optimizing parameters based on different language. It means that our model may not be optimal for some languages, which is the reason why the performance differed a lot from each other. The top languages may have some related properties with Albanian. However, languages like French, Romanian and Latin may not be correctly modeled by our model.

In the low setting of Task 1, we only get 100 training samples for each language. Deep learning may easily overfit and can not generate good results when testing. That is why Haida performs well in high and medium settings while staying at the bottom 10 in the low setting.

5 Conclusion

In this paper, we proposed a character sequence-to-sequence model with global attention to do morphological reinflection and achieved good results in some languages. Due to the time constraint, we only searched for the optimized model based on the Albanian dataset, which may not be suitable for other languages. It might be interesting to add some linguistic features to improve the performance and the generalization of our system.

Acknowledgements

The work presented in this paper is supported in part by National Science Foundation (CNS-1624782) and National Institutes of Health (R01GM110240). The content is solely the responsibility of the authors and does not necessarily represent the official views of the granting agencies.

References

Dzmitry Bahdanau, Kyunghyun Cho, and Yoshua Bengio. 2014. Neural machine translation by jointly learning to align and translate. In *ICLR 2015*.

Rich Caruana, Steve Lawrence, and Lee Giles. 2000. Overfitting in neural nets: Backpropagation, conjugate gradient, and early stopping. In *NIPS*. pages 402–408.

Kyunghyun Cho, Bart van Merrienboer, Caglar Gulcehre, Fethi Bougares, Holger Schwenk, and Yoshua Bengio. 2014. Learning phrase representations using rnn encoder-decoder for statistical machine translation. In *Conference on Empirical Methods in Natural Language Processing (EMNLP 2014)*.

Ryan Cotterell, Christo Kirov, John Walther Géraldine Sylak-Glassman, Ekaterina Vylomova, Patrick Xia, Manaal Faruqui, Sandra Kübler, David Yarowsky, Jason Eisner, and Mans Hulden. 2017. The CoNLL-SIGMORPHON 2017 shared task: Universal morphological reinflection in 52 languages. In *Proceedings of the CoNLL-SIGMORPHON 2017 Shared Task: Universal Morphological Reinflection*. Association for Computational Linguistics, Vancouver, Canada.

Manaal Faruqui, Yulia Tsvetkov, Graham Neubig, and Chris Dyer. 2016. Morphological inflection generation using character sequence to sequence learning. In *Proceedings of NAACL*.

Katharina Kann and Hinrich Schütze. 2016. MED: The LMU system for the sigmorphon 2016 shared task on morphological reinflection. *ACL 2016* page 62.

Diederik P. Kingma and Jimmy Ba. 2014. Adam: A method for stochastic optimization. In *Proceedings of the 3rd International Conference on Learning Representations (ICLR)*.

Minh-Thang Luong, Hieu Pham, and Christopher D Manning. 2015. Effective approaches to attention-based neural machine translation. *arXiv preprint arXiv:1508.04025* .

Einat Minkov, Kristina Toutanova, and Hisami Suzuki. 2007. Generating complex morphology for machine translation. In *ACL*. volume 7, pages 128–135.

Robert Ostling. 2016. Morphological reinflection with convolutional neural networks. *ACL 2016* page 23.

Data Augmentation for Morphological Reinflection

Miikka Silfverberg, Adam Wiemerslage, Ling Liu and Lingshuang Jack Mao

Department of Linguistics
University of Colorado Boulder
`first.last@colorado.edu`

Abstract

This paper presents the submission of the Linguistics Department of the University of Colorado at Boulder for the 2017 CoNLL-SIGMORPHON Shared Task on Universal Morphological Reinflection. The system is implemented as an RNN Encoder-Decoder. It is specifically geared toward a low-resource setting. To this end, it employs data augmentation for counteracting overfitting and a copy symbol for processing characters unseen in the training data. The system is an ensemble of ten models combined using a weighted voting scheme. It delivers substantial improvement in accuracy compared to a non-neural baseline system in presence of varying amounts of training data.

1 Introduction

Natural language processing (NLP) for English is typically word based, that is, words such as **dogs**, **cat's** and **they've** are treated as atomic units. In the case of English, this is a viable approach because lexemes correspond to a handful of inflected forms. However, for languages with more extensive inflectional morphology, the approach fails because one lexeme can be realized by thousands of distinct word forms in the worst case. Therefore, NLP systems for languages with extensive inflectional morphology often need to be able to generate new inflected word forms based on known word forms. This is the task of *morphological reinflection*.

The traditional approach to word form generation is rule-based. For example, finite-state technology has been successfully applied in constructing morphological analyzers and generators for a large variety of languages (Karttunen and Beesley, 2005). Unfortunately, the rule-based approach is labor-intensive and therefore costly. Additionally, coverage can become a problem because systems need to be continually updated with new lexemes. For these reasons, machine learning approaches have recently gained ground.

Results from the 2016 SIGMORPHON Shared Task on Morphological Reinflection (Cotterell et al., 2016) indicate that models based on recurrent neural networks can deliver high accuracies for reinflection. The winning system by Kann and Schütze (2016) achieved an average accuracy in excess of 95% when tested on 10 languages.[1] Based on these results, morphological reinflection could be considered a solved problem. However, the 2016 shared task employed training sets of more than 10,000 word forms for most languages. In a setting with less training data, the reinflection task becomes much more challenging. In an extreme low-resource setting of 100 training examples, a standard RNN Encoder-Decoder system like the one used by Kann and Schütze (2016) will typically perform quite poorly.[2]

This paper documents the submission of the CU Boulder Linguistics Department for the 2017 CoNLL-SIGMORPHON Shared Task on Universal Morphological Reinflection. The task covers 52 languages from different language families with a wide geographical distribution. The task evaluates systems trained on varying amounts of data ranging from 100 to more than 10,000 training examples.

Our system is an RNN Encoder-Decoder (Cho et al., 2014) specifically geared toward a low-resource setting. The system closely resembles the

---

[1] For inflecting lemmas according to a given morphological feature set.

[2] According to experiments performed by the authors, the system employed by Kann and Schütze (2016) delivered accuracies between 0% and 1% for most languages in the shared tasks when using 100 training examples.

Proceedings of the CoNLL SIGMORPHON 2017 Shared Task: Universal Morphological Reinflection, pages 90–99,
Vancouver, Canada, August 3–4, 2017. ©2017 Association for Computational Linguistics

system introduced by Kann and Schütze (2016). However, the novelty of our approach lies in the training procedure. We augment the training data with generated training examples. This is a commonly used technique in image processing but it has been employed to a lesser degree in NLP. Data augmentation counteracts overfitting and allows us to learn reinflection systems using small training sets.

We employ an ensemble of 10 models under a weighted voting scheme. We also implement a mechanism, the copy symbol, which allows the system to copy unseen characters from an input lemma to the resulting word form. This improves accuracy for small training sets. Unfortunately, due to time constraints, we were only able to use the copy symbol in Task 2 of the shared task.

For Task 1 of the shared task, we achieve substantial improvements over a non-neural baseline (Cotterell et al., 2017), even in the low resource setting.

The paper is organized as follows: Section 2 presents related work on morphological reinflection and data augmentation for natural language processing. In Section 3, we describe the shared task and associated data sets. We provide a detailed description of our system in Section 4 and present experiments and results in Section 5. Finally, we provide a discussion of results and conclusions in Section 6.

2 Related Work

Several existing approaches to morphological reinflection are based on traditional structured prediction models. For example, Liu and Mao (2016) and King (2016) use Conditional Random Fields (CRF) and Alegria and Etxeberria (2016) and Nicolai et al. (2016) employ different phoneme-to-grapheme translation systems. Other approaches include learning a morphological analyzer from training data and applying it to reinflect test examples (Taji et al., 2016) and extracting morphological paradigms from the training data which are then applied on test words (Ahlberg et al., 2015; Sorokin, 2016). The results of the 2016 SIGMOR-PHON Shared Task on Morphological Reinflection indicate that none of these approaches can compete with deep learning models. The deep learning systems outperformed all other systems by a wide margin.

The three best performing teams (Kann and

Schütze, 2016; Aharoni et al., 2016; Östling, 2016) in the 2016 SIGMORPHON shared task employed deep learning approaches based on the RNN Encoder-Decoder framework proposed by Cho et al. (2014) and later used for machine translation by Bahdanau et al. (2014). This family of models is intuitively appealing for morphological reinflection because of the obvious parallels between the reinflection and translation tasks. The success of the winning system by Kann and Schütze (2016) highlights the importance of an additional attention mechanism introduced by Bahdanau et al. (2014).

Although the RNN Encoder-Decoder framework has proven to be highly successful in morphological reinflection, an out-of-the-box RNN Encoder-Decoder system performs poorly in presence of small training sets due to overfitting. To alleviate this problem, we employ data augmentation, that is, augmentation of the training set with artificial, generated, training examples. The technique is well known in the field of image processing (Krizhevsky et al., 2012; Chatfield et al., 2014). Even though the technique is used less frequently in NLP, a number of notable approaches do exist. Sennrich et al. (2016) use monolingual target language data to improve the performance of an Encoder-Decoder translation system. They first train a translation system from the target language to the source language, which is used to back-translate target language sentences to source language sentences. The sentence pairs consisting of a translated source sentence and a genuine target sentence are then added to the training data. Other approaches to data augmentation in NLP include substitution of words by synonyms (Fadaee et al., 2017; Zhang and LeCun, 2015) and paraphrasing.

3 Task Description and Data

The shared task consists of two subtasks: (1) generation of word-forms based on a lemma and a set of morphological features (for example, **dog+N+Pl → dogs**), and (2) completion of morphological paradigms given a small number of known forms (see Figure 1).

Systems are evaluated on 52 languages.[3]

---

[3]Albanian, Arabic, Armenian, Basque, Bengali, Bokmal, Bulgarian, Catalan, Czech, Danish, Dutch, English, Estonian, Faroese, Finnish, French, Georgian, German, Haida, Hebrew, Hindi, Hungarian, Icelandic, Irish, Italian, Khaling, Kurmanji, Latin, Latvian, Lithuanian, Lower Sorbian, Mace-

For both subtasks and all languages, there are three data settings, which differ with respect to the size of available training data: *low*, *medium*, and *high*. In Task 1, these span 100, 1,000 and 10,000 examples respectively. However, there is no training set for the high setting for Gaelic. In Task 2, there are 10 example paradigms in the low setting. Most languages have 50 example paradigms in the medium setting (Basque has 16, Haida 21 and Gaelic 23). In the high settings, most languages have 200 example paradigms (Bengali has 86, Urdu 123 and Welsh 133). There is no training set for the high setting in Task 2 for Basque, Haida and Gaelic. All settings use the same development and test sets. Further details concerning the shared task and languages can be found in Cotterell et al. (2017).

lock	–	V V.PTCP PRS
lock	–	V 3 SG PRS
lock	–	V V.PTCP PST
lock	lock	V NFIN
lock	–	V PST

Figure 1: Illustration of Task 2 – the paradigm completion task. The system will fill in missing forms based on the lemma, morphological features and the known word forms.

4 System Description

Our system is an RNN Encoder-Decoder network heavily influenced by Kann and Schütze (2016). The key difference is that our system is trained using augmented data, which substantially improves accuracy given small training sets. We train several models and employ a weighted voting scheme, which improves results upon a baseline majority voting system. Additionally, we use copy symbols which allow the system to process lemmas that contain characters that were missing in the training data.

4.1 RNN Encoder-Decoder with Attention

We use an RNN Encoder-Decoder model with attention proposed by Bahdanau et al. (2014) for machine translation, which was later applied to morphological reinflection by Kann and Schütze (2016). The architecture of our model differs from

donian, Navajo, Northern Sami, Nynorsk, Persian, Polish, Portuguese, Quechua, Romanian, Russian, Gaelic, Serbo-Croatian, Slovak, Slovene, Sorani, Spanish, Swedish, Turkish, Ukrainian, Urdu, and Welsh.

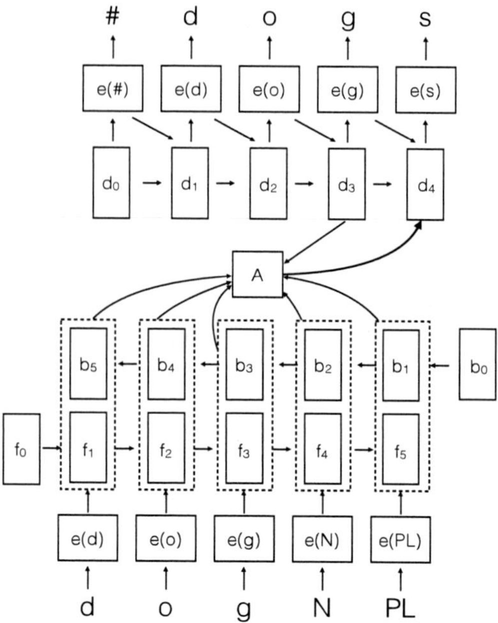

Figure 2: The RNN Encoder-Decoder for morphological reinflection. The system takes a lemma and associated tags as input and produces an output form.

the model proposed by Kann and Schütze (2016) only with regard to minor details.

The high-level intuition of the system is conveyed by Figure 2. The system takes a sequence of lemma characters and morphological features as input (for examples **d, o, g, N, PL**) and produces a sequence of word form characters as output (**d, o, g, s**). It incorporates two encoder LSTMs, which operate on embeddings of input characters and morphological features. One of the encoders consumes the input lemma and features from left to right and the other one consumes them from right to left. This results in two sequences of state vectors, which are translated into a sequence of output characters by a decoder LSTM with an attention mechanism.

More specifically, our system first computes character embeddings $e(\cdot)$ for input characters and features. These embeddings are then encoded into forward state vectors f_i and backward state vectors b_i by a bidirectional LSTM (a combination of a forward and backward LSTM). Each forward and backward state pair $e_i = (f_i, b_i)$ is used as the bidirectional LSTM state at position i. Subsequently, a decoder LSTM generates a sequence of embeddings which is then transformed into output characters by a softmax layer. At each state during decoding, the current state vector of the decoder is computed based on (1) the previous decoder state, (2) the previous output embedding, and (3) all encoder states (f_i, b_i). The simultaneous use of all encoder states is realized by an attention mechanism A which computes a weight $w_{i,j-1}$ for each encoder state e_i given the previous decoder state f_{j-1}. These weights are then normalized into weighting factors $\epsilon_{i,j-1}$ using softmax, that is $\epsilon_{i,j-1} = \exp(w_{i,j-1}) / \sum_{i=1}^{n} \exp(w_{i,j-1})$. The next decoder state f_j is then determined based on the previous decoder state f_{j-1}, the previous output embedding and a weighted average of all encoder states $A(f_{j-1}, e_1, ..., e_n)$ given in Equation 1.

$$A(f_{j-1}, e_1, ..., e_n) = \sum_{i=0}^{n} \epsilon_{i,j-1} e_i \qquad (1)$$

The attention mechanism A is implemented as a feed-forward neural network with one hidden layer and hyperbolic tangent non-linearity (tanh).

For the encoders and the decoder, we use 2-layer LSTMs (Hermans and Schrauwen, 2013) with peephole connections (Gers and Schmidhuber, 2000) and coupled input and forget gates (Greff et al., 2015). We train our system using Stochastic Gradient Descent. Our system is implemented using the Dynet toolkit (Neubig et al., 2017)[4] and our code is freely available.[5]

There are three hyper-parameters in our system: the character embedding dimension, the size of the hidden layer of the LSTM models and the size of the hidden layer of the attention network. We set these to 32 for most languages but use 100 for a number of languages, as explained in Section 5.

4.2 Data Augmentation

In order to counteract overfitting caused by data sparsity in the low and medium data settings of the shared task, we use data augmentation. That is, we generate new training examples from existing training examples.

Our data augmentation technique is based on the observation that in most cases word forms can be split into three parts: an inflectional prefix, a word stem and an inflectional suffix. For example, the English word **fizzling** can be split into **0+fizzl+ing**. In many cases, as in the case

of the lemma **fizzle** and word form **fizzling**, the stem is shared between the lemma and word form. By replacing it, in both the lemma and word form, with another string, we can produce a new training example from an existing one. For instance, we can produce a new example (**sfkekgivlofe+V+PRS+PCP, sfkekgivlofing**) from (**fizzle+V+PRS+PCP, fizzling**) by replacing **fizzl** with **sfkekgivlof**.

Data augmentation requires that we can identify word stems. We approximate this by identifying the longest common continuous substring of the word form and lemma. This strategy can be expected to work well for languages with largely concatenative morphology. In languages with extensive stem changes or stem allomorphy, it can, however, fail.

We experimented with two different techniques for generating new stems:

- Draw each character from a uniform distribution over the set of characters occurring in the training file.

- First, train a language model on the training data. Then, use a sampling-based method to identify a likely character sequence $c_1, ..., c_m$ based on the probability given by the language model to the string $p_1...p_l c_1...c_m s_1...s_n$, where $p_1...p_l$ and $s_1...s_l$ are the inflectional prefix and suffix respectively.

We experimented with two different language models—a simple trigram based model with additive smoothing and a 5-gram model with Witten-Bell smoothing (Witten and Bell, 1991).

The augmented training data generated using the language models seems to be phonotactically superior to the data generated by the uniform distribution over all characters. However, surprisingly, it fails to produce comparable accuracy. Therefore, we only report results for the strings drawn from the uniform distribution.

4.3 Voting

For each language and setting, we train an ensemble of ten models. The most straightforward way of utilizing such an ensemble is *majority voting* which is employed by Kann and Schütze (2016). In majority voting, the output candidate which was generated by the greatest number of models is the final output of the ensemble. In contrast to Kann

---

[4]http://dynet.readthedocs.io/en/latest/index.html
[5]https://github.com/mpsilfve/conll2017

and Schütze (2016), we apply a *weighted voting scheme* to the model ensemble.

In weighted voting, each model receives a weight $w_i \in [0, 1]$. It then uses this weight to vote for the output candidate that it generated. Let S_j be the set of models that generated output candidate c_j. Then the total weight W_j of candidate c_j is given by Equation 2. The candidate with the highest total weight is the output of the ensemble. It is easy to see that setting all model weights $w_i = 1/10$ gives regular majority voting.

$$W_j = \sum_{i \in S_j} w_i \qquad (2)$$

We tune model weights using Gibbs sampling in order to attain improved accuracy. Gibbs sampling is implemented as a function which iteratively adjusts the weight distribution $\{w_1...w_{10}\}$ in order to find weights that result in improved accuracy on the development set. Each adjustment is made by moving some probably mass of size α from a randomly selected weight w_i onto another randomly selected weight w_j as illustrated in Figure 3.[6] The new weight distribution is then accepted or rejected based on the resulting development set accuracy. We initialize the weights using an even distribution, where $w_i = 1/10$.

The development set accuracy a_2 of the adjusted weight distribution is checked against the development set accuracy a_1 of the previous distribution, and the adjusted distribution is accepted with a probability proportional to a_2/a_1. This draws upon the intuition of Gibbs Sampling that an inferior configuration is sometimes accepted in order to account for the non-convex nature of the objective function.

After Gibbs sampling completes, the weight distribution attaining maximal development set accuracy $w_{max} = \{w_1...w_{10}\}$ is returned.

4.4 The Copy Symbol

The decoder of an RNN Encoder-Decoder system can only emit characters that were observed in the training data. This is typically a minor problem when using large training sets because these are likely to contain all frequent orthographic symbols. However, it can become a severe problem when the training set is very small. The problem

---

[6]We test α values in the set $\{.001, .01, .05, .1, .2\}$ and run Gibbs sampling for 10,000 iterations.

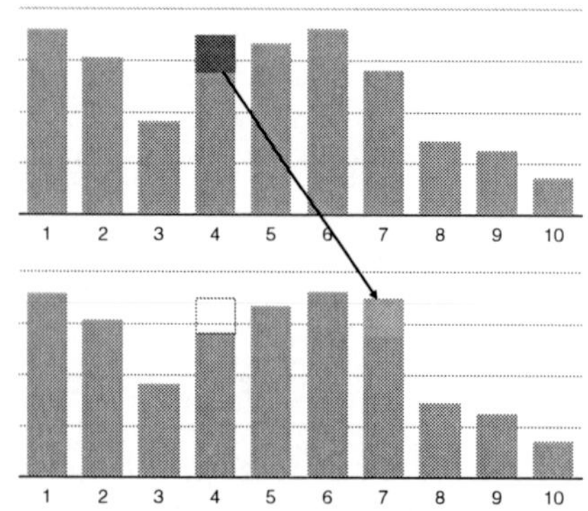

Figure 3: The probability mass is moved from model 4 to model 7 in order to test a new weight distribution

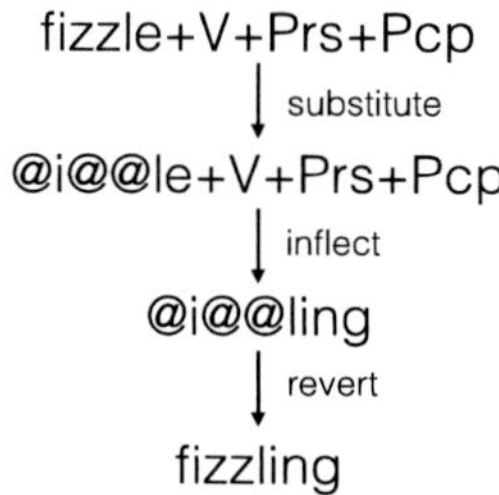

Figure 4: Substitution of unknown characters with copy symbols (@), inflection, and subsequent reversion. In this example, the characters **f** and **z** are missing from the training data.

can have a surprisingly large effect on overall accuracy because reinflection will often fail when even one of the characters in the lemma is unknown to the system.

In order to solve the problem of missing characters, we use a special *copy symbol*. During test time, unknown symbols are substituted by copy symbols and reinflection is performed. After reinflection, each copy symbol is reverted back to the original unknown symbol as shown in Figure 4. Reversion is performed by substituting the ith copy symbol in the output string with the ith unknown symbol in the lemma. If extra copy symbols remain after reversion, they are replaced with the empty string.

Generated stems with copy symbols are added to the training data during data augmentation. This allows the system to learn to copy the symbols from the input lemma to the output word form.

5 Experiments and Results

For Task 1, we train ten models for each language and setting. We then apply weighted voting as explained in Section 4. For most languages, a hidden layer size, embeddings size, and attention layer size of 32 gave reasonable results. For 11 languages, **Faroese, French, German, Haida, Hungarian, Icelandic, Latin, Lithuanian, Navajo, Bokmal**, and **Nynorsk**, we found 32 insufficient, and set hidden layer size, embedding size and attention layer size to 100 instead. Setting the layer size to 100 might improve results for other languages as well. Unfortunately, we did not have enough time to test this.

Data augmentation is used in order to improve accuracy in the low and medium training data settings for Task 1. In the low setting, we add 4900 augmented training examples to the training set, and in the medium data setting, we add 9900 augmented training examples. Given that the original low training data spans 100 and the medium training data spans 1000 examples, this means that the original training data accounts for 2% of the augmented low training set and 10% of the augmented medium training set.

For Task 2, we also use augmented data. In the low setting, we add augmented data until the total size of the training set is 20,000 examples. In the medium and high settings, we add augmented examples until the size of the training set is 25,000. Time constraints prohibited us from using more generated data.

Because of the large variance of the sizes of training sets in Task 2 (for example the low Basque training data spans 4,750 examples, whereas the low English training data spans 50 examples), some languages use substantially more augmented data than other languages. In the high setting, some languages, in fact, draw upon no augmented data at all due to the large size of the training set.

For Task 2, we use the copy symbol as explained in Section 4. This would probably have resulted in improved accuracy for Task 1 as well. Unfortunately, we were unable to run experiments using the copy symbol for Task 1 because of time constraints.

The test results for Task 1 and Task 2 are shown in Table 1. For Task 1, the RNN system achieves average accuracy 45.74% for the low settings, 77.60% for the medium setting and 92.97% for the high setting. All of these figures are substantially greater than the baseline accuracies which are 37.90%, 64.70% and 77.81% for the different settings, respectively.

The RNN system fails to achieve the base-line accuracy for eight languages in the low settings: Dutch (51.90% versus 53.60%), Haida (24.00% versus 32.00%), Hungarian (16.00% versus 21.00%), Kurmanji (79.50% versus 82.80%), Latvian (62.60% versus 64.20%), Lithuanian (19.80% versus 23.30%), Navajo (11.70% versus 19.00%) and Romanian (43.10% versus 44.80%). Additionally, there is one language in the medium setting where the RNN does not achieve the baseline, namely Danish (76.70% versus 78.10%) and another one in the high setting, namely Quechua (90.30 versus 95.40).

For Task2, the RNN system fails to achieve the baseline accuracy for most languages and settings.

6   Discussion and Conclusions

The experiments clearly demonstrate that the system presented in this paper delivers substantial improvements in accuracy over a non-neural baseline for most of the 52 languages in the shared task and in all data settings in Task 1. Due to data augmentation, it improves upon the baseline even in the extreme low resource setting of a mere 100 training examples. In this setting, a conventional RNN system will overfit the training data and, consequently, generalize poorly. Indeed, we found it impossible to train models for the low training data setting without using data augmentation (all models delivered accuracies in the range 0-1%). In Task 1, we did not apply copy symbols due to time constraints. We estimate that this reduces accuracy for the low setting by about 2%.

Even though our system achieves substantial improvements over baseline in Task 1, there are several languages which do not reach the performance of the baseline system in Task 2. One possible cause for this is overfitting due to insufficient variation in the training set. A single lemma occurs multiple times in the Task 2 training data sets because training examples form complete paradigms, which contain dozens (or even hundreds) of word forms. Additionally, the number of unique lemmas in Task 2 training sets is substantially lower than the number of unique lemmas in Task 1 training sets of the same setting. For example, the low setting Task 1 training data for Finnish contains 100 unique lemmas, whereas the Task 2 data set only contains 10 unique lemmas. Finally, time constraints prevented us from training a model ensemble for Task 2. This would probably have improved accuracy for several lan-

| | Task 1 | | | | | | Task 2 | | | | | |
| | Low | | Medium | | High | | Low | | Medium | | High | |
	RNN	Baseline	RNN	Baseline	RNN	Baseline	RNN	Baseline	RNN	Baseline	RNN	Baseline
Albanian	**31.00**	21.10	**89.40**	66.30	**97.60**	78.90	12.19	12.69	82.17	83.87	86.36	89.46
Arabic	**29.50**	21.80	**73.60**	42.10	**90.40**	50.70	**48.78**	42.85	63.01	54.34	**75.54**	55.67
Armenian	**51.30**	35.80	**87.50**	72.70	**96.30**	87.20	75.47	76.18	**86.57**	80.89	**92.04**	86.11
Basque	**4.00**	2.00	**66.00**	2.00	**100.00**	5.00	**1.54**	0.46	**7.35**	4.40	-	-
Bengali	**60.00**	50.00	**95.00**	76.00	**99.00**	81.00	73.38	77.20	19.75	85.86	21.02	87.52
Bulgarian	**57.10**	30.20	**79.90**	72.80	**97.40**	88.80	**35.51**	33.50	49.25	49.58	**78.39**	74.37
Catalan	**66.40**	55.90	**89.50**	84.30	**97.60**	95.50	90.06	94.16	79.69	95.33	90.06	96.03
Czech	**41.90**	39.30	**86.30**	81.50	**92.40**	89.60	16.39	26.56	46.68	56.12	68.36	85.79
Danish	**68.90**	58.40	76.70	78.10	**90.50**	87.80	**53.11**	41.31	64.92	71.15	71.48	75.41
Dutch	51.90	53.60	**74.70**	73.20	**95.60**	87.00	45.57	50.18	60.33	67.71	73.06	78.04
English	**87.80**	80.60	**91.60**	90.90	**95.60**	94.70	**84.40**	76.40	81.60	84.00	84.00	91.60
Estonian	**32.20**	21.50	**74.00**	62.90	**97.10**	78.00	**50.17**	39.81	**61.76**	60.71	**78.29**	77.07
Faroese	**41.20**	30.00	**64.60**	60.60	**85.40**	74.10	46.79	49.78	53.21	59.19	65.62	70.10
Finnish	**15.80**	15.40	**67.20**	43.70	**93.80**	78.20	54.58	60.82	57.14	63.30	**68.78**	68.18
French	**63.00**	61.80	**77.80**	72.50	**88.20**	81.50	84.10	87.09	**85.67**	85.16	89.48	92.63
Georgian	**81.80**	70.50	**92.50**	92.00	**95.40**	93.80	78.86	78.86	81.00	82.42	89.31	90.38
German	**56.60**	54.30	**74.60**	72.10	**89.70**	82.40	68.28	69.83	68.47	70.41	75.82	76.40
Haida	24.00	32.00	**68.00**	56.00	**80.00**	67.00	45.85	47.15	59.63	64.53	-	-
Hebrew	**35.40**	24.70	**77.80**	37.50	**98.50**	54.00	28.83	33.27	**54.89**	42.70	**70.46**	54.09
Hindi	**65.30**	29.10	**93.30**	85.90	**100.00**	93.50	63.62	64.49	61.79	71.11	9.15	96.82
Hungarian	16.00	21.00	**56.20**	42.30	**86.40**	68.50	11.56	17.91	39.68	45.73	**54.95**	53.97
Icelandic	**40.80**	30.30	**67.10**	60.40	**89.10**	76.30	**51.40**	45.79	**56.57**	54.51	63.22	67.36
Irish	**31.30**	30.30	**57.00**	44.00	**88.70**	53.00	26.46	35.95	**44.34**	40.33	**53.28**	47.99
Italian	**56.40**	41.10	**85.90**	71.60	**97.00**	76.90	58.29	66.95	**77.62**	71.86	**89.86**	73.05
Khaling	**10.20**	3.10	**82.90**	17.90	**98.90**	53.70	39.16	42.30	7.53	58.20	**89.64**	79.08
Kurmanji	79.50	82.80	**91.10**	89.10	**94.40**	93.00	65.04	78.43	87.48	88.35	**93.74**	93.39
Latin	**19.30**	16.00	**46.10**	37.60	**80.50**	47.60	22.55	24.45	38.07	39.53	**50.51**	47.58
Latvian	62.60	64.20	**86.00**	85.70	**94.60**	92.10	**74.78**	68.88	**81.99**	79.97	**88.47**	86.46
Lithuanian	19.80	23.30	**58.40**	52.20	**92.90**	64.20	28.19	38.27	61.73	65.92	**64.14**	60.57
Lower Sorbian	**52.30**	33.80	**83.60**	70.80	**95.40**	86.40	27.22	38.20	**71.16**	65.92	80.15	82.27
Macedonian	**59.60**	52.10	**90.40**	83.60	**95.20**	92.10	14.74	42.49	83.12	86.41	**92.56**	89.70
Navajo	11.70	19.00	**40.50**	33.50	**83.10**	37.80	**19.73**	0.00	**32.60**	0.00	**46.30**	0.00
Northern Sami	**18.70**	16.20	**57.00**	37.00	**96.10**	64.00	15.32	15.62	27.93	31.43	**54.61**	45.68
Norwegian Bokmal	**73.80**	67.80	**80.80**	80.70	**91.50**	91.00	**49.06**	41.51	**57.23**	50.94	**70.44**	67.92
Norwegian Nynorsk	**50.50**	49.60	**62.50**	61.10	**87.50**	76.90	39.88	42.33	56.44	60.74	60.74	64.42
Persian	**38.30**	24.50	**86.10**	62.30	**99.50**	79.00	**84.69**	73.42	**94.47**	78.29	25.09	76.44
Polish	**43.70**	41.30	**78.00**	74.00	**90.90**	88.00	55.19	56.72	79.77	80.28	83.10	90.27
Portuguese	**68.40**	63.60	**94.70**	93.40	**99.30**	98.10	89.94	91.71	92.10	95.29	36.23	96.19
Quechua	**30.60**	16.40	**88.20**	70.30	90.30	95.40	79.84	91.33	0.04	91.34	64.45	89.13
Romanian	43.10	44.80	**77.40**	69.40	**85.50**	79.80	10.36	14.20	60.80	61.54	75.00	78.99
Russian	**45.90**	45.60	**81.90**	75.90	**90.80**	85.70	36.66	40.18	82.21	82.98	**87.42**	85.58
Scottish Gaelic	**56.00**	44.00	**74.00**	48.00	-	-	29.96	44.13	**44.53**	41.30	-	-
Serbo-Croatian	**39.20**	18.40	**83.30**	64.50	**92.10**	84.60	27.90	30.07	36.59	36.84	74.40	77.66
Slovak	**46.70**	42.40	**78.00**	72.30	**89.30**	83.30	38.86	44.39	59.00	59.89	68.27	69.16
Slovene	**60.20**	49.00	**86.30**	82.20	**95.80**	88.90	52.15	57.74	**69.15**	67.87	**77.18**	76.48
Sorani	**27.10**	19.30	**71.50**	51.70	**89.10**	63.60	43.53	54.78	67.96	68.30	8.88	72.27
Spanish	**63.60**	57.10	**89.50**	84.70	**96.80**	90.70	79.58	79.75	86.53	92.18	34.63	93.58
Swedish	**60.40**	54.20	**76.30**	75.70	**87.60**	85.40	31.47	43.53	**59.41**	57.35	70.29	78.24
Turkish	**19.70**	14.10	**66.60**	32.90	**96.40**	72.60	**34.89**	20.93	**76.05**	73.26	31.08	85.05
Ukrainian	**50.40**	43.90	**79.70**	72.80	**90.20**	85.40	32.38	43.97	65.71	67.14	72.54	73.97
Urdu	**64.60**	31.70	**96.10**	87.50	**98.30**	96.50	79.56	80.59	67.23	81.02	90.79	95.33
Welsh	**53.00**	22.00	**82.00**	56.00	**98.00**	69.00	**82.72**	51.67	79.05	82.80	81.66	85.25
AVG	**45.74**	37.90	**77.60**	64.70	**92.97**	77.81	47.90	49.63	60.94	65.20	65.11	73.11

Table 1: Results from Task 1 and Task 2. RNN refers to the RNN Encoder-Decoder with data augmentation and weighted voting presented in Section 4. Baseline refers to the non-neural baseline system presented in Cotterell et al. (2017). RNN accuracies which are greater than the baseline accuracy are shown in boldface.

guages.

The overall performance in Task 1 varies greatly between languages especially in the low and medium data settings. For example, the accuracy for Basque in the low setting is 4.00%, whereas the accuracy for Danish is 68.90%. One explaining factor may be the number of distinct morphological feature sets in the test data.

We found that there is a link between low accuracy and the number of distinct morphological feature sets occurring in the test data in the low training data setting, as is shown in Figure 5. A larger number of distinct feature sets correlates with lower accuracy. No such trend exists for the high or medium setting. This can partly be explained by the number of unseen morphological feature sets.

In languages with many different morphological feature sets, the test data may contain a large amount of morphological feature sets which were unseen in the low training data spanning 100 examples. This seems to adversely impact accuracy even though the Encoder LSTM does not treat morphological feature sets as atomic units (for example "V;PRS;PCP") but instead splits them into separate symbols ("V", "PRS", "PCP"). This conclusion is supported by the results for Basque: for the low setting, the system achieves accuracy 4%, whereas it achieves accuracy 100% for the high training data setting. A mere 8% of the morphological feature sets in the Basque test data occur in the low training data of 100 examples. However, 99% of them occur in the high training data containing 10,000 examples.

The present work employs a very naïve form of data augmentation. A new training example is created from an existing one by replacing the longest common substring of the stem and word form with a sequence of random characters from the training data. We also tried to use more sophisticated language models for generating the examples. Interestingly, this failed to bring improvements. In fact, it resulted in reduced performance. This may be due to overfitting because the generated strings too closely resemble existing training examples.

For eight languages (Dutch, Haida, Hungarian, Kurmanji, Latvian, Lithuanian, Navajo and Romanian), the RNN system failed to reach the baseline in the low training data setting. Except for Haida and Navajo, the difference between the baseline and the RNN system is, quite small ($\leq 5\%$). The

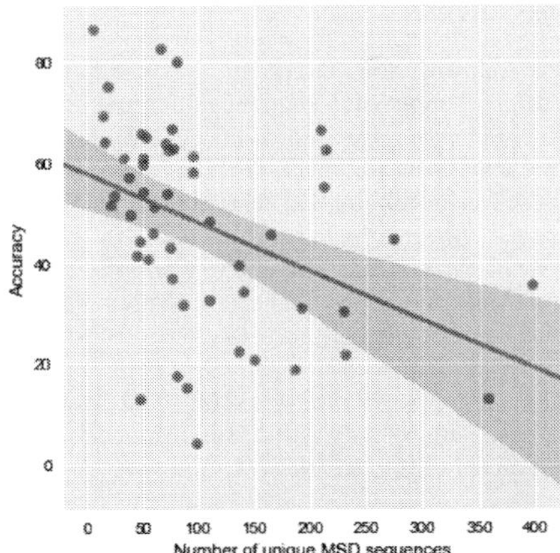

Figure 5: Low accuracy on the dev data (for the low setting in Task 1) trends downwards as the number of unique MSD combinations in a language's dev data increases. The red regression line shows the slope of this trend, with a 95% confidence interval represented as the translucent shadow around it.

Haida test set is very small (100 examples). Therefore, random fluctuations play a big role in the accuracy. For Navajo, the difference of 7.3%-points is substantial. We conjecture that this happens because data augmentation is not effective in the case of Navajo due to the short average length of the longest common substrings (LCS) of Navajo lemmas and word forms. For example, the average word lengths in the low training data for Navajo and Danish are nearly the same: 9.9 and 9.6 characters, respectively. However, the average length of the LCS of lemmas and word forms is a mere 2.9 characters for Navajo but it is 6.7 characters for Danish. Therefore, generated examples for Navajo will contain long substrings that occur in the original training data which may lead to overfitting.

In conclusion, we have demonstrated that an RNN Encoder-Decoder system can be applied to morphological reinflection even in a low resource setting. We achieve substantial improvements over a non-neural baseline in Task 1. However, the system performs poorly in Task 2 due to overfitting. Improving performance for Task 2 remains future work at the present time.

Acknowledgments

The third author has been partly sponsored by DARPA I20 in the program Low Resource Languages for Emergent Incidents (LORELEI) issued by DARPA/I20 under Contract No. HR0011-15-C-0113.

References

Roee Aharoni, Yoav Goldberg, and Yonatan Belinkov. 2016. Improving sequence to sequence learning for morphological inflection generation: The BIU-MIT systems for the SIGMORPHON 2016 shared task for morphological reinflection. In *Proceedings of the 14th SIGMORPHON Workshop on Computational Research in Phonetics, Phonology, and Morphology*. Association for Computational Linguistics, Berlin, Germany.

Malin Ahlberg, Markus Forsberg, and Mans Hulden. 2015. Paradigm classification in supervised learning of morphology. In *HLT-NAACL*.

Iñaki Alegria and Izaskun Etxeberria. 2016. EHU at the SIGMORPHON 2016 shared task. a simple proposal: Grapheme-to-phoneme for inflection. In *Proceedings of the 14th SIGMORPHON Workshop on Computational Research in Phonetics, Phonology, and Morphology*. Association for Computational Linguistics, Berlin, Germany.

Dzmitry Bahdanau, Kyunghyun Cho, and Yoshua Bengio. 2014. Neural machine translation by jointly learning to align and translate. In *ICLR 2015*.

Ken Chatfield, Karen Simonyan, Andrea Vedaldi, and Andrew Zisserman. 2014. Return of the devil in the details: Delving deep into convolutional nets. *arXiv preprint arXiv:1405.3531*.

Kyunghyun Cho, Bart Van Merriënboer, Caglar Gulcehre, Dzmitry Bahdanau, Fethi Bougares, Holger Schwenk, and Yoshua Bengio. 2014. Learning phrase representations using RNN encoder-decoder for statistical machine translation. *arXiv preprint arXiv:1406.1078*.

Ryan Cotterell, Christo Kirov, John Sylak-Glassman, Géraldine Walther, Ekaterina Vylomova, Patrick Xia, Manaal Faruqui, Sandra Kübler, David Yarowsky, Jason Eisner, and Mans Hulden. 2017. The CoNLL-SIGMORPHON 2017 shared task: Universal morphological reinflection in 52 languages. In *Proceedings of the CoNLL-SIGMORPHON 2017 Shared Task: Universal Morphological Reinflection*. Association for Computational Linguistics, Vancouver, Canada.

Ryan Cotterell, Christo Kirov, John Sylak-Glassman, David Yarowsky, Jason Eisner, and Mans Hulden. 2016. The SIGMORPHON 2016 shared task: Morphological reinflection. In *Proceedings of the 14th SIGMORPHON Workshop on Computational Research in Phonetics, Phonology, and Morphology*. Association for Computational Linguistics, Berlin, Germany.

Marzieh Fadaee, Arianna Bisazza, and Christof Monz. 2017. Data augmentation for low-resource neural machine translation. *arXiv preprint arXiv:1705.00440*.

Felix A. Gers and Juergen Schmidhuber. 2000. Recurrent nets that time and count. Technical report. *Istituto Dalle Molle Di Studi Sull Intelligenza Artificiale*.

Klaus Greff, Rupesh Kumar Srivastava, Jan Koutník, Bas R. Steunebrink, and Jürgen Schmidhuber. 2015. LSTM: A search space odyssey. *CoRR* abs/1503.04069.

Michiel Hermans and Benjamin Schrauwen. 2013. Training and analyzing deep recurrent neural networks. In *Proceedings of the 26th International Conference on Neural Information Processing Systems*. Curran Associates Inc., USA, NIPS'13, pages 190–198.

Katharina Kann and Hinrich Schütze. 2016. MED: The LMU system for the SIGMORPHON 2016 shared task on morphological reinflection. In *Proceedings of the 14th SIGMORPHON Workshop on Computational Research in Phonetics, Phonology, and Morphology*. Association for Computational Linguistics, Berlin, Germany.

Lauri Karttunen and Kenneth R Beesley. 2005. Twenty-five years of finite-state morphology. *Inquiries Into Words, a Festschrift for Kimmo Koskenniemi on his 60th Birthday* pages 71–83.

David King. 2016. Evaluating sequence alignment for learning inflectional morphology. In *Proceedings of the 14th SIGMORPHON Workshop on Computational Research in Phonetics, Phonology, and Morphology*. Association for Computational Linguistics, Berlin, Germany.

Alex Krizhevsky, Ilya Sutskever, and Geoffrey E. Hinton. 2012. ImageNet classification with deep convolutional neural networks. In *Proceedings of the 25th International Conference on Neural Information Processing Systems*. Curran Associates Inc., USA, NIPS'12, pages 1097–1105.

Ling Liu and Lingshuang Jack Mao. 2016. Morphological reinflection with conditional random fields and unsupervised features. In *Proceedings of the 14th SIGMORPHON Workshop on Computational Research in Phonetics, Phonology, and Morphology*. Association for Computational Linguistics, Berlin, Germany.

Graham Neubig, Chris Dyer, Yoav Goldberg, Austin Matthews, Waleed Ammar, Antonios Anastasopoulos, Miguel Ballesteros, David Chiang, Daniel Clothiaux, Trevor Cohn, Kevin Duh, Manaal Faruqui, Cynthia Gan, Dan Garrette, Yangfeng Ji, Lingpeng Kong, Adhiguna Kuncoro, Gaurav Kumar, Chaitanya Malaviya, Paul Michel, Yusuke Oda, Matthew Richardson, Naomi Saphra, Swabha Swayamdipta, and Pengcheng Yin. 2017. DyNet: The dynamic neural network toolkit. *arXiv preprint arXiv:1701.03980*.

Garrett Nicolai, Bradley Hauer, Adam St Arnaud, and Grzegorz Kondrak. 2016. Morphological reinflection via discriminative string transduction. In *Proceedings of the 14th SIGMORPHON Workshop on Computational Research in Phonetics, Phonology, and Morphology*. Association for Computational Linguistics, Berlin, Germany.

Robert Östling. 2016. Morphological reinflection with convolutional neural networks. In *Proceedings of the 14th SIGMORPHON Workshop on Computational Research in Phonetics, Phonology, and Morphology*. Association for Computational Linguistics, Berlin, Germany.

Rico Sennrich, Barry Haddow, and Alexandra Birch. 2016. Improving neural machine translation models with monolingual data. In *Proceedings of the 54th Annual Meeting of the Association for Computational Linguistics, ACL 2016, August 7-12, 2016, Berlin, Germany, Volume 1: Long Papers*.

Alexey Sorokin. 2016. Using longest common subsequence and character models to predict word forms. In *Proceedings of the 14th SIGMORPHON Workshop on Computational Research in Phonetics, Phonology, and Morphology*. Association for Computational Linguistics, Berlin, Germany.

Dima Taji, Ramy Eskander, Nizar Habash, and Owen Rambow. 2016. The Columbia University - New York University Abu Dhabi SIGMORPHON 2016 morphological reinflection shared task submission. In *Proceedings of the 14th SIGMORPHON Workshop on Computational Research in Phonetics, Phonology, and Morphology*. Association for Computational Linguistics, Berlin, Germany.

Ian H. Witten and Timothy C. Bell. 1991. The zero-frequency problem: estimating the probabilities of novel events in adaptive text compression. *Information Theory, IEEE Transactions on* (4):1085–1094.

Xiang Zhang and Yann LeCun. 2015. Text understanding from scratch. *arXiv preprint arXiv:1502.01710*.

Seq2seq for Morphological Reinflection: When Deep Learning Fails

Hajime Senuma
University of Tokyo
National Institute of Informatics
senuma@nii.ac.jp

Akiko Aizawa
National Institute of Informatics
University of Tokyo
aizawa@nii.ac.jp

Abstract

Recent studies showed that the sequence-to-sequence (seq2seq) model is a promising approach for morphological reinflection. At the CoNLL-SIGMORPHON 2017 Shared Task for universal morphological reinflection, we basically followed the approach with some minor variations. The results were remarkable in a certain sense. In high-resource scenarios our system achieved 91.46% accuracy (only modestly behind the best system by 3.85%), and in medium-resource scenarios the performance was 65.06% (almost the same as baseline). In low-resource settings, however, the performance was only 1.58%, ranking the worst among submitted systems. In this paper, we present system description and error analysis for the results.

1 Introduction

Processing morphological inflection is a fundamental task for the analysis and generation of natural languages and serves as a building block for many tasks such as machine translation, text analytics, and question answering. Whereas English is morphologically simple and abundant for resources, other languages are often morphologically rich and resource-poor, resulting in severe performance degradation (Tsarfaty et al., 2010). To tackle the issue, the CoNLL-SIGMORPHON 2017 Shared Task hosted a shared task on universal morphological reinflection (Cotterell et al., 2017), in which participants must solve the task for 52 languages and for high-, medium-, and low-resource settings.

Although the shared task comprised two subtasks, we participated only in Task 1. Each data set in Task 1 consists of three columns. The first and second column provides a *lemma* and a *target form*, respectively. The third column lists morphosyntactic descriptions (MSDs), or the features for a target form, where each feature is taken from a universal set of morphological features called UniMorph (Sylak-Glassman et al., 2015). The purpose of the task is to construct a system which can estimate a target form from a lemma and its MSDs. For each of 52 languages, participants cope with the problem under varying sizes of training data (10,000 for high, 1,000 for medium, and 100 for low). The use of external resources are not permitted in the main track, but allowed as a separate track.

To solve the problem, we basically followed Kann and Schütze (2016a), the winner of the Shared Task in the previous year (Cotterell et al., 2016). Unfortunately, our approach experienced severe difficulties in low-resource settings. In high-resource settings, our system achieved 91.46% accuracy, the 12th among the 20 systems. In medium-resource setting, the performance was 65.06%, almost the same as that of the baseline (64.7%). And in low-resource setting, the system achieved only 1.58%. The cause of the problem is that if we decrease the number of examples, at some point, the accuracy of deep learning-based approach drastically drops. For our system, the point is somewhere between 110 and 150; at 150, we still retain the accuracy around 36% but at 110, the result becomes nonsensical (see Section 5).

This paper is organized as follows. In Section 2, we briefly summarize related researches in this field. In Section 3, we describe the system description of our approach. In Section 4, we present environmental settings used in our experiments and the main results of our work. In Section 5, we discuss the error analysis of our results.

Proceedings of the CoNLL SIGMORPHON 2017 Shared Task: Universal Morphological Reinflection, pages 100–109,
Vancouver, Canada, August 3–4, 2017. ©2017 Association for Computational Linguistics

2 Related Work

Morphological inflection has a long-tradition in natural language processing (NLP). The earliest studies used finite-state transducers (Karttunen, 1983; Koskenniemi, 1984; Kaplan and Kay, 1994). The advantages of the approach are that rules are often hand-crafted and thus suitable in low-resource settings and that it is relatively easy and direct to incorporate the linguistic knowledge of specialists. On the other hand, manual crafting of such rules is often expensive and usually language specialists are not easily available. General purpose open-source libraries for this approach include OpenFST (Allauzen et al., 2007) and Foma (Hulden, 2009). In addition, there are several language-specific systems such as TRMorph for Turkish (Çöltekin, 2010) and HornMorpho for the languages of the Horn of Africa (Gasser, 2011).

In this decade, machine learning for morphological inflection became a hot topic. One direction is to exploit the paradigmatic nature of inflection (Durrett and DeNero, 2013; Ahlberg et al., 2015). For example, Durrett and DeNero (2013) proposed a multi-step supervised learning approach. The first phase tries to extract transformational rules from data sets and consists of three sub-steps: the alignment of words in training data, merging spans across the resulting alignments, and rule extraction from these intermediary information. And then the second phase tries to learn the position and the type of transformation application. The advantage of this approach is that we can obtain concrete paradigms of inflection.

Another recent innovation in this field (Faruqui et al., 2016; Kann and Schütze, 2016b) is the use of the sequence-to-sequence (seq2seq) model (Sutskever et al., 2014) (also known as the encoder-decoder model (Cho et al., 2014)). Notably, Kann and Schütze (2016a) applied the attention-based version of seq2seq models (Bahdanau et al., 2015) to the SIGMORPHON 2016 Shared Task (Cotterell et al., 2016) and showed that their system can learn morphological reinflection even for extremely morphologically rich languages such as Maltese and became the winner of the year.

3 System Description

Our implementation is based on the system of Kann and Schütze (2016a). We will release the implementation under a BSD lincense on the GitHub account of the first author [1].

3.1 Basic architecture

3.1.1 Seq2seq model

Fig. 1 shows the basic archicture of our system. The figure depicts how an input tuple (`dun`, `V;PST`) is converted to an output string `dunned`.

In its basic form, the seq2seq model consists of two recurrent neural networks (RNNs), the encoder and the decoder. After the encoder is feeded with a sequence of input symbols, the hidden layer of the encoder is used as an input to the decoder, and finally the decoder emits a sequence of output symbols. In reality, RNNs are substituted by gated recurrent units (GRUs), inputs are encoded as bidirectional sequences, and the decoder also gets an attentional information from a context vector (Bahdanau et al., 2015).

Given an input example which consists of a lemma and a set of features, a sequence of symbols for the system is represented as $\{S_{Start}f^+x^+S_{End} \mid f \in \Sigma_\phi, x \in \Sigma_L\}$, where S_{Start} and S_{End} represents a start symbol and an ending symbol respectively, Σ_ϕ a set of features, Σ_L a set of symbols in a language, and $+$ the repetition of one or more symbols. To improve the predictive efficiency, f^+ should be sorted by some criteria (Kann and Schütze, 2016a), such as lexicographic order (in Fig. 1, `V;PST` is sorted as $S_{PST}S_V$). Likewise, an output string is encoded as $\{S_{Start}x^+S_{End} \mid f \in x \in \Sigma_L\}$.

For more details, see Bahdanau et al. (2015) and Kann and Schütze (2016a).

3.1.2 Loss function

Following Faruqui et al. (2016), we used the negative log-likelihood of the output character sequence for our loss function.

3.2 Differences from previous studies

In this section, we describe the differences between our work and previous researches.

3.2.1 Dimension

We used 300 for symbol embeddings, 200 for hidden layers, and 200 for context (attention) vectors, while Kann and Schütze (2016a) used 300 for symbol embeddings and 100 for hidden layers (the dimension of context vectors was not described). We increased the size of hidden layers because at

---

[1] `https://github.com/hajimes/` `conll2017-system`

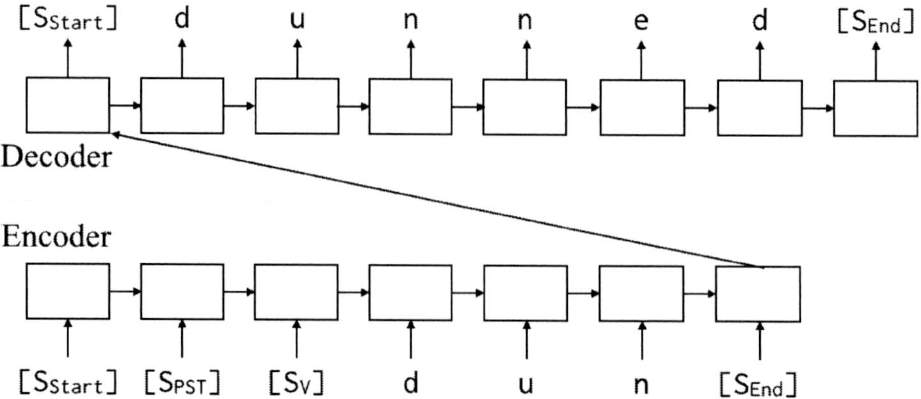

Figure 1: The basic architecture of Kann and Schütze (2016a)'s seq2seq model for morphological reinflection.

least in this task we found that 100 for hidden layers was harmful to predictive performance.

3.2.2 Implementation

We implemented the attention-based version of an encoder-decoder model from scratch with Theano (The Theano Development Team, 2016), while Kann and Schütze (2016a) reused Bahdanau et al. (2015)'s original implementation.

3.2.3 Initialization

We used the Glorot uniform (Glorot and Bengio, 2010) for matrix initialization, while Kann and Schütze (2016a) used the identity matrix.

3.2.4 Optimization / regularization

Faruqui et al. (2016) used AdaDelta (Zeiler, 2012) with L_2 regularization. Kann and Schütze (2016a) also used the same optimizer.

We used the AdaMax optimization algorithm (Kingma and Ba, 2015) with recommended hyperparameters in the paper. The method is a combination of Adam optimization and L_∞ regularization; that is, the bigger the maximum of parameters is, the bigger the penalty for the model is. The reason we used AdaMax is that the method is known for fast convergence. Furthermore, the authors provided recommended hyperparameters, resulting in less hyperparameter calibration.

3.2.5 Iteration number

While Kann and Schütze (2016a) simply used 20 training iterations for any language, we continued training until they are converged: four consecutive no gains in accuracy for development data where

the maximum is 40 iterations (for some languages, we hand-tuned the number of training iterations so this number may vary).

4 Experimental Results

4.1 Environmental settings

We used Amazon Web Services (AWS) and ran our system on an Amazon EC2 `p2.16xlarge` instance, Ubuntu with CUDA 8.0 and cuDNN 6.0. The instance was equipped with the eight cards of NVIDIA Tesla K80 (16 GPUs in total).

We trained our model with purely online learning manner (no mini-batch). Although clock-time for training depends on language, under high-resource setting, usually it took about 7 minutes to train a model by using 10,000 examples (that is, one iteration for high-resource training dataset) with one GPU. Hence Time=30 in Table 1 implies training for the language under high-resource setting took about 210 minutes (using one GPU). We only participated in the main track, so we did not use any external resources.

4.2 Results

Table 1 shows the results of our system, descending order of the results for test data set in high-resource setting.

Morphologically simple languages such as English and Persian seem to give high accuracy. Agglutinative languages such as Turkish also tend to contribute to good results. On the other hand, highly-inflectional languages such as Latin give bad performance.

Language	High				Medium			Low		
	Base	Dev	Test	Time	Base	Dev	Test	Base	Dev	Test
norwegian-bokmal	0.750	0.901	0.896	40	0.590	0.772	0.767	0.417	0.015	0.003
georgian	0.933	0.982	0.974	38	0.900	0.864	0.885	0.793	0.012	0.012
lower-sorbian	0.866	0.960	0.953	37	0.670	0.607	0.591	0.362	0.008	0.012
norwegian-nynorsk	0.610	0.866	0.817	37	0.604	0.588	0.557	0.439	0.003	0.007
ukrainian	0.808	0.900	0.908	37	0.734	0.576	0.572	0.523	0.006	0.007
icelandic	0.617	0.850	0.813	36	0.531	0.384	0.412	0.439	0.006	0.006
irish	0.474	0.834	0.831	36	0.424	0.325	0.319	0.317	0.002	0.000
macedonian	0.942	0.936	0.934	36	0.832	0.752	0.762	0.396	0.005	0.002
slovak	0.777	0.942	0.917	36	0.720	0.614	0.614	0.647	0.010	0.006
kurmanji	0.875	0.917	0.920	35	0.790	0.770	0.762	0.633	0.002	0.002
navajo	0.408	0.853	0.851	35	0.385	0.310	0.318	0.306	0.006	0.007
russian	0.900	0.872	0.861	35	0.830	0.526	0.531	0.412	0.000	0.000
serbo-croatian	0.863	0.870	0.888	35	0.570	0.425	0.418	0.285	0.000	0.001
lithuanian	0.662	0.863	0.860	34	0.615	0.404	0.387	0.536	0.003	0.005
slovene	0.798	0.957	0.952	34	0.767	0.629	0.658	0.616	0.013	0.020
faroese	0.651	0.831	0.814	33	0.559	0.365	0.390	0.513	0.003	0.002
northern-sami	0.562	0.928	0.926	32	0.499	0.346	0.344	0.314	0.004	0.005
danish	0.827	0.924	0.884	31	0.753	0.757	0.750	0.567	0.012	0.012
italian	0.901	0.969	0.960	31	0.839	0.866	0.861	0.769	0.001	0.000
bulgarian	0.819	0.951	0.964	30	0.640	0.683	0.655	0.553	0.006	0.004
estonian	0.581	0.965	0.963	30	0.551	0.687	0.658	0.385	0.003	0.001
latin	0.493	0.740	0.709	30	0.449	0.308	0.307	0.336	0.001	0.000
latvian	0.877	0.926	0.922	30	0.852	0.629	0.619	0.790	0.004	0.000
armenian	0.856	0.952	0.941	29	0.785	0.729	0.732	0.722	0.001	0.000
czech	0.841	0.903	0.906	29	0.610	0.620	0.603	0.307	0.003	0.000
polish	0.794	0.885	0.881	29	0.694	0.497	0.496	0.506	0.000	0.002
portuguese	0.975	0.985	0.979	29	0.969	0.827	0.855	0.951	0.007	0.010
sorani	0.646	0.883	0.873	29	0.661	0.565	0.581	0.534	0.007	0.009
english	0.900	0.954	0.942	28	0.832	0.904	0.904	0.784	0.006	0.011
romanian	0.773	0.835	0.828	28	0.630	0.456	0.460	0.151	0.002	0.000
swedish	0.723	0.868	0.875	28	0.635	0.658	0.680	0.421	0.004	0.002
arabic	0.566	0.918	0.902	27	0.553	0.549	0.536	0.380	0.002	0.002
dutch	0.845	0.954	0.943	26	0.796	0.750	0.731	0.588	0.006	0.005
hebrew	0.547	0.984	0.990	26	0.417	0.656	0.673	0.380	0.006	0.006
albanian	0.942	0.985	0.983	25	0.882	0.594	0.612	0.160	0.001	0.003
catalan	0.965	0.967	0.964	25	0.958	0.787	0.772	0.942	0.004	0.004
turkish	0.825	0.940	0.935	25	0.613	0.596	0.607	0.124	0.000	0.001
finnish	0.709	0.845	0.841	24	0.720	0.490	0.512	0.517	0.000	0.000
khaling	0.840	0.996	0.989	24	0.546	0.718	0.693	0.247	0.005	0.009
german	0.705	0.854	0.857	23	0.662	0.594	0.609	0.610	0.004	0.003
quechua	0.972	0.999	0.996	23	0.973	0.914	0.902	0.973	0.008	0.006
hindi	0.961	1.000	1.000	22	0.746	0.839	0.819	0.698	0.009	0.012
persian	0.889	0.994	0.996	21	0.911	0.743	0.717	0.822	0.006	0.005
french	0.982	0.853	0.811	20	0.893	0.713	0.680	0.864	0.003	0.001
spanish	0.954	0.951	0.950	20	0.911	0.798	0.803	0.787	0.001	0.002
urdu	0.991	0.993	0.996	20	0.680	0.875	0.891	0.670	0.045	0.047
welsh	0.752	1.000	0.980	18	0.693	0.850	0.860	0.601	0.010	0.020
hungarian	0.585	0.815	0.791	16	0.453	0.534	0.528	0.255	0.000	0.000
basque	0.060	0.990	1.000	11	0.051	0.750	0.810	0.040	0.020	0.050
haida	0.690	0.990	0.990	9	0.802	0.890	0.880	0.554	0.010	0.010
bengali	0.847	0.990	0.990	4	0.847	0.950	0.950	0.661	0.010	0.010
scottish-gaelic	-	-	-	-	0.441	0.860	0.800	0.449	0.360	0.320

Table 1: Results of our system. Base represents the baseline system provided the organizers. Dev represents the best result for development data. Test represents the final result of our system. Time represents the number of examples for training convergence (unit: 10k). Note that Scottish Gaelic for the high-resource setting is omitted because the data was not provided.

In high-resource setting, our system achieved 91.46% accuracy, the 12th among the 20 systems. In medium-resource setting, the performance was almost the same as baseline 65.06%. And in low-resource setting, the system achieved only 1.58%.

4.3 Comparison with other systems

A heat map in Fig. 2 shows the accuracy of participants under high-resource settings, with the descending order of the average accuracy. Green color (light color in black-and-white) denotes high accuracy whereas red (purple at the extreme) color (dark color in black-and-white) denotes low accuracy. Note that the ranking is slightly different from the official one, because in this figure, if a system did not participate in some languages, we treated them as zero accuracy.

As we see, it is hard to tell the difference, because top systems achieved nearly 100% accuracy for almost all languages. However, if we carefully examined, almost all systems (which have higher performance than the baseline) have similar color spotting patterns, possibly because these participants used similar systems, that is, the seq2seq model (Faruqui et al., 2016; Kann and Schütze, 2016a; Kann et al., 2016). We also see that the color of the Latin language tends to be yellowish or reddish, which indicates that this language is very hard to process by using the seq2seq model.

Heat maps in Fig. 3 and Fig. 4, which depict the case of medium- and low-resource settings, are also interesting to see.

Let us see the case of low-resource settings. It is easy to recognize the systems of UA took unique approaches. Other systems have similar color patterns—it may indicate they used the seq2seq model—but the intensity of colors gradually degrades according to the ranking of these systems. Then, after crossing a certain point, the color suddenly becomes purple (nearly 0%) for almost all languages (EHU-01-0 and our system UTNII-01-0).

We will release these figures on the GitHub account of the first author [2].

[2]https://github.com/hajimes/
conll2017-stats

5 Discussion

5.1 Convergence speed under high-resource settings

As we see in Table 1, the number of training time for morphological reinflection significantly differs from each language. In the case of Bengali, only 40k (4 iteration for the data set) was sufficient to achieve the best result, whereas Norwegian Bokmål requires 400k (40 iteration). This contrasts with Kann and Schütze (2016a)'s approach where they simply used 20 iterations for any language.

The following table is a list of the top five languages for fast convergence.

Language	Base	Dev	Test	Time
bengali	0.847	0.990	0.990	4
haida	0.690	0.990	0.990	9
basque	0.060	0.990	1.000	11
hungarian	0.585	0.815	0.791	16
welsh	0.752	1.000	0.980	18

On the other hand, training for the following five languages was slow to converge.

Language	Dev	Test	Time
norwegian-bokmal	0.901	0.896	40
georgian	0.982	0.974	38
lower-sorbian	0.960	0.953	37
norwegian-nynorsk	0.866	0.817	37
ukrainian	0.900	0.908	37

5.2 Accuracy under low-resource settings

To test why our system gave catastrophic results under the low-resource setting, we tested more fine-grained analysis as to the size of resources.

We made several new datasets from `english-train-medium` with the size 100, 110, 130, 150, and 500. After we trained our model on these datasets, model-100 gave the best result 0.022 on development data, model-110 0.029, model-130 0.149, model-150 0.356, model-500 0.843, (and model-1000 0.904 as seen in Table 1). It seems that a big trench for our system happens to lie somewhere between 110 and 150 (or 130 and 150)—except Scottish-Gaelic (see Table 1 and Fig. 4). This may explain the reason for big gaps in accuracy with other participants; crossing the trench or not, that is the question. The abrupt decline of predictive performance was also observed by Kann and Schütze (2016b).

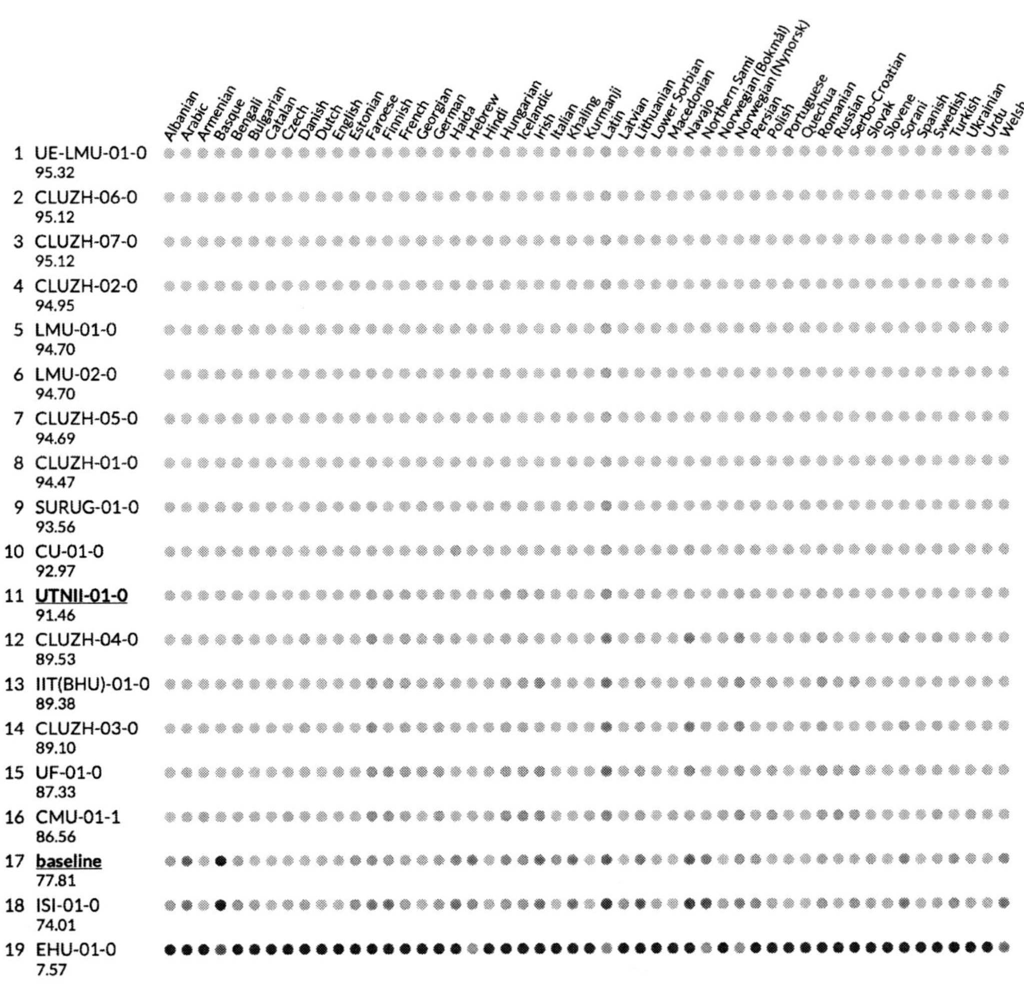

Figure 2: Comparison with other systems under high-resource settings. The signature of our system is `UTNII-01-0`. The ranking is slightly different from the official one, because in this figure, if a system did not participate in some languages, we treated them as zero accuracy. The last number of a system name denotes the usage of external resources (0 = no, 1 = yes).

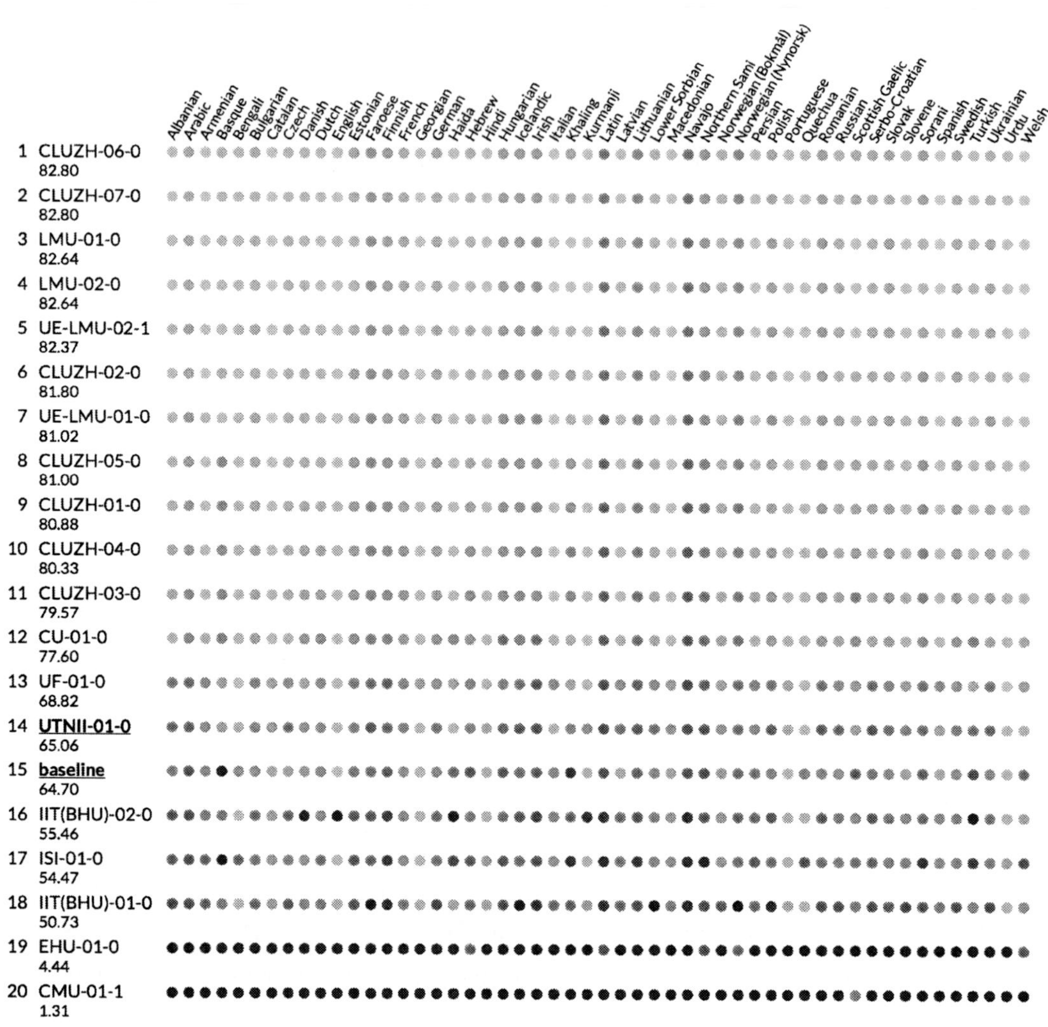

Figure 3: Comparison with other systems under medium-resource settings. The signature of our system is UTNII-01-0. The ranking is slightly different from the official one, because in this figure, if a system did not participate in some languages, we treated them as zero accuracy. The last number of a system name denotes the usage of external resources (0 = no, 1 = yes).

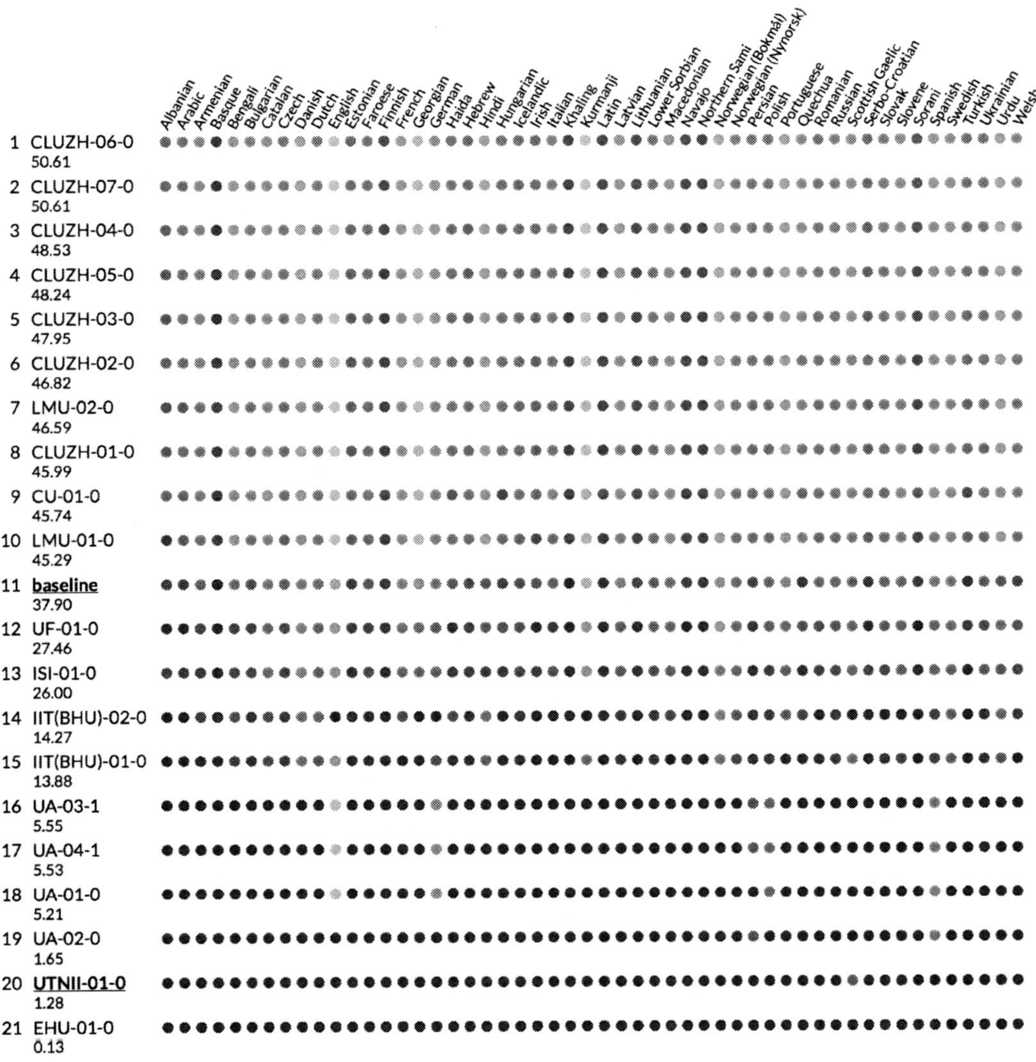

Figure 4: Comparison with other systems under low-resource settings. The signature of our system is UTNII-01-0. The ranking is slightly different from the official one, because in this figure, if a system did not participate in some languages, we treated them as zero accuracy. The last number of a system name denotes the usage of external resources (0 = no, 1 = yes).

One possible solution to mitigate this situation is to use other regularization approaches such as dropout (Srivastava et al., 2014), where different configurations are trained simultaneously and probabilistically, although such techniques alone may not change the inherent nature of our system. We will try to find how we can lower the trench in the future.

It is interesting that our system achieved meaningful accuracy for Scottish-Gaelic even under low-resource settings. Although this tendency is not global, the system of `IIT(BHU)-01-0` also shows relatively good performance on the language, so the robustness for processing Scottish-Gaelic may not be by pure chance. We plan to analyze the language in detail, because it will reveal what kind of linguistic natures determine the "trench" of the required number of training examples for seq2seq systems.

6   Conclusion

In this paper, we presented system description and error analysis for our system submitted to the CoNLL-SIGMORPHON 2017 Shared Task. As the reader sees in our results, pure deep learning approaches have a major disadvantage, that is, their predictive performance drops steeply after crossing a certain point of the number of training examples. We also showed that the convergence speed for training the models of morphological reinflection highly depends on the type of languages, which can be useful information to tackle the task again in the future.

Acknowledgements

This work was supported by CREST, Japan Science and Technology Agency. We are also grateful to two anonymous reviewers for their helpful comments.

References

Malin Ahlberg, Markus Forsberg, and Mans Hulden. 2015. Paradigm classification in supervised learning of morphology. In *Proceedings of the 2015 Conference of the North American Chapter of the Association for Computational Linguistics: Human Language Technologies*. Association for Computational Linguistics, Stroudsburg, PA, USA, pages 1024–1029. https://doi.org/10.3115/v1/N15-1107.

Cyril Allauzen, Michael Riley, Johan Schalkwyk, Wojciech Skut, and Mehryar Mohri. 2007. OpenFst: A General and Efficient Weighted Finite-State Transducer Library. In *Proceedings of the Twelfth International Conference on Implementation and Application of Automata*. pages 11–23.

Dzmitry Bahdanau, KyungHyun Cho, and Yoshua Bengio. 2015. Neural Machine Translation By Jointly Learning To Align and Translate. In *Proceeding of the 3rd International Conference on Learning Representations (ICLR2015)*. http://arxiv.org/abs/1409.0473v3.

Kyunghyun Cho, Bart van Merrienboer, Caglar Gulcehre, Dzmitry Bahdanau, Fethi Bougares, Holger Schwenk, and Yoshua Bengio. 2014. Learning Phrase Representations using RNN EncoderDecoder for Statistical Machine Translation. In *Proceedings of the 2014 Conference on Empirical Methods in Natural Language Processing (EMNLP)*. Association for Computational Linguistics, Stroudsburg, PA, USA, pages 1724–1734. https://doi.org/10.3115/v1/D14-1179.

Çağrı Çöltekin. 2010. A Freely Available Morphological Analyzer for Turkish. In *Proceedings of the Seventh conference on International Language Resources and Evaluation (LREC'10)*. European Language Resources Association (ELRA), Valletta, Malta, pages 820–827.

Ryan Cotterell, Christo Kirov, John Sylak-Glassman, Géraldine Walther, Ekaterina Vylomova, Patrick Xia, Manaal Faruqui, Sandra Kübler, David Yarowsky, Jason Eisner, and Mans Hulden. 2017. The CoNLL-SIGMORPHON 2017 Shared Task: Universal Morphological Reinflection in 52 Languages. In *Proceedings of the CoNLL-SIGMORPHON 2017 Shared Task: Universal Morphological Reinflection*.

Ryan Cotterell, Christo Kirov, John Sylak-Glassman, David Yarowsky, Jason Eisner, and Mans Hulden. 2016. The SIGMORPHON 2016 Shared Task— Morphological Reinflection. In *Proceedings of the 14th Annual SIGMORPHON Workshop on Computational Research in Phonetics, Phonology, and Morphology*. pages 10–22. https://doi.org/10.18653/v1/W16-2002.

Greg Durrett and John DeNero. 2013. Supervised Learning of Complete Morphological Paradigms. In *Proceedings of the 2013 Conference of the North American Chapter of the Association for Computational Linguistics: Human Language Technologies*. Association for Computational Linguistics, Atlanta, Georgia, June, pages 1185–1195.

Manaal Faruqui, Yulia Tsvetkov, Graham Neubig, and Chris Dyer. 2016. Morphological Inflection Generation Using Character Sequence to Sequence Learning. In *Proceedings of NAACL-HLT 2016*. pages 634–643. https://doi.org/10.18653/v1/N16-1077.

Michael Gasser. 2011. HornMorpho: a system for morphological processing of Amharic, Oromo, and

Tigrinya. In *Conference on Human Language Technology for Development*. Alexandria, Egypt, pages 94–99.

Xavier Glorot and Yoshua Bengio. 2010. Understanding the difficulty of training deep feedforward neural networks. In *Proceedings of the 13th International Conference on Artificial Intelligence and Statistics (AISTATS)*. volume 9, pages 249–256.

Mans Hulden. 2009. Foma: a finite-state compiler and library. In *Proceedings of the Demonstrations Session at EACL 2009*. Association for Computational Linguistics, Athens, Greece, pages 29–32.

Katharina Kann, Ryan Cotterell, and Hinrich Schütze. 2016. Neural Morphological Analysis: Encoding-Decoding Canonical Segments. In *Proceedings of the 2016 Conference on Empirical Methods in Natural Language Processing*. Association for Computational Linguistics, Stroudsburg, PA, USA, pages 961–967. https://doi.org/10.18653/v1/D16-1097.

Katharina Kann and Hinrich Schütze. 2016a. MED: The LMU System for the SIGMORPHON 2016 Shared Task on Morphological Reinflection. In *Proceedings of the 14th Annual SIGMORPHON Workshop on Computational Research in Phonetics, Phonology, and Morphology*. pages 62–70. https://doi.org/10.18653/v1/W16-2010.

Katharina Kann and Hinrich Schütze. 2016b. Single-Model Encoder-Decoder with Explicit Morphological Representation for Reinflection. In *Proceedings of the 54th Annual Meeting of the Association for Computational Linguistics (Volume 2: Short Papers)*. Association for Computational Linguistics, Stroudsburg, PA, USA, pages 555–560. https://doi.org/10.18653/v1/P16-2090.

Ronald M. Kaplan and Martin Kay. 1994. Regular Models of Phonological Rule Systems. *Computational Linguistics* 20(3):331–378.

Lauri Karttunen. 1983. KIMMO: A General Morphological Parser. *Texas Linguistic Forum* 22:165–186.

Diederik P. Kingma and Jimmy Lei Ba. 2015. Adam: A Method for Stochastic Optimization. In *International Conference on Learning Representations 2015*. arxiv:1412.6980v8.

Kimmo Koskenniemi. 1984. A General Computational Model for Word-Form Recognition and Production. In *10th International Conference on Computational Linguistics and 22nd Annual Meeting of the Association for Computational Linguistics*. pages 178–181. http://aclweb.org/anthology/P84-1038.

Nitish Srivastava, Geoffrey Hinton, Alex Krizhevsky, Ilya Sutskever, and Ruslan Salakhutdinov. 2014. Dropout: A Simple Way to Prevent Neural Networks from Overfitting. *Journal of Machine Learning Research* 15:1929–1958. http://jmlr.org/papers/v15/srivastava14a.html.

Ilya Sutskever, Oriol Vinyals, and Quoc V. Le. 2014. Sequence to Sequence Learning with Neural Networks. In *Advances in Neural Information Processing Systems 27 (NIPS 2014)*. pages 3104–3112.

John Sylak-Glassman, Christo Kirov, David Yarowsky, and Roger Que. 2015. A Language-Independent Feature Schema for Inflectional Morphology. In *Proceedings of the 53rd Annual Meeting of the Association for Computational Linguistics and the 7th International Joint Conference on Natural Language Processing (Volume 2: Short Papers)*. Association for Computational Linguistics, Stroudsburg, PA, USA, pages 674–680. https://doi.org/10.3115/v1/P15-2111.

The Theano Development Team. 2016. Theano: A Python framework for fast computation of mathematical expressions https://arxiv.org/abs/1605.02688.

Reut Tsarfaty, Djamé Seddah, Yoav Goldberg, Sandra Kübler, Marie Candito, Jennifer Foster, Yannick Versley, Ines Rehbein, and Lamia Tounsi. 2010. Statistical Parsing of Morphologically Rich Languages (SPMRL) What, How and Whither. In *Proceedings of the NAACL HLT 2010 First Workshop on Statistical Parsing of Morphologically-Rich Languages*. pages 1–12. http://dl.acm.org/citation.cfm?id=1868772.

Matthew D. Zeiler. 2012. ADADELTA: An Adaptive Learning Rate Method. Technical report. http://arxiv.org/abs/1212.5701.

SU-RUG at the CoNLL-SIGMORPHON 2017 shared task:
Morphological Inflection with Attentional Sequence-to-Sequence Models

Robert Östling
Department of Linguistics
Stockholm University
Sweden
`robert@ling.su.se`

Johannes Bjerva[*]
Center for Language and Cognition Groningen
University of Groningen
The Netherlands
`j.bjerva@rug.nl`

Abstract

This paper describes the Stockholm University/University of Groningen (SU-RUG) system for the SIGMORPHON 2017 shared task on morphological inflection. Our system is based on an attentional sequence-to-sequence neural network model using Long Short-Term Memory (LSTM) cells, with joint training of morphological inflection and the inverse transformation, i.e. lemmatization and morphological analysis. Our system outperforms the baseline with a large margin, and our submission ranks as the 4_{th} best team for the track we participate in (task 1, high-resource).

1 Introduction

We focus on task 1 of the SIGMORPHON 2017 shared task (Cotterell et al., 2017), morphological inflection. The task is to learn the mapping from a lemma and morphological description to the corresponding inflected form. For instance, the English verb lemma *torment* with the features 3.SG.PRS should be mapped to *torments*. As our model is poorly suited for low-resource conditions, we only submitted results for the 51 languages with high-resource training data available in the shared task (i.e., excluding Scottish Gaelic).

2 Background

The results of the SIGMORPHON 2016 shared task (Cotterell et al., 2016) indicated that the attentional sequence-to-sequence model of Bahdanau et al. (2014) is very suitable for this task (Kann and Schütze, 2016), so we use this framework as the basis of our model.

---

[*]This work was carried out while the second author was visiting the Department of Linguistics, Stockholm University.

A recent trend in neural machine translation is to use back-translated text (Sennrich et al., 2016) as a way to benefit from additional monolingual data in the target language. There is also work on translation models with reconstruction loss, which encourages solutions that can be translated back to their original (Tu et al., 2016). These developments are technically similar to our semi-supervised training below.

3 Method

Our system is based on the attentional sequence-to-sequence model of Bahdanau et al. (2014) with Long Short-Term Memory (LSTM) cells (Hochreiter and Schmidhuber, 1997) and variational dropout Gal and Ghahramani (2016). The main innovation is that our inflection model is trained jointly with the reverse process, that is, lemmatization and morphological analysis. This can be done in two ways:

1. Fully supervised, where we simply train the forward (inflection) and backward (lemmatization and morphological analysis) model jointly with shared character embeddings.

2. Semi-supervised, where supervised examples are mixed with examples where only the inflected target form is used. This form is passed first through the backward model, a greedy search to obtain a unique lemma, and finally through the forward model to reconstruct the inflected form.

Our official submission only includes results from fully supervised training (method 1), due to time constraints, but Section 5 contains a comparison between the two versions on the development set. The system architecture is shown in Figure 1 for the forward (inflection) model. The backward

Proceedings of the CoNLL SIGMORPHON 2017 Shared Task: Universal Morphological Reinflection, pages 110–113,
Vancouver, Canada, August 3–4, 2017. ©2017 Association for Computational Linguistics

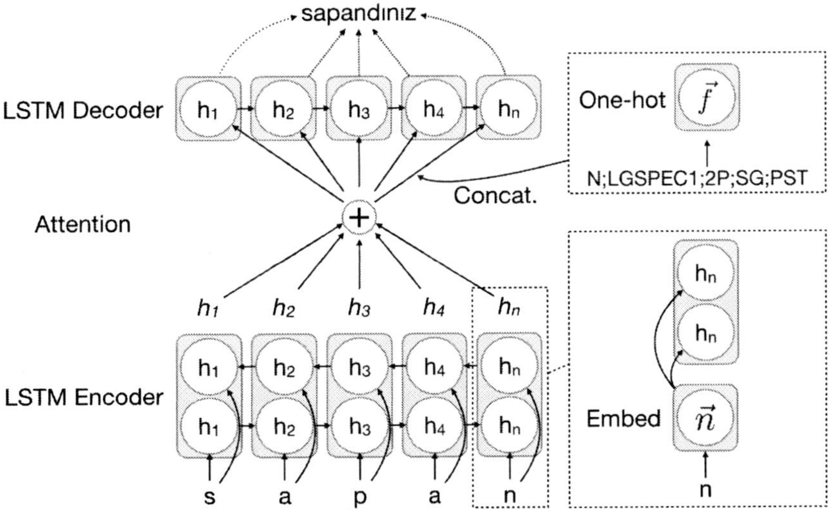

Figure 1: System architecture, consisting of an attentional sequence-to-sequence model with LSTMs.

(lemmatizer) model has separate parameters, except the embeddings, but is structurally identical except for two details: instead of passing the morphological feature information to the decoder (via a single fully connected layer), we predict the features from the final state of the encoder LSTM (via a separate fully connected layer).

Our implementation is based on the Chainer library (Tokui et al., 2015) and available at `github.com/bjerva/sigmorphon2017`.

4 Model configuration

For the official submission, we use 128 LSTM cells for the (unidirectional) encoder, decoder, attention mechanism, character embeddings, as well as for the fully connected layers for morphological features encoding/prediciton. We use a dropout factor of 0.5 throughout the network, including the recurrent parts. For optimization, we use Adam (Kingma and Ba, 2015) with default parameters. Each model is trained for 48 hours on a single CPU, using a batch-size of 64, and the model parameters during this time that give the lowest development set mean Levenshtein distance are saved. For the official submission, we used an ensemble of two such models, using a beam search of width 10 to select the final inflection candidate.

5 Results and Analysis

The system has high performance in general, with a macro-average accuracy of 93.6%, and edit dis-

tance of 0.14. This is substantially higher than the baseline (77.8% accuracy and 0.5 edit distance), and ranks as the 9_{th} best run, and 4_{th} best team in this SIGMORPHON 2017 shared task setting. Furthermore, the difference in scores between our run and the best run overall is low (1.75% accuracy and 0.04 edit distance). Table 1 contains a detailed version of the official results our system on the shared task, in the *high* setting of Task 1.

Notably, the system has an accuracy of 100% on both Basque and Quechua, which indicates that it is capable of fully learning the rules of very regular morphological systems. The relatively high accuracy on Semitic languages (Arabic: 89.8%, Hebrew: 99.0%) again confirms the ability of encoder-decoder models to also handle non-concatenative morphology.

Latin has the lowest accuracy by far, and the reason seems to be that the provided shared task data lacks vowel length distinctions in the lemma but uses them in the inflected forms. This missing lexical information is difficult to predict accurately. Evaluating with vowel length distinctions gives an accuracy of 75.6% (Latin development set), compared to 91.5% without. The latter accuracy score is in line with other Romance languages (French 90.8%, Spanish 94.3%, Italian 97.0%).

We also investigated whether the semi-supervised approach described in Section 3 has any effect on accuracy. The results on the development set, presented in Table 2, indicate that

Table 1: Our system's official results on the SIGMORPHON-2017 shared task-1 test set in the *high* setting.

Language	Accuracy	Edit dist.
Albanian	97.9	0.07
Arabic	89.8	0.39
Armenian	95.6	0.08
Basque	100.0	0.00
Bengali	99.0	0.05
Bulgarian	96.7	0.07
Catalan	97.8	0.06
Czech	92.0	0.15
Danish	93.8	0.09
Dutch	95.9	0.07
English	96.6	0.07
Estonian	96.8	0.08
Faroese	84.6	0.31
Finnish	91.0	0.17
French	87.5	0.24
Georgian	97.6	0.05
German	89.5	0.21
Haida	95.0	0.10
Hebrew	99.0	0.01
Hindi	99.8	0.00
Hungarian	84.8	0.35
Icelandic	86.3	0.25
Irish	87.6	0.35
Italian	96.8	0.09
Khaling	98.3	0.03
Kurmanji	93.8	0.10
Latin	75.3	0.39
Latvian	95.4	0.08
Lithuanian	91.0	0.15
Lower Sorbian	96.9	0.06
Macedonian	96.6	0.06
Navajo	88.9	0.28
Northern Sami	94.5	0.12
Norwegian (Bokmål)	92.4	0.13
Norwegian (Nynorsk)	89.4	0.18
Persian	99.3	0.01
Polish	90.6	0.22
Portuguese	98.8	0.02
Quechua	100.0	0.00
Romanian	86.4	0.42
Russian	89.3	0.31
Serbo-Croatian	90.1	0.24
Slovak	93.1	0.13
Slovene	96.6	0.07
Sorani	88.6	0.14
Spanish	93.5	0.15
Swedish	91.8	0.13
Turkish	96.6	0.11
Ukrainian	94.2	0.11
Urdu	99.7	0.01
Welsh	99.0	0.03
Average	**93.6**	**0.14**

Table 2: Our system's result on the SIGMORPHON-2017 shared task-1 development set, comparing fully supervised training (**Full**) to our semi-supervised method (**Semi**).

Language	Accuracy	
	Full	Semi
Albanian	97.6	97.0
Arabic	93.0	93.1
Armenian	96.9	97.1
Basque	99.0	99.0
Bengali	99.0	99.0
Bulgarian	95.8	96.0
Catalan	98.0	98.3
Czech	92.5	93.1
Danish	95.8	95.9
Dutch	96.8	97.1
English	96.6	96.3
Estonian	97.4	97.6
Faroese	86.7	87.1
Finnish	91.2	91.4
French	89.8	89.3
Georgian	97.9	97.9
German	87.8	89.6
Hebrew	98.8	98.7
Hindi	99.9	99.8
Hungarian	86.8	87.1
Icelandic	88.1	88.6
Irish	89.0	89.5
Italian	97.0	97.2
Kurmanji	92.4	92.7
Latin	75.6	75.9
Latvian	95.2	96.4
Lithuanian	90.3	89.6
Lower Sorbian	97.7	96.3
Macedonian	95.3	95.0
Navajo	88.2	85.2
Northern Sami	94.4	93.5
Norwegian (Bokmål)	91.8	92.7
Norwegian (Nynorsk)	92.3	92.4
Persian	99.5	99.6
Polish	91.0	92.0
Portuguese	98.6	98.0
Quechua	100.0	100.0
Romanian	87.4	88.2
Russian	89.8	88.1
Serbo-Croatian	89.5	89.7
Slovak	95.2	94.8
Slovene	96.7	97.0
Sorani	90.9	90.3
Spanish	94.3	95.7
Swedish	90.9	90.1
Turkish	97.5	97.2
Ukrainian	94.0	92.7
Urdu	99.5	99.2
Welsh	100.0	100.0
Average	**93.9**	**93.8**

there is no systematic effect (the macro-averaged accuracy drops marginally from 93.9% to 93.8%).

6 Conclusions

We implemented a system using an attentional sequence-to-sequence model with Long Short-Term Memory (LSTM) cells. As our model is poorly suited for low-resource conditions, we only participated in the high-resource setting. Our inflection model is trained jointly with the reverse process, that is, lemmatization and morphological analysis. The system significantly outperforms the baseline system, and performs well compared to other submitted systems, showing that this approach is very suitable for morphological inflection, given sufficient amounts of data.

Acknowledgments

The authors would like to thank the reviewers, and Johan Sjons for their comments on previous versions of this manuscript. This work was partially funded by the NWO–VICI grant "Lost in Translation – Found in Meaning" (288-89-003). This work was performed on the Abel Cluster, owned by the University of Oslo and the Norwegian metacenter for High Performance Computing (NOTUR), and operated by the Department for Research Computing at USIT, the University of Oslo IT-department.

References

Dzmitry Bahdanau, Kyunghyun Cho, and Yoshua Bengio. 2014. Neural machine translation by jointly learning to align and translate. *CoRR* abs/1409.0473.

Ryan Cotterell, Christo Kirov, John Sylak-Glassman, Géraldine Walther, Ekaterina Vylomova, Patrick Xia, Manaal Faruqui, Sandra Kübler, David Yarowsky, Jason Eisner, and Mans Hulden. 2017. The CoNLL-SIGMORPHON 2017 shared task: Universal morphological reinflection in 52 languages. In *Proceedings of the CoNLL-SIGMORPHON 2017 Shared Task: Universal Morphological Reinflection*. Association for Computational Linguistics, Vancouver, Canada.

Ryan Cotterell, Christo Kirov, John Sylak-Glassman, David Yarowsky, Jason Eisner, and Mans Hulden. 2016. The sigmorphon 2016 shared task: Morphological reinflection. In *Proceedings of the 14th SIGMORPHON Workshop on Computational Research in Phonetics, Phonology, and Morphology*. Association for Computational Linguistics, Berlin, Germany, pages 10–22.

Yarin Gal and Zoubin Ghahramani. 2016. A theoretically grounded application of dropout in recurrent neural networks. In *Advances in Neural Information Processing Systems 29 (NIPS)*.

Sepp Hochreiter and Jürgen Schmidhuber. 1997. Long short-term memory. *Neural Computation* 9(8):17351780.

Katharina Kann and Hinrich Schütze. 2016. Med: The lmu system for the sigmorphon 2016 shared task on morphological reinflection. In *Proceedings of the 14th SIGMORPHON Workshop on Computational Research in Phonetics, Phonology, and Morphology*. Association for Computational Linguistics, Berlin, Germany, pages 62–70.

Diederik P. Kingma and Jimmy Ba. 2015. Adam: A method for stochastic optimization. The International Conference on Learning Representations.

Rico Sennrich, Barry Haddow, and Alexandra Birch. 2016. Improving neural machine translation models with monolingual data. In *Proceedings of the 54th Annual Meeting of the Association for Computational Linguistics (Volume 1: Long Papers)*. Association for Computational Linguistics, Berlin, Germany, pages 86–96.

Seiya Tokui, Kenta Oono, Shohei Hido, and Justin Clayton. 2015. Chainer: a next-generation open source framework for deep learning. In *Proceedings of Workshop on Machine Learning Systems (LearningSys) in The Twenty-ninth Annual Conference on Neural Information Processing Systems (NIPS)*.

Zhaopeng Tu, Yang Liu, Lifeng Shang, Xiaohua Liu, and Hang Li. 2016. Neural machine translation with reconstruction. *CoRR* abs/1611.01874.

Author Index